Passage To
NIRVANA

To Joanie,
A fellow lover of boots
+ my savior in Miami!
Thanks for all
your help.

J.

Passage To Nirvana

~

A Survivor's Zen Voyage:
Reflections on Loss, Discovery,
Healing & Hope.

Lee Carlson

Henry Chapin & Sons
New York • Tokyo • London

First Edition: August 2010

The author has made every attempt to ensure that all information contained
herein is as accurate as possible. However, the author is not an expert in medicine,
law or finance, and no information given herein is intended as professional advice.
Medical health, especially head injury, is a serious matter, and anyone with a head
injury should immediately seek qualified medical assistance. Similarly, anyone
needing legal and financial advice as a result of head injury or divorce should
consult a qualified attorney and financial advisor.

Lee Carlson is available to speak to groups about Traumatic Brain Injury,
overcoming traumatic life events, Zen Buddhism, and writing as a form of art
therapy. For more information or to book Lee Carlson as a guest speaker at your
event, please contact info@henrychapinbooks.com

Publisher's Cataloging-in-Publication Data

Carlson, Lee.
Passage to nirvana, a survivor's Zen voyage: reflections on loss, discovery,
healing & hope / Lee Carlson.
p. cm.
ISBN 978-0-9826884-6-5 (hardcover)
ISBN 978-0-9826884-7-2 (pbk.)
ISBN 978-0-9826884-8-9 (e-book)
1. Healing—Religious aspects —Zen Buddhism—Personal narratives. 2. Brain
damage —Patients—Biography. 3. Head —Wounds and injuries—Patients
—Personal narratives. 4. Brain—Wounds and injuries—Patients—Personal
narratives. 5. Meditation—Therapeutic use—Personal narratives. 6. Brain
injury—Patients—Rehabilitation—Personal narratives. I. Passage to nirvana, a
survivor's Zen voyage: reflections on loss, discovery, healing and hope. II. Title.

BQ9288.C375 2010   294.3/927092—dc22   2010903488

www.passagetonirvana.com

Manufactured in the United States of America

May penetrating light dispel the darkness,
and the mind flower bloom
in eternal spring.

– Zen Prayer

Heart wisdom has no hindrance of mind,
thus no fear, far beyond all delusion,
Nirvana is already here.

– The Heart Sutra

For Meg,
my muse.

In memory of
Ann Siegfried Carlson

May her ashes float far and wide
on the waters that she loved.

CONTENTS

~

PROLOGUE: A JOURNEY BEGINS

THE BOOK OF PO

WATER

ZEN

CONTENTS

LIFE & DEATH

LOVE & HAPPINESS

CONTENTS

FUN & GAMES

SEASONS

ONE HAND SLAPPING

LAST PO

BRICOLAGE

RUMBLE IN THE JUMBLE

ABOUT THE PO

ENDNOTES

Author's Preface

~

P ASSAGE TO NIRVANA IS A different kind of story. It is a memoir, but not just a memoir; a collection of essays, but not just a collection of essays; a treasury of Zen teachings, yet not just a treasury of Zen teachings; a sailor's yarn, yet not just a simple sailor's tale spun over a glass of rum. The story ranges far and wide, covering many themes: Traumatic Brain Injury, divorce, sailing, Zen, love, compassion, poetry, hope, family, kids, dogs…. Except the story is about more than Traumatic Brain Injury, divorce, sailing, Zen, love, compassion, poetry, hope, family, kids and dogs. At its core, "Passage to Nirvana" is about the poetry of living.

The heart of the story is about healing, about what happens when everything that defines you, everything you are, is totally, completely stripped away. "Passage to Nirvana" is about finding a path to happiness after a traumatic life event. The title's acronym PTN could just as easily stand for finding a path to "Post-Trauma Nirvana," a path that will confront all of us at one point in our lives, whether we're affected by the death of a loved one, a divorce, or an extreme physical trauma—an accident, a debilitating addiction or a life-threatening disease.

The book is a work of nonfiction, based on real life experiences. Even though much of the story revolves around two traumatic brain injuries, there is little discussion of parts of the brain, modern neuroscience, neurotransmitters and other state-of-the-art medical understanding. There are plenty of other good books on those subjects. Instead, using art instead of science, the book conveys what it feels like to live with a Traumatic Brain Injury, or care for someone with a Traumatic Brain Injury. The story gives a sense of the struggle, the darkness, and the joy of finally finding a path out of that darkness. "Passage to Nirvana" is an artist's expedition of discovery into the mysterious oceans of the human mind.

"Passage to Nirvana" is not a conventional narrative. A voyage to nirvana is not easy; the passagemaker moves forward in fits and starts, is sometimes driven backwards by howling storms, and is sometimes becalmed in maddening, airless doldrums. The voyager's route can fetch up against impassable reefs so the voyager must double back and set a new course. "Passage to Nirvana" mimics that process. Part I, "Prologue: A Journey Begins," is an introduction that lays the framework and sets the course for the journey, providing keel, ribs, fasteners, planks, charts, parallel rules and compass. Part II, "The Book of Po," finishes the fitting out and puts to sea, providing the necessary equipment: sails, masts, paint, winches, ropes, anchors, caulking, bunks, portholes and hatches for gazing at the sky, provisions for nourishment and sustenance. "The Book of Po" is the log of the voyage.

Part III, "Bricolage," is like fine adornment: varnish, brass lamps, decorative rope work, cinnamon and nutmeg in the coffee, things that give the voyage another layer of enjoyment. Some people consider these components essential enhancement, while others consider them unnecessary, extra ornamentation. Personally, I consider man's urge to expand his world to be a fundamental need. As my father often quoted to me, "Variety is the spice of life."

"The Book of Po" is designed so that one can read sequentially, like a conventional memoir, or by titles that catch one's fancy, such as "New England Nirvana" or "Lover's Lament," since each chapter is a self-contained essay. The chapters are like pieces of a jigsaw puzzle; by putting them together the picture will slowly come into focus, but there is no "right" order in putting together the pieces.

If you have ever talked to a brain-injured person, you know it can be a frustrating, challenging experience, with the level of frustration dependent on the degree of the person's injury. The brain injury survivor can get angry, can say inappropriate things; they sometimes have trouble focusing on the conversation and sticking with any one thread of thought. They can just stop in the middle of the conversation, lost, or they can simply be slow on the uptake. "Passage to Nirvana" mimics not only the course of a path to nirvana, but also the way the traumatic-brain-injured mind works, having trouble concentrating on one thing for any length of time, jumping from unruly shaped puzzle piece to unruly piece, dancing back and forth from the present moment to memories to future possibilities and back again, searching for a way to make sense of the chaos.

But dealing with a brain-injured person can also be an immensely rewarding experience. The brain-injured person can be thankful, upbeat, just happy to be alive. They often operate without guile or falsehood. There can be an energy around them that is infectious. For the "normal" person who is dealing with a brain injury survivor, one usually needs to bring an attitude of patience and compassion, otherwise you may be driven crazy. Coming face to face with a brain-injured person can be an experience that teaches you about yourself. "Passage to Nirvana" mimics that odyssey as well.

I had a philosophy teacher in high school whose classroom had a clock on the front wall that had stopped working. She refused to call maintenance, saying that since she taught existentialism, having a classroom where normal rules didn't apply, where time stood still, fit right in. I feel the same way about "Passage to Nirvana." It does not follow the "normal" rules for how a book should behave. This difference can be exasperating, it can be challenging, but it can also be enlightening, forcing you to slow down and rethink your assumptions. Since this is a story about existence, having a narrative that operates without guile, that relishes the joy of being alive, that energetically jumps forward, backwards and then sometimes stands perfectly still while it makes sense of the chaos is not a thing that needs fixing.

–Lee Carlson, March 2010

Prologue

~

A Journey Begins

God moves in a mysterious way,
His wonders to perform.
He plants his footsteps in the sea,
and rides upon the storm.

– William Cowper,
British Poet & Hymnodist, 1731–1800

A Thousand Steps

~

T HE CHINESE PHILOSOPHER LAO-TZU WROTE that a journey of a thousand miles begins with a single step. While that may be true up to a point, as an inveterate traveler and travel writer my own experience is that a journey of any mileage begins with a thousand small steps. There are the conscious undertakings: guidebooks, magazines, web sites and travel brochures to be read; plane and train tickets to be bought; car and hotel reservations to be made; clothes and equipment to be purchased; traveling companions to be communicated with; and family, friends and coworkers to be notified of one's absence and plans. Then there are the subconscious influences that have led to a voyage: the postcard sent by grandparents years ago from Africa that fueled a yearning for far-off lands, the childhood family ski trip to New England that fostered a love of athletic adventure, the unhappy breakup of a young love affair that sent us off in search of a happier time and place.

The journey described in "Passage to Nirvana" began with a number of steps, both large and small, conscious and subconscious; it arose from the ashes of a series of sweeping personal tragedies, as well as a thousand more mundane influences. It began with despair, like the breakup of a young love affair, but it also began, like all journeys, with hope, aspirations, ambition and excited expectations for something better—otherwise why embark on the voyage?

On the morning of May 15, 2002, I was standing in a car wash in Riverhead, New York, on the Eastern End of Long Island. I was on my way to meet a potential new client, an elegant female real estate developer who was interested in cashing in on the booming New York City real estate market. I was forty-four, a professional writer, and had been doing copywriting for prominent New York developers, writing big, expensive, glossy marketing brochures, and my friend David, who was a construction contractor, thought I could give this developer a tour of the up-and-coming areas of Brooklyn, where old warehouses and factories were rapidly being turned into luxury condominiums, popping up like mushrooms after a long rain.

It was a messy time in my life: my wife's business was failing, and even though I had pumped huge amounts of time, money and energy into helping her make it succeed, she still blamed me for its failure. After fourteen-hour days of sweeping floors, shipping orders, fighting with creditors and trying to convince investors to put more money into the company, I would come home not to a place of refuge, but to a spouse who would scream at me, telling me how awful I was as a person, a husband, a father and businessman. Maybe she had a point, maybe not, but the undeniable reality was that the stress of a failing business had soured a once-loving relationship.

There had been a time when Belinda would paint cards for me with a simple abstract watercolor on the outside and a message inside, something like "Thank you so much for everything, if it falls apart we'll move to the Caribbean and live happily every after! Love, B." But that was all in the past. Now, in spite of two years of couples therapy, we were headed for an acrimonious divorce, which would separate me not only from my wife, but from our two young boys, ages eight and five, who were everything to me. The business failure had left us financially destitute, on the verge of bankruptcy and in danger of losing our house. As if that were not enough trauma, my mother had recently suffered a serious accident, leaving her an incapacitated invalid, a shadow of her former vibrant self at the young age of sixty-seven. As a result I had spent a great deal of time traveling back and forth to Buffalo, New York, where I had grown up, helping my father and sisters with my mother's care.

Things were looking up in my business life, however. I had a number of good new writing clients, both commercial and editorial; I had just returned from working for NBC Sports at the Salt Lake City Winter Olympics. One of my favorite new clients was the Environmental Defense Fund, where I felt I was doing work that also had some redeeming social value. I had recently begun doing marketing copywriting for Lavazza Coffee, and there was talk of my traveling to Italy to visit the company headquarters and get a real sense of how important the Italian idea of la dolce vita, the sweet life, was to the company's philosophy and products. Hope and rejuvenation were in the springtime air as I drove along the country roads from my house toward Manhattan, marveling at the beauty of apple orchards in full bloom and farmers' fields filled with bright green shoots and flowering crops.

I was scheduled to pick up David and the developer in Manhattan on that May morning, and since I had two small boys, as well as an energetic golden retriever, the car was full of dog hair and lollipop wrappers and other assorted detritus; it was not clean enough for chauffeuring an important prospective client around town, especially a sophisticated businesswoman. So I stopped at a car wash that would clean and detail the inside of my dark blue Nissan Pathfinder. Apparently I had just gotten out of my car when a car wash attendant backed a large Ford SUV out of the detailing shop and, speeding in reverse without looking behind him, ran me down. I had my back to the speeding car, and never heard it coming over the din of the car wash. As one of the eyewitnesses later told the police, I "never had a chance."

I say "apparently I had just gotten out of my car" because I have no memory of that day, or the days afterward, or, strangely enough, of the weeks leading up to the accident. I hit my head violently on the pavement, fracturing my skull and losing consciousness. Cerebrospinal fluid oozed from a crack in my skull behind my left ear. I was taken by ambulance to a local hospital, where they did an MRI and realized my injuries were too severe for them to treat. Depending on who was reading the films, the diagnosis was either a subdural hematoma or a subarachnoid hemorrhage, or both, on the left side of my brain. I was rushed to Stony Brook University Medical Center, which had a world-famous neurological trauma unit. Regardless of what the MRI diagnosis was, there was no doubt I was in a light coma and had bleeding and swelling in my brain. The Stony Brook doctors diagnosed what the medical profession calls a Traumatic Brain Injury, or TBI. In the pre-political correctness days, it would have been called simply brain damage, or being kicked in the head by a horse.

David was left standing in Manhattan with the developer, looking at his watch, assuring her that I was usually very punctual. He called my cell phone numerous times and kept getting voice mail. When I didn't call back he finally started the tour of Brooklyn without me. Later that day he called Belinda to see if she knew where I was.

"He got run over by a car in a car wash and he's in the hospital," she told him, laughing. "He's okay. He's got a concussion or something. Can you believe how stupid he is? Only he could do something like that. What an idiot!"

Months later, when I was finally well enough to ask questions about what had happened that day, David described this conversation to me; he was still marveling at her reaction. "She was just laughing the whole time, I couldn't believe it," he said.

Certainly my wife's reaction was extreme, her perceptions colored by our impending divorce, but many TBI patients have similar problems with family: you look fine, you're talking, you appear alert. So you got a bump on the head? So what? There's nothing the matter with you; why can't you just get on with life? So you've got a headache? So what? We all get headaches. Snap out of it!

My wife's response to the accident would just be the beginning of many such reactions from people who didn't understand the magnitude of what had happened to my brain.

Medically I was lucky; the bleeding stopped, the swelling receded and surgery was avoided. While serious, it appeared that my injuries would not be life-threatening. Belinda brought Chas and Niall to the hospital, where these two small boys found their father trussed up with tubes and monitors and his head resting on a blood-soaked pillow. It was scary for them to see their father this way, especially since they had recently seen their grandmother lying in a hospital bed, unconscious from a head injury, unable to speak or walk. Fortunately I appeared well enough to the casual observer. I was talking and appeared alert.

Appearances were, however, deceiving. I was ranked in the middle of the Glascow Coma Scale, a measure of consciousness. Like most people, I assumed from watching medical dramas on television that a person was either in a coma—lying in a hospital bed, eyes closed, unaware—or out of a coma: awake, talking, moving. But there is a whole range of in-between states in which the patient is still considered to be "in a coma." On a scale of one to fifteen, the deep, unresponsive comatose state is a three on the Glasgow Coma Scale and the fully awake, conscious state is a fifteen. I was somewhere in the middle.

David called my sister Debbie in Buffalo to tell her what had happened, and her first thought was, "Oh God, this can't be happening again. First Mom, and now Lee!?" Debbie called the hospital and a sympathetic nurse told her to get down here, now, after seeing the way Belinda treated me. Debbie left her husband and children, got on a plane and rushed down to help care for her injured brother.

When David came to visit the day after the accident, I was lying awake in bed. Knowing how much I liked to read, he had brought with him several magazines. He told me later that as he entered the intensive care unit, he was amazed and angry that the hospital had put me in a bed with old, dirty sheets. He couldn't believe how dirty the pillowcase was behind my head. It was only upon coming closer that he realized that the "stains" were really blood and fluid that still oozed from my skull. David is a tall, lanky, bespectacled, preternaturally calm person. For him to say he was shocked is a momentous thing.

In the years since the accident, what happened next has become one of his favorite stories, and he never tires of telling it.

The story starts with me beckoning him over to the bed with my finger. "Come here, I have to tell you something," I say in a conspiratorial whisper.

He bends his ear closer.

"You have to get me out of here," I whisper, barely audible.

"Why?"

"I met my mother out in the bay last night, and we unloaded a shipment of guns from her boat onto mine."

David and I had been friends since childhood; we had grown up down the street from each other in a suburb of Buffalo and our parents had been good friends. Our grandparents had been good friends. He knew my mother well; Ann Carlson was a respectable, solid Midwesterner; she did not run guns. He also knew about her accident and that there was no way she had been out in the bay on a boat. If my mother had been able, she would have been in the hospital by my side.

"Oh, I see, and what are you doing with the guns?"

"We're going to sell them in a yard sale on Sunday."

"Oh."

The image of my mother as a gunrunning moll coming in under cover of darkness on a tramp steamer with boxes full of AK-47s brought a chuckle to David's lips, as did the image of my mother and me selling them off tables in my driveway on a sunny spring Saturday morning. I have no idea where this outlandish fantasy came from, but it showed how out of it I really was. I was completely serious about the whole gunrunning story and at this point David realized that although I appeared fine, there were some very real problems with my cognitive functioning. He told Debbie that instead of magazines he could have just brought me a paragraph; since I couldn't remember anything I could just read the same paragraph over and over again.

There were other strange and weirdly comic moments in those first few days. The doctors asked me their standard neurological questions to determine my cognitive functioning. They asked me questions such as where I worked, was I married, where did my wife work? I told them she worked for Ralph Lauren, which had been true at one point in our lives, but she had not worked there for eight years. Another standard question asked of all patients in neurological intensive care is "Who is the president of the United States?"

"George Bush," I correctly answered. What the doctors didn't realize is that I was thinking of George Bush Sr., who had been president nine years before, at the same time my wife had worked at Ralph Lauren, and not the current president, George W. Bush. You'd think that smart, educated doctors would come up with a better question.

Another odd occurrence was that the car right behind mine, the primary witness to the accident, turned out to be my wife's divorce lawyer. He had never met me or seen me, so didn't know who I was until the police pulled my wallet from my pants as I lay unconscious, read the name off the license and asked if anyone knew me.

"Oh my God," my wife's lawyer said, "if I wasn't already suing him I'd be following the ambulance to the hospital to get him as a client!"

You can't make this stuff up.

When David heard that my wife's lawyer had been first on the scene, he jokingly asked if I had seen an envelope stuffed with cash change hands between the lawyer and the car wash attendant. This was, after all, Long Island, land of Amy Fisher, the Long Island Lolita who shot her lover Joey Buttafuoco's wife. It was also the general locale of the famous Woodward murder case where a wealthy socialite shot her husband, which was the basis for the book "The Two Mrs. Grenvilles," and the scene of the famous "Murder in the Hamptons" where multimillionaire financier Ted Ammon was killed by a electrician who turned out to be his wife's lover. Stranger things had happened on Long Island than envelopes of cash changing hands in car washes. I was not a multimillionaire and my wife had no money to bribe car wash attendants, so of course my sister, David and I knew this was just a stupid accident, but his joking helped ease the tension of my lying in an intensive care unit with a fractured skull and a fractured home life.

Even though that lawyer didn't follow me to the hospital, another lawyer showed up in those first few days. Apparently he had been sent by my own divorce lawyer. He was a seemingly decent person, but he was also an ambulance chaser. It was surreal to have a total stranger in a suit sitting by my bedside pretending to care about my well-being, when he was really there for the money. The last thing I needed at the moment was to worry about lawsuits, money, etc. I needed to concentrate on my health. The next day when Belinda brought our boys to the hospital, the boys were chanting, "We're going to own a car wash, we're going to own a car wash," as my sister just rolled her eyes, indicating to me that she had nothing to do with where they were getting their view of what was important.

In the days that followed the accident my wife's behavior continued to be so lacking in compassion and understanding that the doctors told my sister they would not release me until they knew I was going somewhere where I would be properly cared for, far away from my wife, who would be "poison" to my recovery. So when I was discharged from Stony Brook after five days in the intensive care unit, my sister helped me into a wheelchair, then into a waiting hired black car with driver, then wheeled me onto a plane and flew with me to Ft. Myers, Florida, where she handed me off to my father, who could care for me and drive me to various doctors, specialists and therapists every day: cognitive therapists, physical therapists, neurologists, neuropsychologists, vestibular therapists, occupational therapists, psychologists and others.

Unfortunately my father knew all about traumatic brain injuries from my mother's accident, which had been more serious than mine. On Friday evening, September 28, 2001, eight months before my accident, my mother had fallen down a flight of basement stairs while looking for the bathroom at a dinner party in an unfamiliar house. She had opened a door, stepped into the darkened space and tumbled down the steps, landing on her head on the concrete floor. She was rushed unconscious by ambulance to the hospital, where surgeons were forced to remove the part of her brain that had been critically damaged. She was in a deep coma—the dramatic television kind—for weeks.

When my mother regained consciousness after a month she was severely disabled, confined to a wheelchair, unable to walk, talk, feed herself, go to the bathroom by herself, bathe herself or perform the thousands of other small daily domestic tasks we all take for granted. I spent the months after her accident helping my father and sisters with my mother's care, traveling back and forth to Buffalo. After several months of therapy in a nursing home, my mother was mobile enough to travel, and I helped my father wheel my mother onto a commercial jetliner for the flight down to their winter home in Naples, Florida. The house was a single-story, two-bedroom old-style Florida bungalow, with a white pea gravel driveway, carport and a combination living room/dining room. My father slept alone in the master bedroom while the second bedroom became a hospice room for my mother, where round-the-clock caregivers bathed her, dressed her and watched over her while she slept. The house also had a small porch where my mother could sit outside in her wheelchair, looking at the water in the small canal behind the house, watching birds flit from orange tree to avocado tree to palm tree while caregivers spoon fed her and wiped spittle from her mouth.

Just when our family was recovering from the shock of what had happened to this vibrant matriarch, my accident occurred, and my father suddenly had the burden of being the caregiver not only for his wife of forty-six years but also for his forty-four-year-old son—both with traumatic brain injuries.

In the next few months my wife abandoned me, sold our house to her boyfriend, took our two sons and moved to Wisconsin, leaving me with no money, no health insurance and no home—no place to sleep other than my parents' living room couch. (It sounds like a bad joke, but it's all true.) My mother continued to deteriorate until her body finally gave out and she mercifully died in her sleep, leaving my father and me both grieving and grateful for her death. One of my most vivid memories is of the parallel tracks left in the white pea gravel by the coroner's gurney, and my father in the driveway with a rake, smoothing out the gravel, erasing the evidence of her long passing.

When my doctors finally released me from rehabilitative therapy in Naples after a year, I moved back to Southold, New York, on Long Island's North Fork, one town over from my previous home, and I spent the next five years trying to work my way back to some sort of normal life: renting and furnishing a house so I could have a home for my children when they visited; trying to find work and get back to writing; trying to find a woman who would accept me as I was and be supportive and loving not only to me but to my children.

In the midst of trying to regain some sense of normalcy, my brother-in-law Kevin, who was married to my other sister, Kristan, and who was also a good friend, was diagnosed with throat cancer at age forty-seven. He was a vibrant, intelligent person, a lawyer who had forgone entering private practice to instead help the poor and underprivileged. While many lawyers become public defenders for a few years after law school and move on, he had stayed with the public defender career path, choosing public service over private financial gain. He took a personal interest in helping his clients, acting like a social worker as much as a lawyer. Why had cancer targeted him?

I returned to Buffalo to help Kristan, who had two young children, while she went to the hospital every day. I would take the kids to Buffalo Bisons baseball games (Buffalo's minor league team), or play with the kids in the backyard—basketball, street hockey—or help Elizabeth, who was only six, throw the ball for my golden retriever Henry, trying to do whatever I could to take their minds off a dying father who looked like a skeleton, his emaciated body and hollow eyes staring out like a ghost from his hospital bed in the terminal patient ward at Roswell Park Cancer Institute.

His dying was prolonged and painful, leaving all of us emotionally drained and leaving my sister a widow with two young children.

Then only a few months after Kevin's death my Aunt Leslie died of ovarian cancer at age fifty-nine. She had been a successful chef in New York City, the first woman ever hired at the Waldorf Astoria, a personal favorite of James Beard and a well-known innovator and food personality who had been featured on television and had written several successful cookbooks. I had often visited my aunt and Uncle Phil's home in Bronxville with my boys, laughing around the dining room table as we shared family stories and home-cooked meals. How could cancer have taken her too?

The cost of my mother's care nearly bankrupted my father, and my accident did bankrupt me. All the dying and illness and loss in our family left me physically, emotionally, psychologically and financially drained. It was a difficult time.

Forgetfulness of Things Present

~

WHEN I RETURNED TO SOUTHOLD one of the most severe lingering problems was memory loss. I would forget people's names, forget the way to a friend's house, even though I'd been there hundreds of times. I'd leave food burning on the stove, or stand in my living room with car keys in hand, confused and forgetful about where I was going or what I was doing next. But the biggest problem was work. I tried to get back to work as a writer, but I would write a marketing brochure for a client and by the time the client had reviewed the copy days later and given comments for revisions, I would have totally forgotten what I had written. I would sit and stare at the words, wondering where they had come from. Had I written them? I had no idea, no recollection at all.

The accident had changed my ability to be who I once was. One of my best friends who owned a design firm and who had given me freelance copywriting work before the accident was looking to grow his business and hired me full time. He fired me after a few weeks when it became apparent I could not do the work. I had never been fired from a job in my life. It was devastating to me and not an easy thing for him.

TBI is a huge and little-understood problem in the U.S. and can have profound effects on people's lives. According to the Brain Injury

Association of America, 1.4 million people sustain a traumatic brain injury in the United States every year, of which 50,000 die, 235,000 are hospitalized and 1.1 million are treated and released from an emergency room. The number of people who sustain a brain injury but receive no care is unknown. To help put that number in perspective, the American Cancer Society estimates that in 2009 there will be 1.5 million new cancer cases, roughly the same number as the 1.4 million new TBI cases. Cancer kills many more people—approximately half a million a year— than TBI, which has annual death rates similar to motor vehicle crashes (although some TBI deaths are also motor vehicle deaths). The lower death rates for TBI mean there are many more TBI survivors living with ongoing disabilities. With cancer you can be "cured" or at least in remission. Usually that is not the case with TBI, where the resulting disabilities can cause lifelong impairments.

The leading causes of TBI are falls (twenty-eight percent), motor vehicle-traffic crashes (twenty percent), struck by/against events (nineteen percent) and assaults (eleven percent). Blasts are a leading cause of TBI for military personnel in war zones. TBI has been more in the news due to the wars in Iraq and Afghanistan, as well as the many athletes who are suffering head injuries. Males are about 1.5 times as likely as females to sustain a TBI. The two age groups at highest risk for TBI are children aged zero to four and teenagers aged fifteen to nineteen. African Americans have the highest death rate from TBI.

Direct medical costs and indirect costs such as lost productivity totaled an estimated $60 billion in the United States in 2000. The Centers for Disease Control and Prevention estimates that at least 5.3 million Americans currently have a long-term or lifelong need for help to perform activities of daily living as a result of TBI. According to one study, about forty percent of those hospitalized with TBI had at least one unmet need for services one year after their injury. The most frequent unmet needs were improving memory and problem solving, managing stress and emotional upsets, controlling one's temper and improving one's job skills. TBI can cause a wide range of functional changes affecting thinking, language, learning, emotions, behavior and/or sensation. It can also cause epilepsy and increase the risk for conditions such as Alzheimer's disease, Parkinson's disease and other brain disorders that become more prevalent with age.

As might be expected Traumatic Brain Injury is not the sole source of sudden-onset brain damage and brain-damage-related disabilities. Stroke can have similar debilitating effects, as can Alzheimer's, repeated concussions (Chronic Traumatic Encephalopathy), brain tumors and other brain-related diseases.

In many cases TBI survivors live in a kind of Through-the-Looking-Glass world where normalcy is a relative concept, and since their disabilities are not readily observable to the untrained eye, friends, relatives and acquaintances don't understand why the TBI survivor is so forgetful, or can't be more organized, or has problems with time, or hearing in a crowded restaurant or a myriad of other subtle problems. I was standing with a group of people at a party several years after my accident, people I didn't know well and who didn't know I was a TBI survivor, and they were talking about another person who didn't remember people's names and how rude he was because of this. I wondered what other people must think of me, since I often couldn't remember people's names; at that very moment I had forgotten the names of the people I was standing with. I didn't want to be judged, to be seen as rude or uncaring; all I wanted to do was leave the conversation and slink off into a corner.

Several years later I was sitting at the bar at Claudio's Restaurant with Bob, a strapping young ex-marine who suffered a Traumatic Brain Injury when his vehicle was hit by a bomb blast in Iraq. Even though we're a generation apart, there was a common bond between two people who understood what it is like to have survived a Traumatic Brain Injury. That, and we were both sailors with a common love of the sea. Claudio's is at the foot of the old pier in Greenport, the next town over from Southold, and claims to be the "oldest same family owned restaurant in the United States," having opened its doors in 1870. The long classic wooden bar, with its brass cash register, high ceiling, old mirrors and slowly turning ceiling fans was the perfect place to drink a beer or a ginger ale, eat some chicken wings and watch a football game. There is even a trap door behind the bar where bootleggers hoisted cases of booze up from boats underneath the wharf during Prohibition. My mother would have felt right at home smuggling her guns here.

"You know, I always feel like I'm being judged by others who don't know what happened to me," Bob said.

"I know exactly what you mean," I said. "It's as if the Queen of Hearts is constantly passing judgment, yelling 'off with their heads!'"

We clinked glasses, and drank a toast to being somewhere we could just eat, drink, watch football and not be judged.

There was one group, however, that didn't seem to be judging me unfairly. The doctors and therapists understood. They were judging me by TBI standards, not by conventional "normal" standards. My doctors kept encouraging me to write a memoir of my experiences. Writing would be therapeutic, it would help me heal. It was the next logical extension to John Cheever's famous dictum, "I write to make sense of my life." But I would not be writing to make sense of my life, I would be writing to save my life. I would be writing to heal a battered brain, a wounded psyche, a mind and soul laid low by physical infirmity and psychic loss. Writing as therapy. Writing as catharsis. Writing as a healing art. But writing about my journey would also be something I could give back to the community, helping raise awareness of this illness in our society, as well as helping patients, family and caregivers to deal with the aftereffects and challenges of TBI. As someone who was a TBI survivor and had been a TBI caregiver, I had a unique perspective on how TBI affects both patients and family. And since I was a professional writer and journalist, I would be able to put it all together in a way that could truly communicate the magnitude of the problem. I was one of the lucky ones: I had not only survived, but through hard work and luck I had regained most of my faculties and would be able to write intelligibly on the subject of TBI. My doctors believed in me, and that in itself was incredibly healing.

There were several problems, however. First, the memory issues that were preventing me from writing simple short marketing brochures made it impossible to write a full-length book, no matter how good my note taking and file keeping. Second, the subject was so emotional that just sitting down to write about it would exacerbate my post-traumatic-brain-injury disorder, setting my heart racing, my palms sweating, my head pounding. The stress would intensify my memory problems, and I would sit at my desk, staring at the computer screen, stuck as I tried to remember a simple word. Sometimes I would burst into tears at this inability to perform so simple a task.

So I looked for a different way to write, a different way to tell the story.

Zengine of Ingenuity

~

I HAD BEEN A STUDENT OF Zen Buddhism prior to the accident. My spiritual path had begun twenty-five years before, when I had stumbled across a wonderful book, "The Snow Leopard," by Peter Matthiessen, which had just won the National Book Award. The book chronicled Matthiessen's search for meaning through Zen and Tibetan Buddhism after his wife's death from cancer, culminating in a trip to the Himalayas where he searched for the elusive snow leopard, as well as the elusive wisdom embodied by reclusive Buddhist monks at the remote and mysterious Crystal Mountain monastery. Reading that book led to taking a comparative religion course, where my professor, Dr. Joel Smith of Skidmore College's Philosophy & Religion Department, not only taught us in the classroom about the world's great religions, but took us to a Buddhist monastery in the Catskills for an optional weekend retreat. As much as those influences had intrigued me, in my adult life I had been a spiritual dabbler; family, children, work and a wife who didn't approve had all been obstacles to my becoming a more serious student.

The crisis in my marriage before the accident had turned me into someone I barely recognized. I would respond to my wife's taunts by becoming angry and yelling back at her. I would be short and cross with the kids. This was not the calm, peaceful, loving person I wanted to be. I was an agitated, emotional mess. I had reached a turning point in my life that caused a newfound search for meaning, for happiness: Who was I? Who did I want to be? From my previous exposure to Zen Buddhism I thought that finding a meditation group might help calm my emotions. I sought out a meditation group near my home and was amazed and delighted to find that Peter Matthiessen had a small country zendo, or meditation center, about an hour from where I lived, which he called The Ocean Zendo. In the years since he had written "The Snow Leopard" he had become even more immersed in Zen and had become a Zen roshi, or master priest. I sent him a letter, and received a gentle and wonderful invitation to join his sangha, or Zen congregation. So I began to make the hour-long drive once or twice a week to the zendo, where I would meditate, join discussion groups on Zen Buddhist philosophy, and receive regular instruction from several of the teachers. At the same time I set up a small altar with black meditation cushions in a corner of my home office, and I would get up early each morning, before the children or my wife were awake and meditate for a half hour.

All of this had a steady hand in helping me deal with the crises in my life: a failing marriage, a failing business, a mother's crippling accident. I was in the midst of this new path when my own accident occurred. Would Zen and meditation also help me deal with this new crisis? How would an ancient belief system coexist with modern medicine, if at all? Would the two complement or contradict each other?

In one of my first meetings with my neurologist, Dr. Mark Rubino, in Naples after the accident, I gingerly asked him about my Zen meditation: I told him of my Zen practice, and my daily morning meditation sessions that had been a regular part of my life before the accident. Dr. Rubino was the lead physician in the pantheon of doctors and therapists who had become the focus of my daily existence. He always took time to listen and to answer my questions fully. He was also my mother's neurologist. I liked and trusted him.

"Can I still meditate?" I warily asked. "Would meditation be good or bad for my recovery?"

Even though Dr. Rubino was young—I guessed somewhere in his early thirties—and bright, insightful, energetic, wonderfully funny and seemingly open-minded, I fully expected him to be dismissive, since such irrational hocus-pocus as Zen would seem to be inconsistent with modern, rational scientific medicine. I grew up trained in a Western, rational mindset, and I fully expected a similarly trained Western doctor to pooh-pooh meditation as ancient Eastern superstition. Meditation had little in common with modern medicine and its emphasis on brain chemistry, drugs, machines—treatment modalities that had all been carefully researched and tested. I even feared that since Zen meditation emphasizes non-thinking, and since my whole problem was getting my brain to start thinking clearly again, that perhaps meditation would be detrimental to my recovery.

Instead I was surprised by his answer.

"That's great," he said, "it will be good for you. A lot of research has shown that meditation can help with anxiety, concentration, memory and other cognitive functions. Go for it."

That early encouragement to integrate ancient Zen practice into modern rehabilitative practice had a profound effect. It meant that Zen would not only help my brain heal, but would continue to be a vital part of my life, to grow and flower in ways that I would never have thought possible and ultimately to become part of how I would write the book that Dr. Rubino had been encouraging me to write.

Ever since I discovered Zen in college I had been fascinated by the beautiful brevity of its art forms, from the mysterious energy of the calligraphic brushstroke in an *ensō*—the circle of enlightenment—to the freshness of a Japanese haiku, which opens slowly in the mind like a flower opening to the morning dew. So after my accident, as I searched for a way to tell my tale in a way that would be creative, beautiful, enlightening and helpful to others, I began to envision a way to write that was in the footsteps of this great and ancient tradition, a way to tell a story that owed much to the sensibilities of venerable Japanese poets such as Matsuo Basho or more modern poets such as Soen Nakagawa Roshi, one of the first Japanese Zen teachers to come to the United States. Basho's "Narrow Road to the Interior" is one of the best-loved books of Japanese literature and tells the story of a five-month, 1,233 mile journey Basho undertook on foot as a wandering poet, accompanied by his friend Kawai Sora. This thin, spare book is written as a travelogue, combining both prose and poetry into a single, cohesive whole.

Soen Roshi did not write a book, per se, but the book "Endless Vow: The Zen Path of Soen Nakagawa" is a collection of his poetry, letters and calligraphy. It is travelogue of sorts in both poetry and prose, although it covers much more ground, from his youth in Japan to his voyage to America to his role in founding Dai Bosatsu Zendo, the first Japanese Zen monastery in the United States in New York's Catskill Mountains. I felt a certain kindred spirit with Soen Roshi, not only from his writings, but because he himself suffered a Traumatic Brain Injury in his mid-fifties when he fell from a tree in Japan.

Exactly what happened to Soen Roshi is unclear, but according to the stories, he was missing for several days at the monastery. This in itself was not unusual, as he was known to be a bit eccentric and would often disappear for long stretches of time. In monasteries, someone going off alone into a quiet corner for meditation and solitude is the norm. But after he failed to show up for several meals and services, the other monks went searching for him and found him lying unconscious beneath a large tree, supposedly with a sharp piece of bamboo piercing his skull. The stories say that he had been unconscious for three days. The words Traumatic Brain Injury are never used in these accounts, but in 1967 TBI was little understood. It was assumed that Soen Roshi had fallen out of the tree, although what he was doing up in its branches nobody knew for certain. He could have been meditating, sitting in a crook of the tree, or he could have just climbed up to enjoy a better view. That's the kind of person he was.

In later years Soen became a hard drinker, likely an alcoholic, and eventually drowned in his own bathtub, drunk. His drinking was said to be an attempt to deaden the constant pain he felt as a result of the brain injury, however Matthiessen Roshi has wondered how true this story is since he spent much time with Soen Roshi and never saw a scar on Soen's shaved head. Matthiessen Roshi has wondered whether the story might be an apologia for Soen Roshi's hard drinking, since sake is an integral part of Japanese culture, even among spiritual leaders. Even if the bamboo stake is an embellishment, I have no doubt about the brain injury part of the story. The narrative is too detailed to be fabricated out of whole cloth. And I understand only too well the pain, both physical and mental, that can result from a Traumatic Brain Injury. Darkness, depression and despair are some of the very real symptoms that many people who suffer a Traumatic Brain Injury experience, symptoms that stay with them for the rest of their lives. Quite a few TBI sufferers have been known to succumb to depression and take their own lives. This is one more possibility I have to guard against, one more outcome I shall always worry about. If a devoted, enlightened Zen monk could not escape the ravages of depression brought on by a Traumatic Brain Injury, what hope do I have?

And yet I refused to sink into despair. Partly out of kinship with forefathers like Basho and Soen Roshi, I began writing my own short poetry, something that could focus on the beauty of life. But partly because my cognitive functioning was so diminished, so childlike, all I could write were very short, very focused little compositions, often no more than a few words, even shorter than a haiku. My interest in short poetry had already existed before the accident, but now the allure of short verse took on a new urgency. These diminutive poems were something I could still write—and remember. Here was a way of doing something I loved—playing with words—that was still within the grasp of my flawed memory. Here was something I could throw myself into to help alleviate the pain of losing my children, my mother, my home, my own sense of self. Here was something that might stave off future pain, keeping me from sinking beneath the waves of a bathtub in my later years. Writing these poems was a form of therapy, a joyful celebration of what was possible.

To help me remember what I had been thinking when I wrote these short poems, I would write notes to go with them—reflections on life, my life, the human condition, brain injury—and a book-length narrative began to take shape, an odyssey comprised of both poetry and prose, a travelogue recounting my own journey from the hellish depths of despair and hopelessness to the Olympian heights of contentment and peace. It was a story more about healing than about accidents; a story where one could easily substitute other personal hurdles for the words TBI: cancer, divorce, childhood abuse, depression or a thousand other afflictions; a story that would help others searching for meaning in the face of great personal difficulties.

At first, the short poems were a necessary result of my brain injury, but over time, as I healed, I came to see their simplicity as a gift, an art form unto themselves, and I continued to write them. I could have said goodbye to them as vestiges of my brain damage, like therapists to be left behind once my cognitive functioning had improved, but they seemed to have value beyond just a record of my recovery. They were the world's shortest poems, but they carried a universe of meaning.

In a strange way my disability made me much more aware of the nuance and power of each individual syllable and punctuation mark. I did not need umpteen words to tell a story. I developed a sixth sense for the emotional power of simple word relationships and the coupling between words and the human heart that I had only vaguely glimpsed before my accident. I felt like someone who has lost the use of their legs but finds new strength in their arms for, say, rock climbing. I talked to Dr. Rubino about how I felt and he said, "You've only injured certain parts of your brain, and other parts will now become stronger to compensate. You're like the Stevie Wonder of writers."

Nirvana or Bust

~

THE STORY IS TITLED "PASSAGE TO NIRVANA," because, like many survivors of near-death experiences, I was given a newfound appreciation for the joy of being alive, heightened by my Zen meditation and my brain's compensating for the loss of other faculties. Who knows, maybe the appreciation was even heightened because I had one of those out-of-body, life-after-death experiences, where one sees the incredible bright light and hears angels singing. But since I can't remember anything about the accident I'll never know. Just my luck.

In any event thanks to the accident I became acutely aware of the beauty of the world we live in, the nirvana that is there if only we choose to see it. This revelation did not happen overnight. My Aunt Leslie and I were in her backyard garden one summer day about a year before she died. She was busy digging and pruning and brushing a strand of hair out of her eyes, her hands covered with dirt. Her small backyard was a veritable Garden of Eden, overflowing with flowers and tall grasses and herbs and vegetables.

"You know what's weird?" I said. "Even with everything that has happened I'm starting to feel like I'm incredibly blessed."

My boys were helping my Uncle Phil set the backyard table for lunch; Niall was sticking potato chips out through the holes in his smile where he'd recently lost some baby teeth, crossing his eyes and making goofy faces while Phil put hot dogs and ketchup on the table—a simple, delicious backyard American summer boyhood meal with one of the greatest chefs in America.

"Even with Mom's death and my accident and my continuing cognition problems and everything I've lost, I often feel joy at just being alive. Not all the time; there are plenty of days when I still feel depressed and miserable, especially when the boys leave, but I still have glimpses of real happiness."

My aunt didn't know she was dying then; that would come months later. At this moment she knew she had beaten the cancer once, and probably thought she would do so again, even though it had returned. She nipped some dead flower heads with her fingers and looked at me with a beatific smile.

"Yes," she said, "the epiphany happens slowly."

So "Passage to Nirvana" is written as a kind of slow travelogue, a leisurely journey of a thousand steps whose waypoints are as much psychological as they are physical; a journey with traveling companions: my dogs, my children, my new partner Meg, my Zen teachers; an epiphanic journey of heart, spirit and mind.

There is also a double entendre in the title. While I had been working on the book for more than five years after my accident, it really came together in its final form after spending a year living on a sailboat that Meg and I had made our new home. Meg and I had first met several years before my accident when I had taken my boys to a daytime Halloween party at a friend's house. There were probably a hundred children running around outside on the lawn, all in costumes, while costume-clad adults supervised bobbing for apples or candy hunts, or popped out of coffins in the haunted basement. There was a full-sized Indian tepee on the lawn, with an Indian maiden fortune-teller inside, a clutch of enthralled children sitting around her. The fortune-teller was a beautiful blonde in a buckskin dress, with creamy skin, painted face and a feather headdress. That was Meg. She was married, and so was I, but I couldn't help noticing her radiance, and how wonderful she was with the kids and how they responded to her.

Now it was five years later and we were both divorced. We'd reconnected and had been dating for a year and a half. We were serious about each other. She seemed to have an adventurous spirit; after all she was an Indian maiden. Although she hadn't grown up around boats, she loved the water. I had taken her sailing on a little seventeen-foot used sailboat I had bought when I moved back to Southold after my accident. The boat was a way of soothing my brain, of doing something I loved with my kids. That fall, after they left, Meg and Henry and I had sailed to a small local island, walked a long curving sand spit, reveled in the beauty of the green and yellow seaweed waving in the shallow water at low tide, of the orange and yellow jingle shells scattered on the sand.

So I had an idea. I had grown up around boats, mostly sailboats, and had worked as a professional captain on and off since my teens. Both my mother and brother-in-law were avid sailors who had dreamed of living on a boat and sailing to far-off lands, but both died without realizing their dreams. So partly as an homage to their indomitable spirit, partly because I knew the positive life lessons boats can impart to children and families, partly because I believed the tranquility of sea and sky would have a salutary effect on my recovery (and Meg's recovery from her own divorce), and partly because I didn't want to die one day not having realized my own dreams, I said to Meg, "Life is too fleeting, too fragile; what are we waiting for? Let's buy a boat and sail away."

This idea may have been further evidence that my brain wasn't thinking clearly, but she didn't see it that way, so with almost no money and no clearly defined path for what would happen next, we took the plunge. We bought a twenty-five-year-old, sixty-foot, dark-blue-hulled sailing ketch big enough to hold my two children, Meg's two children and our two dogs. My personal mantra was "Proceed as way opens," a sagacious saying from the Quakers. So we proceeded. The boat's name? We christened her "Nirvana."

I had a photography teacher in high school who referred to photographs that came out much better than expected as "happy accidents." I feel much the same way about the tragedies in my life: they turned out much differently, much better than I would have expected. It may seem incongruous to call being hit by a car and suffering a Traumatic Brain Injury a "happy accident," but despite enormous loss, I do feel blessed. Without the accident there would have been no heightened awareness of the splendor of existence, no new appreciation for the power of simple words, no slow epiphany, no passage to nirvana.

Po-etic Past & Present

~

I LIKE TO THINK OF THE short poems in Book II as a new genre of poetry, and as such they deserve their own name, like haiku, or sonnet or *ruba'i*. I call these short poems "po." A single one is a po, and the plural form is also po, in keeping with the simplicity of the form. A book of these little gems can be called a Book of Po.

Po is a shortened form of the word poem. There are many other meanings for po. There is a river in Northern Italy named Po, as well as a river in Virginia. Po is the symbol for the chemical element Polonium (element number 84, discovered by Marie Curie and named for her native country, Poland). In Korean, po can mean a type of traditional overcoat or a kind of meat or fish jerky. For a little pop culture fun, Po is the name of one of the Teletubbies (the red one), as well as the hero of the film "Kung Fu Panda." (My son Niall, now twelve, gave me a high five for knowing that allusion.) Po can be an abbreviation for post office, petty officer, purchase order or put out (a baseball term). My two favorites are po's relationship to po' boy, a mouthwatering oyster sandwich from New Orleans, and Li Po, the ancient Chinese poet.

My friend Neil O'Keefe, who is an acupuncturist and t'ai chi teacher, and who helped us rebuild Nirvana, pointed out another meaning of po. In ancient China the soul was believed to be divided into two parts, *hun* and *p'o,* which were associated with yang and yin. The *hun* was the higher, spiritual soul associated with the rational mind and also with yang energy, while the *p'o* was the more earthly aspect of a person correlated with yin. Over the centuries this belief has morphed many times. In some views these two parts of the soul were believed to split after death, with the spiritual soul ascending to heaven and the base *p'o* descending to the underworld. In another view the *p'o* was created at birth and extinguished at death, while the *hun* lived on. What persisted is the belief that these two forces balance each other in the living human. I appreciate this view of the world, and while I aspire to develop and nurture the spiritual side of my soul, I am well aware that I live in the everyday, mortal world. So I am pleased to know that at one level these little poems are associated with our everyday, down-to-earth life.

I don't think these meanings would mind being joined by another, literary meaning, and I doubt these meanings are in general use, except among residents who live along the River Po, or among chemists or fans of costumed children's characters. So perhaps these groups will let lovers of words have our own little meaning for the word po.

There are seventy-three po in "Passage to Nirvana." Like most collections of creative works, some are more successful than others. Not every reader will agree on which po are best, which the worst. As with most things in life, we all have our own personal preferences. As the product of a childlike, cognitively impaired brain the po are like a group of unruly children: some will be charming, some annoying, some quiet and demure, some loud and boisterous. Some will set your teeth on edge, while with some you will, hopefully, go "ahh..."

Some po may run wild in your brain, unwilling to leave, like an annoying jingle, while others are more subtle, sneaking up from behind when you least expect it, welling up into your brain days later. Their simplicity can be deceptive; they could be viewed as a cheap parlor trick, an overly clever way of playing word games, but that would be what Buddhists call "wrong understanding." If you are willing to search for something more, to climb higher in the tree, you may get glimpses—or even full panoramas—of the expanding universe behind the words.

There is more about po's rules, history and development in Part III, "Bricolage." But now it is time to get to the heart of the story.

THE BOOK OF PO

With words as with sunbeams,
the more they are condensed,
the deeper they burn.

– Robert Southey,
British Poet, 1774–1843

WATER

Nirvana

Our boat
floats.

~

HERE IS SO MUCH HERE. There is the concrete reality of the joy Meg and I felt seeing Nirvana, our new home, being slowly lowered into St. Martin's Simpson Bay Lagoon after six weeks of sweaty work in a steamy, mosquito-infested boatyard, and having her actually float. Nirvana had been sitting in a sandy hole for two years in a corner of the boatyard when we found her, slowly rotting in the fierce Caribbean sun. She was like a nautical Humpty Dumpty, having fallen from her watery perch, and now she sat cracked and broken on the hard land. But we were determined to disprove the old nursery rhyme and put her back together again. We had fixed cracks in the hull, replaced chainplates (the metal tangs that hold the stays that hold up the mast), installed new instruments and done a thousand other small and not-so-small repairs, but most importantly we had replaced all the thru-hull fittings, seacocks, hoses, the cutlass bearing, the propeller shaft, depth sounder transponder—basically everything below the waterline—and we were keeping our fingers crossed that nothing would leak. Meg smashed the traditional bottle of champagne against the bow, and as the hoist lowered Nirvana and she settled into the water we threw ourselves below, pulling up floorboards, listening for the sound of running water, looking for any telltale signs of the ocean entering the hull. Mercifully we heard nothing. Everything held.

Then there is the abstract reality, the realization that true nirvana is just enjoying being alive, a state of peace and bliss unencumbered by day-to-day worries and cares. A state in which our personal boat—our body, life and soul—floats freely.

I was exhausted from all the work in the boatyard, and there were times when my damaged brain had seemingly shut down, and I would be confused and forgetful, but not as much as I had feared, and not so much that other people would really notice anything other than a mild spaciness. We were behind schedule, which is not unusual in a project like this, but I'm sure the delay also had something to do with my not being nearly as productive as I had been before my accident.

The boat was named Prima Donna when we found her. She had been owned by a German couple—a former German naval officer and his younger wife—and they had lived on board while plying the charter trade in the islands. The captain had died unexpectedly of a heart attack, and his wife had walked away from the boat, putting her up on the hard in the boatyard and returning to Germany.

We had planned to have several months to work on Prima Donna/ Nirvana before relaunching her, but it turned out the boat's ownership was tied up in German probate court. By the time we got all the legal hassles straightened out (thanks to the former captain's German sister-in-law who had been raised by missionaries in New Guinea and who spoke perfect English), several months had passed and we only had six weeks until hurricane season. Our insurance company insisted we be in the water and on our way north, out of the hurricane belt, by June 1. This left us little time, and it meant we would be forced to hire local help to do much of the work I had planned to do myself. It also meant that finding the right local help would be a challenge; most of the better yard workers were already employed on other projects and would not be available until it was too late. On May 4th I got on a plane to St. Martin, fairly certain that the boat would be ours in a day or two, but still apprehensive that something could go wrong at the last minute after all the hassles with getting the boat out of German registry. As soon as I received word from our lawyer on May 9th saying the boat was finally ours, I put the word out that we were looking for qualified mechanics, electricians, fiberglass repair people, woodworkers, painters and general help. In the next few days, as I began ripping out old hoses and rotting wood, filling black plastic garbage bags with mildewed curtains and old clothes left behind in drawers, piling it all in a growing garbage heap beside the boat, a small but steady stream of people came by, looking for work.

There was Hartmut, an ex-Stasi (East German secret police) agent who once protected Mother Theresa and who now lived on his own sailboat with his Brazilian girlfriend and a pet monkey and two small dogs, and who became our diesel mechanic. He was tall, muscular and blond, with a heavy German accent, and had the typical German love of all things mechanical. There was Ralf, a wiry, white, former crack addict South African, who had sailed all the way from Cape Town on a replica of Joshua Slocum's famous sloop Spray, and who was known around the island as a skillful electrician, but also a willful eccentric. He claimed to have been on the bow of the Spray in the middle of the Atlantic and seen a fish that was really his father, which somehow caused him to become a devotee of Shinto with its emphasis on animism, although his drug-addled version of Shinto varied greatly from the traditional Japanese variety. Ralf was always in a constant state of manic motion and would show up, work for a few hours, then disappear, then materialize hours later ... or not. Sometimes he didn't reappear until days later.

One morning after I'd been working on the boat for a few days, a huge young black man walked up to the base of the ladder.

"I hear you're looking for help," he said.

"Yes, what can you do?" I asked, wiping dirt, motor oil and sweat off my bare arms.

"Well, I've worked on some other yachts; I sailed here from Trinidad, and now I'm living on St. Martin."

He didn't offer any particular skills, such as diesel mechanic or electrician, but he looked like he could lift the entire thirty-ton boat out of the hole she rested in by himself. His name was Dominic. I had no idea exactly how I was going to use him, but I knew there would be a lot of heavy lifting.

"You're hired," I said, "when can you start?"

"I've got a few things I need to finish up, and then I can be here tomorrow morning."

The next day, and every day after that, he was the first one on the boat, often arriving before I did, bringing with him some morning coffee for both of us. It wasn't until a few weeks later that I discovered he was living in an abandoned shipping container in a far corner of the boatyard, unknown even to the boatyard owner, where he had created a small, organized home with a mattress on the floor, milk crates for storage and a rope strung across the container as a clothesline.

In another corner of the boatyard, an old wooden Portuguese fishing schooner, the Saudade, was being completely rebuilt. The new owners had hired a crew of experienced local boatwrights, mostly carpenters, and they were completely tearing the boat apart and then rebuilding her, replacing rotten ribs and hull planks and decking. Their project made ours look like child's play. It was obvious their time frame and budget was much different from ours; the boat looked like it would be at least a year away from getting back in the water. I spoke to the foreman, explained my deadline problem to him and asked if he had any extra workers he could spare for a few weeks. He said he needed his guys forty hours a week, but if they wanted to work overtime in the evenings and weekends, he'd send them my way. That afternoon a wiry black man covered with sawdust climbed up the ladder.

"I hear you lookin' for some help," he said with big, yellow-toothed grin, a cigarette dangling from the corner of his mouth, enormous silver chains dangling around his neck and a white rag wrapped around his head to keep off the sun.

"My name's 'Eyes.' Everyone calls me Eyes on account of my eye." One eye looked straight at me with the wisdom and smarts from years of surviving on the margins of society; the other stared straight ahead, not moving. Weeks later, when I had gotten to know him better, he explained that his father beat him when he was younger: "He broke my eye," he told me then, looking up from fiberglassing a hole in the deck.

But there was no time for small talk now. "We need to get her in the water before hurricane season, and we have a lot of work to do."

"How much you payin'?"

"We'll pay the going rate, but we're not rich. I'm more concerned that we get good, quick, efficient work for what we pay. We can't afford the work to go on forever like it sometimes does in the islands."

"I got a hardworking crew, we can all work for a few hours every day after we finish with Saudade."

And so the next day we gained four new workers: Eyes, Biggie, Rufus and Shaun. Eyes also lived in a corner of the boatyard, although he had a veritable palace compared to Dominic: an old sailboat he had bought for almost nothing, surrounded by weeds and other abandoned boats. Eyes did all the talking, but Rufus was really in charge. A big, taciturn man, he was a skilled carpenter and started right in repairing our teak decks, giving instructions to Biggie and Shaun, who were the junior members of the crew. He had a real home somewhere up in the hills and drove an old, small green pickup truck to work every day, bringing Biggie and Shaun with him.

In the evenings, as we were finishing our twelve-hour days, a carload of young black women would pull up, friends and girlfriends of Biggie and Shaun, and watch us work, waiting for their men to finish, clean up and go out on the town.

At some point we were joined by Rakeesh, a young Guyanese of Indian descent who did all manner of boatyard work. Along with Rakeesh came his cousin Ian, who had never worked on a boat before but made his living as a carpenter. They were invaluable. Ian would crawl into dark corners of the engine compartment, cleaning, painting and installing new sound insulation. Rakeesh and Dominic started tearing out parts of Nirvana's interior and unbolting the chainplates, which were old and cracked and needed to be replaced, from the hull.

We also had one woman in this ragtag boatyard crew besides Meg. Liana was a young Brazilian who worked as a waitress at night, but also had extensive experience working on boats in the islands. She was small, energetic and strong, and I'll never forget the sight of this pretty, stylish, exotic woman with her hair pulled up in a bun, covered with oil and grease as she cleaned out the deepest parts of the bilge with a shop vac and oily rags.

We rigged blue tarps as awnings to keep out the scorching sun, making it easier to work in the heat, and the boat was soon crawling with workers sawing, scraping, sanding, painting, fixing and generally making a huge, filthy, chaotic, exuberant mess.

Into this pandemonium parachuted first Meg, then my old high school friend Neil, the acupuncturist and t'ai chi teacher, then my Australian friend Russell and finally my old sailing friend since childhood, Peter. They were almost as varied a group of characters as the ones I found in the boatyard and had all flown down from the States to help get Nirvana in the water and sail her north. They all knew the travails of my life the past few years, and were determined to help however they could. Meg is a writer from Eastern Long Island who teaches writing to college freshman. Neil lives in Steamboat, Colorado. Russell is an award-winning winemaker and vineyard owner from Eastern Long Island and Peter owns a marine insurance agency that is one of the largest on the Great Lakes.

Peter's arrival in St. Martin was a welcome opportunity for celebration. He appeared in the boatyard one evening at quitting time, straight from the airport, with a present for one of our hardest workers; Dominic had implored us to ask one of our northern crew to find him a used guitar in a stateside pawn shop. Guitars were expensive in the islands and Dominic had left his old guitar behind in Trinidad. Cold beers were quickly procured from a nearby store, an impromptu party broke out as Peter presented Dominic with his new instrument, and any barriers between races, classes and backgrounds quickly melted away.

These northern friends had gotten more than they bargained for, since we were so far behind. They threw themselves into the maelstrom with amazing good humor and energy, especially considering they had been recruited with promises of balmy tropical breezes, cold rum drinks and sailing in the tropics, a way to soak up some sun after a long winter. They managed to blend right in with the boatyard crew and soon were also covered with dirt, grime, fiberglass dust and sticky black caulking.

In the midst of all this bonhomie there were moments of stress, anger and anxiety, especially as the days dragged on, more necessary repairs were found, the mess got worse instead of better, and it seemed as if Nirvana would never be ready in time to meet our deadline. Hartmut disappeared (he was hiding from the police after getting into a bar fight); Ralf showed up one morning drunk, singing and balancing a beer can on his head, having not yet gone home. Neil, Russell and Peter nearly mutinied, and went looking for a vaguely rumored all-night bonfire party on the far side of the island, and Dominic disappeared entirely the last few days before we launched the boat. His container was locked up tight and we assumed he had blown us off entirely, especially since he had said he needed money, had asked for an advance, and we had given it to him.

Important parts disappeared, leading to angry thoughts of theft, but then would materialize under a pile of debris. Late afternoon rain squalls would sweep the boatyard, soaking everything and shutting down production. The need for one particular size bolt or particular thickness Lexan porthole would necessitate a day-long search throughout every chandlery and hardware store on the island. There were moments, hours, days, when we thought we would never get Nirvana back in the water. And then the final clincher: on the morning we were ready to launch, a flirtatious French con woman, who had provided some finish carpenters to help with interior cabinet joinery, threatened to call the police and have Nirvana impounded, claiming that we owed her more money. We thought our own workers were going to murder her on the spot.

But in spite of (or perhaps because of) all the mayhem and madness, we managed to put Nirvana back together again, stronger, sturdier and more seaworthy, leading to that magical moment when Meg christened Nirvana's bow, the travel lift winches groaned, the slings lowered her navy-blue hull into the water, and Nirvana settled into her natural element.

Man is a social animal, and modern research into happiness tells us that the happiest people tend to be the ones with close coworkers, friends and family—the people who have the most positive social interaction. I know that my spirits—my own personal boat—were buoyed by the presence of these workers who had quickly become friends, the presence of old friends who had quickly become workers, and by the companionship of my new life partner, Meg.

And Dominic? He had been in jail after getting into his own bar fight; he felt terrible that he had not been around to help during our last days on the island. We felt terrible that we had doubted his honesty. But all was not lost. He retrieved his guitar, got a dingy ride out to Nirvana and serenaded us on our new home as she—and we—finally lay floating peacefully at anchor, bathed in the golden glow of the sunset.

The Sea

Waves,
I'm saved.

~

AFTER ALL THE CRAZINESS IN the boatyard, we sailed Nirvana north from St. Martin to Bermuda and finally to Greenport, New York, on the eastern tip of Long Island, a trip of some three weeks and 1700 miles. We left St. Martin's Marigot Bay on a beautiful, typical Caribbean day, the trade winds blowing fifteen knots out of the east, gentle swells rolling in from the Atlantic. We rounded the western tip of Anguilla and headed north, leaving the low-lying, uninhabited Dog Island to port, and the rocky coral and scrub of the Prickly Pear Cays to starboard. As we headed north into the open ocean, Nirvana blissfully charging up and down the waves for the first time since we'd owned her. I was struck by the immense difference in how I felt being in nature, on Nirvana, feeling the waves beneath her, the wind in her sails, the connection to the planet we live on, versus how I felt back in St. Martin, stuck on land in a filthy, airless man-made boatyard, sleeping in a tiny boxed-in rental house.

The difference between those two environments was sharp and stark, so that there could be no doubt that nature is man's true element, rather than a desk, or a cubicle, or a factory floor or even a living room with television noise drowning out the more subtle sounds of nature: wind, birds, and in this case, waves. I am a water person, and I know that water is not for everyone. Some people are happier on land—walking in the woods, tending their gardens or working on their lawns. Others are more at home in the desert, or the mountains. Water is my home, and I'm thankful to have discovered that truth at a young age. Some of us never do find our true homes. On this day, as we sailed into the vast open horizon, I knew I was going to be okay; I was home.

It reminded me of my first memory in the hospital. Dr. James Davis, the head of neurology, and come into my room, trailed by a retinue of interns and residents. He was a big gentle bear of a man, with a salt and pepper beard and a calming, soothing bedside manner. I must have been holding on tight to myself up until that moment, scared and anxious that I would end up like my mother, waiting for the next thing to hit me. But his reassuring words, tone and demeanor put me at ease; I felt my entire being let out a big, long sigh. I knew I would not spend the rest of my life as an invalid in a wheelchair like my mother. I knew I was going to be okay. I was going home.

Yet Dr. Davis and the other doctors could only do so much. They came into my life for only brief moments. Nature was the best therapist, the best doctor I had. She was always there, any time of the day or night, and I always knew where to find her. She always had time for me, didn't keep me cooling my heels in stuffy waiting rooms. It didn't cost a penny to go for a walk on the beach, or just down the street, looking at the trees, bushes and grasses in all their diverse colors, shapes and sizes, watching the birds sitting in the branches or hunting for food on the lawns. And now, several years after the accident, she was still with me.

All throughout that first summer living on Nirvana, I marveled at that feeling of being immersed in nature, being surrounded by water and sun and wind during the day, and by stars at night, and how different that feeling was compared to when we were in our house, furnace on in winter, air conditioning on in summer, doors and windows closed, no movement underfoot, no wind blowing my hair, feeling totally cut off and disconnected from the natural, healing world.

Water Wisdom

Shower body,
Empower soul.

~

EARLY ONE MORNING AS WE lay at anchor I thought about the Japanese love of soaking in hot baths and the enchanting communal hot spring baths, or *onsen*, I had visited in the Japanese Alps, with steam rising off the obsidian water while snow fell from the infinite sky. I was thinking about the haiku I had just read by the Japanese poet and Roshi, Soen Nakagawa:

Sound of mountain
sound of ocean
everywhere spring rain

All of this got me ruminating on the importance of water, how it nourishes us: soaking in it, drinking it, sailing on it, floating in it, letting it cleanse us, hearing its sounds: roaring waves, babbling brooks, trickling rivulets. How we are made up of 55–60 percent water, how a steamy shower can soothe, wake and refresh us. We don't rough it on Nirvana; she has a hot water heater and carries 600 gallons of fresh water, so hot showers are possible, although they are much shorter than on land. Living on a boat teaches conservation of precious resources.

When I was undergoing rehab in Naples I would rise every morning before dawn and take my *zafu* and *zabuton*—black meditation cushions—and walk out onto the dock behind my parents' house and meditate for a half hour, while fish gently rose to the surface, herons waded in the shallows and a gentle morning breeze riffled the water's surface and played over my skin. Then I would go to the nearby beach on the Gulf of Mexico and take a long walk, listening to the healing sound of the waves washing the beach. Pelicans flew across the tops of the waves; terns stood at the water's edge; I would see a handful of other people walking or jogging. Occasionally I would see a manatee swimming along the shoreline or dolphins playing offshore.

At first I could not go into the water; I had severe vertigo from my brain injury, and my neurologist had told me that I could become so disoriented that I could drown in only three feet of water. This was hard to believe for someone who had spent his life in and around the water and was a strong swimmer. At one point when I was younger I even had my lifeguard certification. Several days after that conversation with my neurologist I was walking the wide Gulf beach and decided to wade into the warm waters and float on my back, feeling the soothing, healing, salty embrace. I stayed in the shallows, only going up to mid-thigh. I lay back, dipping my head in the water, and suddenly my head started to spin. I had no idea which way was up or down. I struggled to my feet and somehow staggered to shore and fell to my knees in the sand, panting heavily, vowing never to doubt my neurologist again. For the next few months I just walked the beach, never daring to enter the water. But just being near it, seeing it, hearing it, smelling the salt air and putting my toes in the ocean had a powerful restorative effect on my brain and body, which was still wracked with pain.

Eventually I was able to swim, and to lie on my back, floating in the Gulf's warm, caressing waters. Then I would come back to the house and shower, feeling refreshed and empowered and ready to face the often painful day of therapy that lay ahead.

Sailing

Wind:
Friend.

~

THIS THOUGHT CAME WHILE WALKING my golden retriever Henry in Greenport, at the end of the summer, just after a huge nor'easter had Nirvana (and us in her) bouncing all over the water at Preston's dock. S.T. Preston & Sons is a wonderful weather-beaten old marine chandlery where we had pulled in for several weeks to escape the fall storms. It's the kind of place where during a severe nor'easter, when the wind, waves and high tide conspire to push water up through the worn wooden floorboards, the staff just dons rubber sea boots, picks up any stock off the floor, puts it on the shelves and goes about their business, sloshing through the store while the storm rages outside. Even with the wind and waves tossing Nirvana around, throwing her against the fenders and wooden pilings, her inch-thick dock lines creaking and straining to hold her, fenders squeezed almost to bursting, water coming up over the dock, the tempest screaming in the rigging, there was something familiar and soothing about the wind, an old friend.

I was reminded of a time when I was only tw
and I was working as the production manager fo.
mercial glazing company. The job was incredibly st
for a young, inexperienced boy/man fresh out of colleg
pressures were immense, the dollar amounts staggering
all the glass windows, doors, atrium and facing on a new
or a new bank headquarters in downtown Buffalo. The   ne
stress of trying to get the most efficient production out of ιny union
employees in spite of a union business agent who would scream at me
about work rules, how the men didn't work for me, they worked for
the union, etc. I knew he was testing me because I was young and
inexperienced, and because I was the boss' son, but knowing that
didn't make things any easier. Then there was the added challenge of
having to get it all done before the winter snows came, a fact of life in
the northern climate of Buffalo.

At the end of the day I would drive the half hour to my local sailing beach, put together my windsurfer, don my wetsuit and head out
onto the water. For the first half hour or so I would fall constantly—
the stress of the day had totally knocked me off center, both physically
and emotionally—but after half an hour of falling into the cold waters
of Lake Erie, climbing back on the board, pulling up the sail, starting to move, wrapping my cramped hands around the boom, trying
to balance the pull of the wind with my weight, falling back into the
cold water, climbing up again, refusing to quit, I would slowly feel my
mind and body relax, become centered, and off I would go, sailing for
hours without falling. I would skim the wave tops, speeding over the
water, forgetting everything except the wind, until sunset finally sent
me back to the beach, where I would flop down, spent and content.

There have been many other times in my life like that, where fate's
vicissitudes knocked me around, battering and bruising me, but sailing and the wind have always been there to calm, to soothe. One of
the most common forms of Buddhist meditation is to concentrate on
one's breath—you slowly breathe in, then slowly breathe out, the flow
of your breath like the rhythm of gentle waves washing up and down
a sandy shoreline, cleaning away all thoughts and cares. In sailing you
concentrate on the breeze—the breath of the world we live in, the
steady, calming breath of sea, earth and sky.

Ocean Storm

Gale,
Pale.

I WAS AGAIN WALKING HENRY, DURING the height of yet another gale in Greenport, remembering all the white-knuckled times sailing through fierce gales at sea. I have been in storms so violent that crew members were screaming we were going to die; storms so powerful that I have been forced to tie seasick crew members into their bunks. The words of "Ocean Storm" are a triple entendre: the white pallor of skin after drenched days and nights spent in wet clothes, salt water trapped against soaked, wrinkled skin by foul weather gear (which is supposed to keep the water out!); the wan faces of seasick shipmates; and the pallid, sunless, stormy sky. Even the sea is pale during a gale, not bright with sunlight reflecting off the waves. The depths are not a dark aquamarine blue, but a ghostly greenish-grey topped with milky foam, spray and whitecaps. I think galeing should be an adjective, like storming, only it would be more descriptive, more evocative of the bleak skies, roaring seas and howling, shrieking winds that sometimes blow through our lives.

Morning Meditation

Seagulls cry,
Sigh...

~

A T PRESTON'S, MOST MORNINGS ARE not filled with fierce storms but are peaceful and calm. Every morning I meditate in the cockpit as the sun comes up and seagulls whirl overhead putting forth their plaintive cries, surrounded by mirror-surfaced water, old fishing trawlers, ferries, and the sun rising through the mist over nearby Shelter Island. On the pier to the east is a two-story, wire-frame sculpture of an osprey, wings outstretched, alighting silently on a perch made from girders taken from the World Trade Center. Every day tourists walk out on our dock to view the sculpture, a memorial to all that is great about nature and terrible about man. The tourists think nothing of walking up to Nirvana and peering at us, as if we, too, are a tourist attraction. Having a steady stream of staring strangers can be a bit unnerving, but in the early morning, when we have the dock, the seagulls and the osprey to ourselves, our neighborhood is incredibly atmospheric and beautiful ... my soul sighs.

Bahama Nirvana

Palm trees,
Kind breeze.

~

WE SPENT A WINTER LIVING in the Bahamas on Nirvana. The Bahamas are an amazing place for anyone to visit, but are especially enticing to someone on a boat. There are thousands of islands, many of them uninhabited or with only a few residents, spread over an area slightly larger than New York state. In one day you can sail from the hustle and bustle of Nassau, where you stock up on provisions, to a quiet, deserted island paradise where you can ruminate, reflect and write. For anyone looking to calm and focus the mind, the Bahamas are, indeed, a kind of nirvana.

Returning to the Bahamas was also a return voyage to the innocence of childhood, a voyage to rebuild my shattered sense of self. I first visited the Bahamas when I was only fourteen, when my father bought a used thirty-four-foot sailboat, the Lollipop, with an old friend who lived in Miami and also had a boy my age, and we sailed from Miami to Bimini for a long weekend. I will never forget crossing the Gulf Stream for the first time, enthralled by the magic of the ultramarine blue water, the iridescent purple sails of the Portuguese Man o' War riding the ocean currents and silver flying fish skimming across the wave tops.

The Gulf Stream and Bimini were an exotic adventure for a kid from Buffalo. In Bimini we dined at the Compleat Angler Hotel, with its collection of Ernest Hemingway memorabilia lining the walls, including photos of Hemingway with huge marlin and letters in his own hand. That trip was my first glimpse of the possibility of another world, the world of the writer, adventurer and sensualist. I read "The Old Man and the Sea" and "Islands in the Stream" and was transported to a world of struggle, triumph and losing with dignity, the world of manhood I was on the verge of entering.

During the next several years we took more trips during school vacations, sailing on board the Lollipop to the Bahamas with my father, mother, myself and two younger sisters. We explored deserted islands, snorkeled with schools of flashing fish, were startled by iguanas charging out of the underbrush where the littoral met the scrub woodlands, and met islanders who taught us how to clean conch, enjoy drinks without ice and see the world in an entirely new way.

I loved the Bahamas, but our island paradise turned into a drug smuggler's lair; the Lollipop was sold, and I hadn't been back in many years. The boy I first sailed with across the stream was now a middle-aged man like me, and had remained one of my best friends. He, his mother and brother still lived in Miami, and we stopped to visit them on our way south. So it was that Meg and I found ourselves sailing Nirvana across the Gulf Stream from Miami to Bimini with Meg's sixteen-year-old son Nolan, our two dogs, and a whole winter ahead of us. The Gulf Stream still rolled blue, Man o' War still sailed, and flying fish still jumped. My life may have taken many strange turns in the intervening years, but nature had barely changed.

Bimini, however, was a different matter. The Compleat Angler had burned down. The northern end of the island had been bulldozed for a huge new development, and the docks of the marinas were mostly empty and decaying. Hemingway had changed too, at least in my mind. In the intervening years I read his biographies, learned the details of his suicide, became aware of a backlash against him among academics as overly macho, shallow, even cartoonish. I had learned that many people felt "Islands in the Stream" was a lousy book, cobbled together after his death from remnants of an unfinished novel he wrote after his talent left him.

A large part Hemingway's fall from grace as an insightful genius, from winner of the Nobel Prize in literature to dreadful hack, seemed to be that he wasn't really a perceptive innovator, but instead an inept dullard, evidenced by his boorish public antics, uninspired writing in later works and finally his suicide. But in reading his biography I came to understand what had happened to Hemingway and to feel an even greater affinity with him. While in Europe to cover World War II he sustained head injuries in two different motor vehicle accidents. In London in the spring of 1944 his head hit the windshield and doctors took two and a half hours and fifty-seven stitches to close his head wound. He was hospitalized with intense post-accident headaches. Then in August he was in a jeep accident that caused another "concussion," more headaches and double vision. A year later back in Cuba he was still complaining of headaches, slowed speech and memory problems. Then he was in another car accident in Cuba, hitting his head again. At the time he was working on a novel set in Bimini. Finally in 1954 while on safari in Africa Hemingway was in a serious plane crash. Cerebrospinal fluid leaked from a crack in his skull. He temporarily lost his hearing and eyesight. Newspaper reports describe his head as being "swathed in bandages." Undoubtably Hemingway had sustained multiple TBI's.

Before his suicide in 1961, Hemingway suffered from bouts of depression so severe that he told his doctors that he would sit at his desk, weeping, because "the words just wouldn't come." In one of life's odd coincidences, our next door neighbor in Buffalo was the daughter of one of Hemingway's doctors at the Mayo Clinic in Minnesota. One day when I was in my twenties, the doctor was visiting his daughter, and I met him when our two families got together for dinner.: "We knew Hemingway was going to kill himself," he said. "But he was so depressed, there was nothing we could do about it."

The early sixties was well before the use of antidepressants had become widespread, drugs such as Wellbutrin, Prozac and Lexapro, drugs that I had been given after my head injury. Instead with Hemingway the doctors had tried electroshock therapy, probably further exacerbating his brain trauma. Thankfully for me electroshock therapy is a thing of the past, but twenty years after that seemingly innocent cocktail party banter with Hemingway's physician, I had found myself sitting at my computer, sobbing because the words just wouldn't come.

So in the first years after my accident, I had, in addition to my other problems, the added burden of wondering what would happen to me as a writer: Would the words ever come back? Or would I end up like Hemingway: depressed, unable to write, consumed by such despair at this loss of my creativity that I would end up killing myself?

Thankfully, due to modern medicine's better understanding of how to treat Traumatic Brain Injuries, thanks to Zen meditation and thanks to better luck than Hemingway (one accident, not four), I had been able to start writing again. I started with po, expanding them into essays as the words came. I was writing, not sobbing. Here on Bimini seven years after my accident, I wrote every day on my laptop. Even though the Compleat Angler was gone and the bulldozers were savaging one end of the island, the people of Bimini were still friendly, the wide beach along Bimini's western shore was still a fine powdery white where palm trees swayed in the breeze, and the sun still shone on roadside fish stands and laughing children playing in the schoolyard.

We stayed in Bimini for almost two weeks. We had drinks in the Blue Water Hotel, a house that was the model for the main character's home in "Islands in the Stream." We sailed to the Berry Islands, then to Nassau, then down into the Exumas, some of the most beautiful islands in the world, where we snorkeled, explored deserted islands, watched iguanas playing on the shore, ate conch, walked the dogs on the beach, wrote every day, met new people and reveled in the beauty of the Bahamas.

Not that this watery Shangri-La was without its dark moments: during the winter cold fronts swept through with maddening regularity, bringing chill north winds that howled like banshees in the rigging for days on end. Just getting the dogs into the dinghy and to the beach for a walk could be an adventure. Keeping the laptops charged or protected from the salt and moisture was a challenge. Learning to live with such adversity and realizing that it too is a blessing is part of the beauty of the Bahamas. But on this day there was no need for such difficult mental gymnastics; the palm trees undulated gently like dancers and a warm Bahamian breeze worked like a patient masseur to ease the kinks out of a psyche knotted with the stress and cares of being a TBI survivor, to ease the kinks out of a life gone somehow off the tracks.

Saltwater Reverie

Green, blue,
Soothing hues.

~

COLORS IN THE BAHAMAS ARE truly spectacular, ranging from the azure blue of the open ocean where it presses close alongside the Great Bahama Bank, to an incredible luminescent emerald green over the sand bars, where the sun reflects off the white sandy bottom, infusing the water with light. Anchored off the verdant cays, or small islands, I would sit in the morning in the cockpit, sipping my tea and marveling at the thousands of different shades of green in the softly waving foliage along the shoreline, from the ethereal light-yellow, translucent leaves of the sea grape, backlit by the sun, to the rich, dark green tangled shadows of the mangroves. The colors had sound: the soft rustling of the viridescent Silver Top Palms, the gentle lapping of the turquoise water against the hull. And the sky: so blue, so vast, so all-encompassing, dotted here and there with towering white cauliflower heads of cumulous clouds rising off the Bahama banks as the sun warmed the shallow waters.

Even seven years after the accident, even with a regimen of meditation, yoga, biofeedback and anti-anxiety medication, I still suffer from post-traumatic stress disorder. I am like the proverbial canary in a coal mine: even the smallest stressor can trigger an anxiety reaction where I feel the muscles in my neck, shoulders and chest contract, my skin crawl and my brain go fuzzy as the stress chemicals, especially cortisol, begin to kick in. Driving, crowds, loud noises, violent movies, television, nasty ex-wives, screaming children—all can start the stress hormones flowing. I am hypersensitive to any environmental factor that causes what the medical profession calls the "fight or flight response," a vestigial part of the human animal from the days when we roamed the African veldt, needing to either stand and fight or run like hell when a big beast or a human from a rival tribe crossed our path.

The flip side is that I am also profoundly aware of the palliative impact the natural world has on our bodies and minds. In a way we all know this, or at least sense it, some of us more consciously than others. Thus the human urge to vacation at the beach, ski in the mountains or walk in the park. The great Zen masters have always known this; Zen literature and arts are filled with references to nature, from cherry blossoms to nightingales to snow-capped mountains. The masters are certainly not alone; many great thinkers have contemplated the enlightening effects of the natural world, especially some of our most cherished American minds like Thoreau and Whitman. But we tend to forget the importance of the natural world to our well-being, as we increasingly spend our days in office buildings and cars and malls and houses with the doors and windows shut tight so the air conditioning or heating systems can keep our climate carefully controlled.

Day after day on Nirvana in the Bahamas I would feel the stress slowly, inexorably, drain out of me, until I reached a state of centered harmony, a sense of being one with all existence that was almost impossible to achieve back in the "real" world, surrounded by speeding cars and ringing phones and blaring televisions. I would achieve a state of quiet joy, a reverie of appreciation for the beauty of life. There were moments that were so true, so right, so absolutely without falsehood that tears would come to my eyes. I realized then how much I believe in the truth of beauty, and the beauty of truth, embodied by the simple colors of white, green and blue.

Lagoon Sunrise

Saline
Dream.

I N THE MORNING I WOULD often go for a swim, climbing down
the ladder and slipping quietly into the water's salty somnolence.
I can no longer dive head first into the water—the shock of forehead hitting water causes headaches and confusion—but a quiet,
relaxing dip suits me just fine. I grew up spending summers swimming
in Lake Erie or smaller freshwater ponds, so I am still blown away by
the saltiness of the ocean. I would swim on the surface, then dive to the
sandy bottom to look at a starfish and then just float on my back—my
body and spirit buoyed by the soothing, healing waters.

There are the inevitable comparisons with time spent in the womb,
nurtured by our mother's salty saline fluid, protected and living in a
blissful dream state. But in the womb, with our mind as yet undevel-
oped, we are not aware of the grandeur of the world we are about to
enter. As I lay there on my back, looking up at the dome of sky, tast-
ing the saltiness on my lips, my mind was acutely aware of floating in a
watery, dreamy paradise.

Tribute

Hail! Hail!
One white sail.

~

WE WERE SAILING BACK IN the spring from Shroud Cay in the Exumas to Nassau, working our way back north to the States. It was an absolutely picture-perfect sailing day: ten to fifteen knots of wind out of the Southeast, seas one to two feet, air temperature about eighty degrees and a clear blue sky with white fluffy cumulous clouds; no squalls or rain clouds in sight. We were on a compass course of 319 degrees true, which meant we were on a broad reach, a perfect point of sail for Nirvana. She is a ketch, so the wind filled all three sails, pushing us along at seven knots with no heel and very little rolling since the seas were so small. The dogs lay in the shade of the cockpit, Meg napped, stretched out on a cockpit cushion, and I steered, pointing our bow toward home.

Emotions are always mixed at a time like this; you are both sad about leaving someplace so beautiful and yet excited about returning to your home port. Having hours to do nothing but steer to the wind and waves gave me time to contemplate the transient nature of things.

Ahead and to port of us several miles away on the horizon a lone white sail shone bright in the sunlight, mirroring the towering white clouds above her. The sailboat was headed in the same direction and I could use her as a point of reference as I steered to keep us on course, since there was no land ahead to steer by, only the vastness of the water under the blue vault of the sky. At times like this you can almost see the curvature of the earth as the horizon line stretches across your field of vision.

There was something about that tiny white triangle surrounded above, below and on all sides by the infinity of sea and sky that awed me, and I thought about what it meant to put to sea in such a tiny speck on the vastness of the ocean, to leave home and venture forth into the unknown. The sail represented for me all that is great about sailboats and the people who venture forth in them: freedom, independence, a desire to be one with the wind, an inclination to be patient and go slow instead of racing around at high speed burning fossil fuels, a willingness to embrace voyaging and impermanence, while at the same time understanding the importance of home.

"Hail! Hail!" is a double entendre; in the days of sailing ships, when two boats met at sea they would pull alongside and hail each other for information on weather, whaling grounds, news from back home, etc. It was known as "having a gam" from the sailor's word for large schools of whales, or gams. After months at sea alone, cut off from the world, in need of some new social interaction, seamen relished the ability to meet other humans at sea. In modern times sailors sometimes do the same thing, although they more likely do it by radio. The word "hail" is still used, as in: "This is the sailing vessel Nirvana hailing the sailing vessel Mistress on channel 16, come in Mistress." The other meaning of hail is to give tribute, such as "All hail Caesar" or "Hail to the chief." So the hail is both a greeting and a salute.

The second line comes from a wonderful picture book I read to my boys when they were little. The book was called "One White Sail." It was a simple counting poem ("One white sail on a clear blue sea, / Two orange houses and a slender palm tree," etc.) illustrated with beautiful, simple paintings that reminded me of Matisse's late "cutouts." My boys absolutely adored this book, and would ask me to read it to them every chance they got, and I never tired of sitting at home, a boy on my knee, opening the cover, pointing at the beautiful illustrations and reciting the rhymes: "Five blue doors in the baking hot sun, / Six wooden windows let the cool wind run." Then getting to the end and starting all over again, pointing to the nine steel drums singing a soft sweet tune or ten boats riding at anchor under a full moon and asking, "How many?" Even though each page and each rhyme was beautiful in and of themselves, there was always something about the beginning of the book that set the stage for everything that came afterward, something that set the mood and instantly transported father and child to someplace special: "One white sail on a clear blue sea..."

There is something magical, mystical and mysterious about that one white sail: Who is on board? Where are they going? Where is the crew from? The captain? What kind of boat is it? How big is she? What is her name? Her home port? This is an homage to boats that harness the wind and the people who sail in them and all they represent.

Snorkeling Spirituality

Buddha,
Barracuda.

~

ONE OF THE MOST FAMOUS koans in Zen is "Does a dog have Buddha-nature?" So, does a barracuda have Buddha-nature? Many times I have been snorkeling on a reef, and seen a barracuda floating completely still, like a monk meditating, except for the eyes that follow my every movement. In Buddhism one of the primary goals is to be totally, completely aware. Matthiessen Roshi always says that the goal while meditating facing the wall in the zendo is to be so still, so completely aware that if a tiger entered the zendo you would be instantly aware of it and know how to react. I'm not exactly disagreeing with Roshi, but my own feeling is that I would like to be so aware, so full of Buddha-nature that I would sense the tiger before it even entered the zendo, be mindful of the tiger's presence when it was prowling around outside, and quick get up and bar the door before it got inside. I have no desire to be eaten by a tiger.

So, does the barracuda have that kind of awareness? That kind of energy, that kind of presence? Is it the tiger or the monk, or both? The barracuda is not like a clownfish, darting to and fro, or like a shark, slowly gliding, or like a jack, speedily flashing by. The barracuda hovers, motionless, while it waits for its prey.

In college I took an acting class where the teacher had us all choose an animal we would like to be, and then told us to go out and walk around the campus for the entire hour, not saying a word, pretending we were that animal. Without being overt about it (in other words, if we were a snake, we didn't have to literally slither along the ground), we were supposed to move, think, act and react like the animal we had chosen. (I think one of the greatest examples of this type of acting is Zero Mostel's portrayal of a man turning into a rhinoceros in Ionesco's "Rhinoceros," a role for which he won a Tony award on Broadway and then reprised in the film of the same name.) I choose to be a deer, and I still remember walking around the wooded campus, my senses heightened and completely transformed just by the suggestion that I might be a totally aware animal instead of a clueless college student.

Being in nature for any amount of time can have that same effect. In high school I had committed one too many transgressions for the administration's taste, and it was recommended that I go on a three-week Outward Bound wilderness expedition the summer of my junior year. The expedition I chose was in Colorado's San Juan Mountains, and one element of the course was a three-day solo, all alone on a mountainside, with no human contact, a time to do nothing but sit, feel and think. At age seventeen it was a truly unique experience to be by myself for the first time in my life, no teachers, phones, friends, family, cars, television, radio, stereo, billboards, roads or other signs of civilization and humanity. I was as close to the "primitive" world of nature and animals as one could get, and I remember well that heightened state of awareness, that sensitivity to the world around me. Snorkeling can give much the same feeling: the immersion in the natural world, the falling away of our human veneer, the sheer naturalness of being in the water nearly naked, aware only of our immediate surroundings. One can just simply hover, and float, like a buddha-barracuda.

I enjoy that the two words are so similar—Buddha, barracuda: the alliteration, the rhyme—and I find something compelling in the juxtaposition of these two beings that most people would think are so antithetical, yet in reality have so much in common.

ZEN

Mourning Meditation

Doves coo,
I too.

~

THE HOUR JUST BEFORE DAWN, and the hour after, is my favorite time of day. While most people are still sleeping, I awake, meditate for at least half an hour in the cockpit, then focus on simple domestic chores: putting clean dishes back in the cupboards, picking up the boys' wet towels, sweeping up dog hair, all while trying to stay completely mindful, totally aware of my surroundings, concentrating on what I am doing, not letting the mind wander down fruitless paths. This is the essence of Zen, to be totally mindful and aware of this very moment, to be conscious of every breath.

After meditating and doing chores I will read, or write. Whatever I do, it is a beautiful, calm, peaceful time, before the demands and cares of modern life—work, family, dogs, obligations—begin to take over my day and add to the general stress level. It is a time to set my body and mind on the right path for the rest of the day, to be mindful and calm no matter what curveballs get thrown my way.

When I was in Naples, undergoing rehab, sleeping on my parents' couch, living in the same house with my invalid mother, having lost my home and family, it certainly seemed as if more than one curveball had crossed my home plate. While some of the issues facing me were more abstract, my mother's sickness was a constant, in-your-face nightmare. She needed round-the-clock care, which I helped with as best I could. But I felt guilty not being able to help her more since I spent most of my day in rehab clinics working on my own recovery, and at night my brain was too exhausted from my various therapies to be of much help.

I would talk to her, even though she couldn't talk back, telling her about my day, her grandchildren, how much I loved her. I'd massage her gnarled hands, or read to her or try to get her to choose a red card from the playing cards on the table in front of her; anything to stimulate what was left of her brain. But she continued to deteriorate, her organs giving up one by one, and then my mother finally died.

It was a time of deep mourning, but also a time of healing. The nursing staff disappeared, and my father and I were suddenly alone, which made it easier to have some quiet meditation time to myself at sunrise, before he awoke. Every morning I would hear the mourning doves cooing through the open windows; such a soothing, wonderful sound. It was not a sound that I heard growing up in Buffalo, or living in Manhattan as a young writer. It was not even a sound I remembered hearing when I moved from Manhattan to Eastern Long Island—I was too caught up in the pressures of work and family; I was still unaware of my surroundings, living in what Buddhists call samsara—and so the doves' cooing was all the sweeter in Florida for its novelty.

When I moved back to Eastern Long Island I heard the Mourning Doves every morning as I meditated and spring came to the fields and vineyards. After my mother's death and my own near-death experience, I had learned to appreciate the precious, fleeting nature of the world around me; I had learned to hear the mourning dove's call. The sound was a lovely morning song of peace, the perfect way to start the day.

"Do you want to sing with us?" they called.

"I do, I do…."

I also relish the play on words: is it a morning dove or a mourning dove? For me it was—and is—both. I was mourning the losses in my life while also cooing inside with the awakening joy of new beginnings.

Core Koan

Be
Lee.

~

THIS IS THE KOAN GIVEN me by Matthiessen Roshi in *dokusan* (a private meeting between teacher and student) as I struggled after my accident and divorce at age forty-six to make the transition to my real, true self. It's something we all struggle to do, and yet few achieve. How to truly, truthfully be oneself, with absolutely no falsehood, no matter what the pressures from society, family, peers, work, finances and our own psyches.

It was shortly after I had returned to Eastern Long Island following my year of rehabilitation, and was trying to pick up the pieces of a broken life and start over. All the things that had defined me were gone. I was no longer a husband; even though the divorce was not final, I knew that part of my life was over. I was no longer the day-to-day father of two small boys. Before the accident I had put my sons on the school bus in the morning, or driven them to school or day care, and was there when they got off the bus in the afternoon, or I picked them up from school. During the summers I coached soccer games, took them fishing, played with them on the beach. We built a tree fort together in the woods behind our house. It had four walls, a roof, an outdoor deck, windows, a trap door and a bucket and pulley for hoisting things up. Henry would sit at the base of the tree and bark, wondering why he couldn't come join us in our boy's aerie.

At night, when we were too tired to play outside, we would have dinner together, watch television or play a game, and then I would read to them, hug them and tell them I loved them before putting them to bed. But now all that was gone. I had always expected to come back to Long Island after rehab and, even though we would not be living together because of the divorce, we would at least see each other on a regular basis. I would go to their sports games, attend parent-teacher conferences, help them with their homework. I would have bedrooms for them when they spent the night or the weekend at my house. We would play outside. But I had returned to Long Island and my children were no longer there. My wife had told a judge I had abandoned my children and moved to Florida, then she took the children and moved to Wisconsin. I never had a chance to tell a judge I was undergoing rehab for a Traumatic Brain Injury and would be returning as soon as my doctors allowed. I was no longer a loving, daily dad. I was no longer a husband. Who was I? How could I just "Be Lee?" What were the fundamental traits that made Lee Carlson?

On top of that, I still couldn't write; as hard as I tried the words just wouldn't come, or when they did I would look at my work the next day and not remember what I had written, since the brain injury had so affected my memory. I was no longer a working professional writer. On a daily basis, practicing Zen and trying to write were all I had.

Roshi would see me around the zendo, say hello, ask how I was doing, but the one question he often asked in his quiet, gentle voice was, "Are you writing?" He knew exactly the right thing to say at exactly the right time in my life, just three little words, but absolutely the right words. That is one of the traits that makes him a Roshi. (Did he have this trait throughout his life? Is it one of the things that defines who he is? Or did he acquire this ability after becoming a Roshi? I do not know, since I did not know him before.)

Roshi said to me, as I struggled with the question of who I was, to just "Be Lee." So simple, yet so difficult. This is really his po.

Zen Hello

Welcome home,
Gnome.

~

THERE IS A GREAT SPIRITUAL tradition of leaving home to spend time meditating, searching for answers. Jesus wandered in the wilderness; Buddha withdrew to the forest for five years; Mohammed retreated to a cave. After being away from the Zendo for many months, partly because I felt a need explore the reality of the universe on my own terms, I returned one morning for meditation. I was worried that my absence would be problematic and cause a rift between Roshi and me, or at best some uncomfortable moments. But Roshi, upon seeing me, said simply, "Welcome home." He did not actually call me a gnome, and physically I do not resemble one, but one of the goals of meditation is to change the self-centered view of the world most of us are burdened with. With the letting go of ego, with the attainment of what Zen masters call "non-self," I have learned how small and insignificant I am, a gnomish speck on the horizon.

And yet, and yet.... I have also learned how large I am as part of the greater whole, our true home. The ultimate paradox.

Zendo Dawn

Power
Hour.

~

SITTING IN BED ON MARCH 17, 2007, the 100th anniversary of Soen Nakagawa Roshi's birth, I read some of his haiku and thought of Zen and early morning sittings in the Ocean Zendo in the still darkness, as the world begins to wake, birds begin to sing and golden light slowly fills the air.

The moment of sitting and reading, the moment of sitting and remembering, and the moment of sitting and meditating are all equally powerful times, whether they last a second, a minute, an hour, or whether they transcend the bounds of time and space. In the zendo, the bell rings, we sit silently, unmoving, for thirty minutes, then the bell rings and we do a five minute *kinhin*, or walking meditation, then the bell rings again and we sit and meditate again for another half hour until the bell rings once more. I have had those half hours last seemingly forever, and I have had times when the entire hour goes by in the blink of an eye. Either way, that time is a very powerful time, a time when the energy of the earth bears witness to the power of silence.

Philosophy I

Disregard
Kierkegaard.

~

Anxiety is the dizziness of freedom.
Wherever there is a crowd there is untruth.
—Soren Kierkegaard (1813 – 1855)

KIERKEGAARD INSISTED THAT GENUINE THOUGHT and action must always arise from the self, without support from others. He then went on to assert that the only appropriate emotional response to this supposed condition of total human freedom is angst, or anxiety and despair. Knowing oneself, and thinking and acting from that place of centered wholeness is important, but Kierkegaard's theory is only right if one is merely aware of half the picture. Realizing our complete and total connection with all sentient beings, with all things in the universe, is equally important.

The myth of the great rugged American individualist, the John Wayne character who rides off alone into the sunset, is one of our society's greatest fictions. It is not just an American myth, but a Western society myth, perpetuated not only by philosophers but by artists, actors, politicians, sports heroes, entrepreneurs and adventurers.

Before my accident I was one of those people who bought into the myth. While I had many friends, the things I enjoyed most were solitary pursuits: writing, ocean sailing, fishing, skiing. But the accident and the divorce brought home to me the importance of relationships, the web of subtle and not-so-subtle bonds that connect us, that support, nurture and heal us all.

First there were the numerous networks of professionals—doctors, therapists, insurance agents, lawyers—without which I would not have healed and without which my mother's last days would have been a misery. Certainly these professionals had a job to do and were being paid to do it, but in them was also a genuine compassion that transcended merely practicing a trade, and to know they were there when and if I needed them, to know that those safety nets were there to save me if I stumbled—that was incredibly healing all by itself.

There were the connections with family—my sisters and father who helped me physically, my father and aunt who helped me financially. There were connections with people who lent helping hands, such as my friends Michael and David who took care of my car and then shipped it to Florida when I could finally drive; my friends Debbie and Steve who gave me a place to stay when I visited Cutchogue to see my children; my friends Michael and Paula who gave me a place to stay and helped me find a house to rent when I returned to the North Fork. There were friends who came to Florida on vacation and took the time to look me up, take me out to lunch or dinner. There were countless other friends who called me, sent me e-mails, cards and letters. Just knowing they were there for me if I needed them was comforting and helped ease the anxiety caused by my world being turned upside down.

But there were also relationships with the many people I barely knew whose small acts of kindness helped lift my spirits every day. There were the friendly people at the Pack and Post store who knew about my accident and cognitive problems and helped me send small gifts to my boys, or legal documents to lawyers, or letters to friends. There was the man at the IRS who told me "not to worry and just get better" when I went to the IRS office to explain that I hadn't filed my taxes because I couldn't think clearly enough to gather all my receipts and do the math. And there were many, many more.

One of my favorite Buddhist images is something called "Indra's Jeweled Net." Indra is a Hindu god given importance by Buddhists as the protector of the young Buddha when he was born, but his other significance is as the owner of the jeweled net of existence in his capacity as Supreme God of all the other gods. For Zen Buddhists this is all just a metaphor, rather than an actual belief, but the jeweled net is like a multidimensional spider's web with a beautiful jewel (in actuality a sentient being—a human, a golden retriever, an osprey) at each node of the web. The jewels are infinite, and their surfaces are polished and multifaceted, so that each jewel reflects the light from every other jewel, creating a sparkling, glowing interconnected web of existence, a celebration of the truth of the crowd of life.

In my case that crowded net, that web of existence—filled with doctors, friends, acquaintances, dogs and even strangers—alleviated my suffering, gave me the truth of hope, friendship, support and safety. When one truly becomes aware of the interconnectedness of all things, the glistening jeweled net, the "interbeing" of Buddhism as it is sometimes translated, then the emotional state achievable by humankind is exactly the opposite of anxiety and angst: a state of pure joy, bliss, peace and unconditional love.

Philosophy II

Say no
to Nietzsche.

~

One can promise actions, but not feelings, for the
latter are involuntary. He who promises to love forever
or hate forever or be forever faithful to someone is
promising something that is not in his power.
　　　　　　　–Friedrich Wilhelm Nietzsche (1844–1900)

A S LONG AS WE'RE HAVING the courage to dis great Western
philosophers, why not go after one of the biggest? The man
who proposed the ideas "Superman" and "God is dead?"
　　　When you live on a boat tied to a public pier, you get
to overhear all sorts of interesting conversations. It's as if hundreds of
strangers are walking through your living room each day, talking to
each other. They come to look at the boats, at the water, at the osprey
statue that commemorates 9/11. They come for the atmosphere and the
smells, sights and sounds. One Saturday afternoon as I was sitting in

Nirvana's cockpit reading, a group of five middle-aged women walked down the dock and stopped in front of Nirvana.

"What a beautiful boat."

"Yes, I wonder where she's from."

At this point, Henry always rouses himself from the cockpit floor, stretches languidly and walks over to the gate in the lifelines, wagging his tail, looking for a little attention.

"Oh! Look at the dog!"

"Oh, how cute!"

"Hello sweetie, aren't you adorable?"

He usually sticks his head through the lifelines so total strangers can pet his head and scratch his ears. He is a total flirtation hound. People think nothing of reaching onto the boat to pet him. Sometimes they ask if it's okay, sometimes not. Living on a boat you become part of the public psychic seascape.

From their conversation, I gathered they had just finished lunch at Scrimshaw, the restaurant at the head of the pier with outdoor tables in a roped-off area on the dock. They were having a pleasant girls' day out, enjoying themselves with good wine, good food, sunshine and sea air. I heard them talking about their husbands, their children, their jobs. Nirvana, as she always does, brought up a wistful longing in these strangers for things to be different: for far-off exotic lands, for a different lifestyle, different relationships. Suddenly one of the women said in a plaintive voice to her companions, "How do you stay in love with your husband after all these years, and how do you get him to stay in love with you?"

They all nodded in agreement. One woman rolled her eyes and said, "Tell me about it!"

At that moment I felt like a kid in eighth grade, sitting in the back of the classroom, frantically jumping up and down in his seat and waving his arm in the air, "Pick me! Pick me! I know! I know!"

I wanted to jump out on the dock and talk to these women, to tell them, "First, you get hit by a car...."

But seriously folks, Ba Da, DA, DUM!

The Dalai Lama has written extensively on love and happiness, but when I read his books and hear him speak, I always think, "Yeah, but this guy's never been married, never had kids; let's see him talk so glibly about love and happiness after he's tried marriage and parenting!" Certainly I have great respect for the Dalai Lama, his message of peace, his incredible patience and fortitude in the face of what the Chinese have done to his country, his role in teaching Buddhism to the West, but I still sometimes wonder how he would handle a couple of fighting prepubescent kids that were his own offspring. And then I think, how would he handle a spouse who is screaming invective? What would his response be to years of verbal abuse and angry, personal attacks right in his own bedroom? Attacks from someone he loved and trusted, as opposed to a impersonal foreign threat? Would he find a way to promote love in such difficult circumstances? How would he do it? Would he know how to do it? How would he stay in love with his partner?

So how do you hold on to love in a relationship? How do you nurture love, make it grow and flourish in spite of all the stresses and obstacles of modern life? How do you keep loving your partner and encourage them to keep loving you? Do we have the power to promise to love forever, constantly, daily? Or are we doomed to be like a small boat on the great sea of emotion, buffeted, battered and becalmed by the fickle winds of love, anger and indifference? When we promise to love someone forever, are we, as Nietzsche said, promising something that is not within our power?

I think first you need to define your terms. What is love? Is loving someone the same as being in love with them? I think so. It is different, however, from puppy love, or infatuation, or obsession. True love is deep, calm, patient and kind. It is not a flash in the pan. It is something that grows, that needs to be watered, tended and nurtured. I think loving your partner is the same as being in love with your partner, although ideally you are both "in love with" each other, so you are both together in the same deep well of love and understanding. You're both on the same page.

Secondly, you have to make the commitment. A vow that you will love someone, love the world, love yourself. It's a choice one makes. Not an easy choice, not a self-evident choice, but a choice just the same. A choice to embrace a certain world view. When Chas and Niall ask me about the divorce, I try very hard to walk the fine line of not denigrating their mother, while at the same time teaching them my values.

One day Niall and I were talking. "Dad, you didn't want the divorce, did you?" he asked.

"Well Niall," I replied, carefully weighing my words. "I think people should find ways to love each other, no matter how hard that is. Whether they're Jews and Palestinians, Christians and Muslims, kids fighting in school, or husband and wife. People will always have disagreements with each other, but it's what you do about those disagreements that matters."

I joke about "first you have to get run over by a car," but I think there is some truth to the fact that facing one's mortality can give one a different outlook on life. Most of us think we will live forever, and we have plenty of time to work on things like loving someone. There is no sense of urgency. Love gets put on the back burner while we work, or watch TV, or take care of the kids. But when you suddenly come face to face with how quickly it all can end, you feel a need to live every moment to the fullest, to love every moment, to love your partner every moment, to be loved in return every moment, before it all slips away.

I know a psychiatrist in Manhattan who says that the majority of his practice is working with adults who had difficult relationships with their parents, and then their parents died. Invariably deep down these patients longed for some sort of reconciliation, some parental love, but they never did the hard work because the parent was always there, would seemingly always be there. And then one day the parent is gone and the child is left with remorse, anger, guilt, no sense of resolution or closure, no parental love and a huge therapy bill.

When the moment of near-death happens, you suddenly realize how quickly everything can be gone.

A bad divorce can do that as well. Seeing what it does to children, to each spouse—being aware of the wounds the divorce inflicts and the scars that it leaves—can make you want to work hard to ensure something like that never happens again.

So first you get run over by a car and then you get divorced? Not a good solution; I wouldn't wish it on anybody.

How do we make love stay? Staying in love with someone is certainly not easy, and it takes hard work, but I believe undying love is within our grasp. It starts with defining your terms, but really comes to fruition with commitment, a vow to love not only another person, but to love yourself, to love where you are. Charity starts at home. I promised myself if I got out of this brain injury thing in one piece I would make that commitment. Every day when I awake, before I even get out of bed, I promise myself that I will do my best to love: the world around me, Meg, Chas and Niall, Meg's children, friends, family, people I meet, Henry and Owen. It is a conscious decision, a promise I make to myself and to all creation. Do I ever break that promise? Every day, in a thousand little ways, but I try my best.

Then I get up and meditate for half an hour. After meditating I usually say a prayer taught me by one of my first Buddhist teachers, the Venerable Kurunegoda Piyatissa Maha Theroa, a Sri Lankan monk who taught a course at The New School in Manhattan. It begins by praying for oneself:

> May I be well and joyful,
> May I be free from anger,
> May I be free from suffering.

Then I turn the prayer outward:

> May all beings be well and joyful,
> May all beings be free from anger,
> May all beings be free from suffering.

Finally I make the prayer all-inclusive, celebrating Indra's Jeweled Net:

> May we all be well and joyful,
> May we all be free from anger,
> May we all be free from suffering.

Sometimes I say the prayer silently, sometimes I whisper it under my breath, and sometimes I'll say it more loudly. It depends on my mood, and whether others—Meg, the children, guests—are asleep.

Sometimes I'll vary the prayer, so it doesn't just become rote, forcing me to really concentrate on the prayer's true meaning:

> May I be well and joyful,
> May I be filled with love,
> May I be filled with wisdom.

> May all beings be well and joyful,
> May all beings be filled with love,
> May all beings be filled with wisdom.

> May we all be well and joyful,
> May we all be filled with love,
> May we all be filled with wisdom.

Or:

> May I be well and joyful,
> May I be filled with love and peace,
> May I be filled with wisdom and compassion.

> May all beings be well and joyful,
> May all beings be filled with love and peace,
> May all beings be filled with wisdom and compassion.

> May we all be well and joyful,
> May we all be filled with love and peace,
> May we all be filled with wisdom and compassion.

Afterwards I often read a chapter from a book on faith or love or compassion. Sometimes it's a Buddhist book, sometimes a Christian or American Indian or Hindu/Yoga or secular book. Sometimes I'll get back into bed with Meg so when she wakes I'm there, filled with love, ready to kiss her good morning and hug her and touch her, making real our bond.

What matters is that every day I tend my boat and check the set of my sails, multiple times a day, maintaining my boat and my course and adjusting the canvas that drives me. Love does not come easy, it does not come cheap. It comes because you adopt a philosophy of love, and then you work at it, every day. Sometimes the work is hard, grueling, even backbreaking, but the rewards are worth the struggle.

And how do you get someone else to make the same commitment to you? All I know is to take care of my own boat, set a good example, point my bow towards love and hope that my partner will follow. One thing I know is you can't sail someone else's boat for them; you can only show them how to set the sails, if they're willing to listen. Sometimes they are ready to listen, sometimes their own boat just isn't ready to set sail.

What happens when we really take care of our own boat? What kind of shape does our boat need to be in? If it's leaking and rusting and about to sink, obviously that's no good. On the other end of the scale, if the brass is polished and gleaming, if the paint is so clear and perfect that the sparkling light of the water dances and reflects off the curve of the bow, if the hull and masts and sails are strong and sturdy, if all the lines are properly coiled and stowed, then people will naturally be pulled to her, will naturally want to put to sea aboard her.

In Ayurveda, the ancient Indian medical tradition that focuses on balance and harmony in the body, mind and heart, there are three kinds of beauty. *Roopam* is the Sanskrit word for outer beauty, the traditional Western "beauty is only skin deep." Inner beauty is *gunam*, which is achieved by being, among other traits, joyful, compassionate, loving and wise. Lasting beauty, the kind that keeps you looking young and beautiful well into your old age, is *vayastyag*. *Roopam* is what Western culture focuses on. Just pick up any women's or men's magazine and look at all the ads for makeup, hair products, skin products, exercise machines, beauty-enhancing clothing, even cosmetic surgery. Many people would be surprised to find that this ancient spiritual tradition of Ayurveda, the tradition in which the Buddha was raised, does not teach that outer, physical beauty is unimportant. Most people would assume that a spiritual tradition would teach that inner beauty is more important than outer beauty. But in Ayurveda, this is not the case. In Ayurveda, it is the balance of outer and inner beauty that is important. When *roopam* and *gunam* are in balance, only then will a person achieve *sat chit ananda*, or purity of soul and total bliss, a condition that leads to lasting beauty, or *vayastyag*. Someone who is in that pure, beautiful state is attractive to others, in the same way that Nirvana attracts people to her at the dock, just sitting there, because she has both an obvious well-found inner strength and an outer beauty.

One afternoon I was talking to Roshi Matthiessen, sitting in a wooden chair on his back porch, sipping a cup of coffee. He has a gorgeous back-yard, with a lawn sloping down to a lily pond, surrounded by trees, filled with flowers and birds. Even though McMansions have sprouted like weeds in the potato fields that used to surround the house, Peter's yard, gardens and house are shielded from the view of nearby houses by tall trees. I had been meditating regularly, been to several day- or weekend-long meditation retreats, and had achieved a depth in my practice that I had never experienced before, a place of serenity, acceptance and joy that I would have heretofore thought impossible. I was telling him about this, and about other seemingly mysterious results of my practice.

"One of the strangest things is how animals are responding to me," I said. "I was at my friend's loft in Brooklyn the other day, and her cat came up and started rubbing up against my leg. Then it jumped up in my lap and just curled up there, purring loudly. My friend couldn't believe it; she said her cat normally hated people, especially men, and wouldn't go anywhere near any visitors. She said she'd never seen anything like it."

"Yes, you're giving something off," Roshi said. "I like to tell people the story of years ago, when I was a student at Dai Bosatsu in the Catskills. I'd gone there for a long weekend retreat, and several people that I drove up with had very intense *kensho* [an opening, or enlightenment experience] during the retreat. On the way back we drove through a rough section of the Bronx, and there were these really rough characters standing on a street corner, the kind that when you saw them they'd be so menacing that you'd roll up your windows and lock your doors. But as we drove by their faces lit up and they smiled big smiles and waved at us. It was amazing. We were giving something off too."

As a creative writer, I'm always getting crazy ideas for stories. I once had an idea for a comic book about a superhero called "Buddha Boy," whose secret weapon is a kind of ray that he could project all around him, a force field of compassion, love and peace so powerful that it would cause the bad guys to give up their weapons and drop to their knees weeping, to change their scowls to smiles, their hostility to harmony. One of the most famous Buddhist stories is the tale of how the Buddha tamed the vicious highway robber Angulimala, who had killed 999 people and was looking for his thousandth victim. Instead of stealing jewels, Angulimala would cut off one of the victim's fingers and add it to his macabre souvenir necklace. The Buddha decided to put an end to this wanton destruction and went walking in the forest where Angulimala hunted his victims. The Buddha didn't just sit passively, he took action. Upon seeing the Buddha, Angulimala chased after him, running furiously, but could not catch and kill him, even though the Buddha was walking slowly. Angulimala could not penetrate the Buddha's aura of compassion. This ruthless killer decided to give up his evil ways, repent and become one of the Buddha's most devoted disciples. The Buddha was definitely giving something off.

If we were the Buddha, perhaps we could get someone to love us forever, to promise to be faithful forever. Perhaps we would give off enough of that special something, that *sat chit ananda,* to make such a dream happen. Of course we are not the Buddha; we do not give off force fields of love and compassion so powerful that we can convert vicious criminals just by walking through the forest. We are just unenlightened human beings, struggling to love others and be loved in return. But we can take an active role in at least trying with all our might to promise to love forever or be faithful to someone forever. We can tend our own boat. We can meditate and pray until we are giving off something. We can be activists for love.

Perhaps if I had known that ten years ago my personal love life would have turned out differently, perhaps I wouldn't have ended up divorced and living on my parents' couch. But I do know it now and I am determined to not let the same thing happen again.

What is the alternative? To just throw in the towel and say such a thing is not in our power, as Nietzsche believed? Nietzsche went insane in his later years, and while no one knows with certainty the cause of his mental afflictions, some people have theorized that his madness was a result of the hopelessness brought about by his own philosophy. (Meg says what he really needed was just a good dog.)

So which would you choose? A Western Nietzchean world view that promotes anxiety, despair, madness, faithlessness and an inability to promise love forever? Or a Zen Buddhist philosophy that teaches the possibility of finding happiness, truth and love every day, every moment, for the rest of your life?

Zen I

I.
Eye.

~

Zen II

You.
Mu.

~

Zen III

We

Be.

~

I N KEEPING WITH THE SPIRIT of Zen, there are no reflections (other than this) for Zen I, Zen II and Zen III; these po are koans, mysterious sayings to be meditated on until one realizes their true meaning. The only "explanation" for English speakers is that *mu* is a Japanese word that has no direct English translation, but is variously translated as "emptiness," "no," "none," "null," "without" or "no meaning." It is often used as a mystical, monosyllabic, illogical focus in meditation. *Mu* is a mantra, much as Om is used in Hinduism, or even as amen is used in some meditative Christian prayers and hymns. In all three cases the short syllables with their long vowel sounds are drawn out, so the vibration of the word resonates throughout the body. Interestingly, amen comes from the Hebrew word for "truth" or "certainty."

The ultimate truth of the universe, the certainty of the vast emptiness of space and time, are considered one and the same in the Zen tradition.

Amen to that.

Zen Love

I,
You,
Love.

~

THROUGH THE SIMPLE REARRANGING OF words, and by making the punctuation as important as the words, you can subtly
yet profoundly alter the meaning of a simple, well-known
phrase such as "I love you."

"I love you" sets up a dynamic whereby someone is doing something to someone else. It's a one-way street. It also represents a very
egocentric idea, where the "I" becomes prominent and important, and
it implies a separateness between two people.

Whereas "I, You, Love." represents a much more inclusive scenario,
whereby two people exist side by side, in equanimity, with love as their
partner as a force that pervades the universe.

It is a much quieter, and ultimately much stronger statement, where
two people can sit in peaceful bliss, where time is not a factor, neither
acting on the other, but simply enjoying the love that includes them,
not separates them. It is a very peaceful po.

"I, You, Love." is, in English grammar terms, three equal nouns, as opposed to the subject, verb and object in "I love you." And that ability of language to represent two vastly different but related ideas, just by the simple rearranging of three words and slightly different punctuation, is fascinating to me in its nuance.

There were other options. Should the construction instead be:

I.

You.

Love.

Or:

You,

I,

Love.

Would periods instead of commas convey a greater sense of each individual as their own entity? Was putting myself, the "I" first too egocentric? How to convey the more circular sense of a truly loving relationship, where neither partner is more important than the other? Should both "I" and "You" be on the same line?

I, You,

Love.

Or:

You, I,
Love.

In the end I just liked the pyramidal structure of the po:

I.
You.
Love.

With Love as the foundation, and I and You working together to reach toward the heavens, I think this is the purest expression of the reality of love. I showed this to Meg, and she felt the same way.

Night Light

Full moon,

swoon.

~

HOW IS IT THAT THE full moon can have such an effect on our souls? After years of Buddhist meditation, where emotions are supposed to be more even, I still feel ecstasy at the sight of the full moon bathing the water in silver light as I sit on Nirvana, anchored in a peaceful harbor, or sailing at night, slipping along a shadowy coastline, lights twinkling in the darkness, the landlubbers blissfully warm and snug in their homes. Some of my most memorable times on the water have been sailing at night, sitting in the cockpit at three a.m. with a good friend and a warm mug of coffee, talking about deep thoughts we would never dare voice at other times. The moon pulls our feelings out of us, like it pulls the tides. I get that same feeling of ecstasy on land, walking Henry across moonlit fields—such ecstasy that I feel knees weaken and body tremble, a huge breath filling my lungs. In Zen we talk of the moon being enlightenment, and Zen only being the finger pointing at the moon. How true, how true....

Ego

My

I.

~

LOVE THIS. QUITE PROUD OF IT. (Doesn't that just fit with a po called "Ego?") This po is about as short as a thought in the English language can possibly be: a three-letter title, with only three letters and one punctuation mark in the po. But still this po conveys a large and deep meaning, a reflection of our self, like a placid but fathomless mountain lake.

It is shorter than any of the previous world's shortest poems: "Fleas" (Adam/Had 'em), also known as "Lines on the Antiquity of Microbes," written in the 1920's by the U.S. poet Strickland Gillian, or Muhammad Ali's "Whee!/Me!", his paean to his own supersized ego (see "Ancestor Wordship" in Bricolage for more information about the world's shortest poetry). I think "Ego" wins the award for the world's shortest poem.

It welled up from my id (or was the "My" a controlling product of my superego?) while meditating at a *zazenkai,* a day-long meditation retreat, at the Ocean Zendo on October 23, 2007.

Earth Insight

Realm of Gods,
I Nod.

~

I was raised a Presbyterian, and church was always a factor in my life as I was growing up, although not the dominant factor. One of my earliest memories is of visiting my father's Sunday school classroom at the local church where he taught in Richmond, Indiana. The kids all seemed so adult and grown up and my father was such a presence as their wise old teacher. I laugh now to think about it; I was probably four or five, the kids were only about twelve and my father only in his late twenties. There was something special, however, about that room: an aura of spirituality, a presence; it was my first glimpse of the power of, dare I say it? God?

When I was older I actually wanted to attend Sunday school, as well as after-school Bible study. (Okay, maybe "want" is too strong a word, but I didn't fight it either.) I would ride my bike from elementary school to our small-town, white-steepled church in Orchard Park, a country suburb of Buffalo, stopping at the local drugstore along the way for a quick candy fix. I learned the stories of the Bible, absorbed Christian morality in spite of myself and became well versed in the Christian concepts of God, heaven, hell, angels, devils, resurrection and other cornerstones of Christian theology.

So the ideas of God and heaven have been with me since I was a child, and like most people of the Christian faith, I was taught and believed that heaven was someplace else, a place one went after death, the realm of God and St. Peter and the angels. I was taught that if I prayed and behaved well and followed the Ten Commandments and the golden rule that I would go to heaven.

But nobody really ever taught me how to pray. I was given the words, and told to bow my head and clasp my hands, but that was about it. And as far as getting to heaven, well, that seemed remote at best, given my proclivity for getting into the usual—and sometimes more than usual—young boy trouble.

There were a number of things that first attracted me to Buddhism many years after those first spiritual lessons. Partly it was a college professor who made Eastern philosophy come alive, partly it was a well-written book that spoke to me, and partly it was a family member who had already taken a Buddhist path. But one of the most important qualities was its sheer practicality, a very American trait: sit a certain way with legs folded, spine straight and hands in your lap; breath a certain way, cast your gaze a certain way; repeat daily and you too can see the heaven that surrounds you every moment of every day. No need to wait for death, no obligation to suffer needlessly through this life, heaven on earth—nirvana—is real, tangible and attainable to anyone willing to work for it.

It didn't happen overnight, but thanks to meditation the change in how I saw the world did come. Now I can hear a bird singing in a tree, or smell the fecund aroma of a shoreline at low tide, or see a baby crying or a kid riding their bike and know that we do indeed live in an earthly paradise, the realm of gods. The harder thing is to watch one's mother or brother-in-law die a tragic death, or watch one's children suffering after a divorce, or to have a fight with one's spouse and still go beyond the sadness and regret to see that these, too, are all part of our heaven on earth. But it can be done. Every day I see at least one thing that reminds me how fortunate we are to live in this nirvana, and I smile and nod my head imperceptibly in its direction, an acknowledgment of the winsomeness and wisdom of the world.

Worth Insight

Glowing Pearl,
Floating world.

~

THE GREAT CHINESE ZEN MASTER Gensha, who achieved enlightenment somewhere around 873 CE, would say, in order to instruct people, "All the universe is one bright pearl." Before becoming a monk, Gensha had been a fisherman on the Nandai River, and so used an analogy firmly rooted in the natural marine world with which he was familiar.

Once, another monk asked him, "I hear you have said all the universe is one bright pearl. How can I gain understanding of this?"

Gensha said, "All the universe is one bright pearl. What need is there to understand it?"

The next day Gensha subtly changed the question. He asked the monk, "All the universe is one bright pearl. What is your understanding of it?"

The monk answered, "All the universe is one bright pearl. What need is there to understand it?"

"I know now," replied Gensha, "that you are living in a ghost cave in the mountain of darkness."

I have struggled with this dichotomy my entire life: how to pare down to the essence of The Pearl, to simply see, feel and appreciate the world's worth, while still leaving open the door to instruction, explanation, dialogue and understanding? How to balance these two opposites so as not to be living in a ghost cave in a mountain of darkness?

There is a dichotomy between what Zen refers to as the "Absolute" and the "Relative" worlds. The Absolute is perfect, glorious, unchanging—the glowing pearl of universal mind, something to be felt, and possibly beyond man's capacity to "understand" from an intellectual standpoint, while the Relative is the world we live in every day, a world of ups and downs, joys and sorrows, tragedy and comedy—a ghost cave in the mountain of darkness. In Japan's Edo Period (1600–1867) the term "Floating World" described the pleasure-seeking aspects of the relative world in Edo (modern Tokyo) including geisha, brothels, tea houses, kabuki theaters, sumo wrestlers and samurai. This floating world was seen as a mask, the seeming gaiety a way of hiding the suffering of the human condition. The term "Floating World" was also an ironic allusion in Japanese to the homophone "Sorrowful World," the earthly plane of death and rebirth from which Buddhists sought release. But floating freely can also be the essence of the glowing pearl, a world in which one exists in a state of suspended animation, unfettered by the bounds of time and space, free of cares, worries, sorrows and emotions. A world in which one defies the very laws of nature, a world in which inanimate objects glow magically from within. And "floating world" can certainly describe living on a sailboat, with its leaking hatches, stormy seas, mildewed cushions, but also its glorious sunny days on the water, its laughter, family trips to the Bahamas and stunning sunsets.

In the "Sandokai," a Japanese Zen text whose title is often translated as "The Identity of Relative and Absolute," there are these lines: "Light and darkness are like the foot before and the foot behind in walking. Each thing has its own place and relation to everything else in form and function. The Relative fits the Absolute as a box and its lid. The Absolute meets the Relative like two arrows meeting high in mid-air."

Understanding both the Relative and the Absolute, the ghost cave and The Pearl, the floating sorrowful world and the floating nirvana world and how they are really two sides to the same coin—this is a key to understanding the universe's true worth.

Rothko A Gogo

Orange and gold,
Meaning unfolds.

~

THE OLD CLICHE ABOUT YOUR life flashing before your eyes at the moment just before the car hits you may or may not be true—since my amnesia stole any memory of the accident, I don't know if that flash-before-your-eyes moment happened. But I do know that in the weeks and months following the accident I had the luxury of time, the luxury to ask, "What have I done with my life? Who am I? What is important to me? What are my values? As I rebuild my life and sense of self, what are the cornerstones of the human being known as Lee Carlson?"

When you come face to face with death, you begin to look back at your life, trying to make sense of who you really are, what you have accomplished and what you want to do with the precious time you have left. In my own case, I could see the thread of spirituality, creativity and Zen-like minimalism that ran through my life like a golden, gossamer thread. I could see as I looked back my interest in the spiritual path: Sunday school as a youth, classes in existentialism and philosophy in high school, classes in Eastern Religions and philosophy in college, trips alone to various churches as an adult. I could also see how I had put those urges on the back burner to keep peace in my marriage and to focus on making money to support a family.

Another thread that ran through my life was creativity. Other early memories had to do with art classes—drawings and paintings created, ceramics made, stories written. I had been a natural-born draftsman, and my mother, recognizing my talent, had taken me to weekend art classes at the Albright-Knox Art Gallery, the public museum in Buffalo with its world-renowned collection of modern art. I was fortunate to attend a high school that celebrated the arts; I continued drawing and painting, and in the spring of my senior year, having fulfilled all the requirements for graduation, I spent the last few months creating large abstract color-field canvases in an old squash court that had been converted into a painting studio. At graduation I received the Headmaster's Award and was given a copy of Rollo May's "The Courage to Create" instead of a plaque or citation.

After high school I landed a job at the Albright-Knox. I would spend my lunch hour sitting in front of a single painting by Clyfford Still, Robert Motherwell, Helen Frankenthaler, Richard Diebenkorn or my favorite, an orange and gold "multiform" painting by Mark Rothko. As a young painter, I was fascinated by the deceptively understated squares of Rothko, feeling that his was the real genius of abstract expressionism as opposed to Pollock's frenetic multilayered canvas. There was a preternatural calm, an ethereal mystery that called to me.

The museum's director introduced me to the work of artists such as Walasse Ting, the Chinese abstract painter who was also a poet, and Motherwell's illuminating essays based on his background in philosophy, which showed me the possibilities of creative interconnectedness between the visual arts and the written word.

In my mid-twenties I did the grand European tour with money I saved up from my first "real" job as production manager of a construction company. I wanted to see all the great art of Europe and the Middle East that I had only seen in textbooks. I wanted to travel to southern France and see and feel what Gauguin and Van Gogh had seen and felt. I wanted to explore Paris and sit in Notre Dame at sunset and listen to the organ as the last rays of the sun lit up the windows. I wanted to visit Rome and Athens to experience firsthand the genius of the classical painters and sculptors. I longed to visit Egypt and connect with the work of artists who lived three thousand years ago, to view with wonder and appreciation their paintings on tomb walls, to stand in awe of their vast monumental sculpture. It was a trip of both discovery and ancestor worship, a trip backward through time.

My first stop was London, and I was eager to see the great museums and the London theatre scene I'd heard so much about. I wanted to walk the same streets as Shakespeare and Dickens and Sir Arthur Conan Doyle, to see the warehouses along the Thames where Oliver Twist and the Artful Dodger had woven their intricate bond. On my first full day in London I visited the Tate Gallery, wandering through the galleries on a quiet midweek day. I was eager to see Bacon and Turner and Blake and the museum's famous collection of nineteenth- and twentieth-century art. I was in awe of Turner's late landscapes, no more than simple atmospheric fields of color. As I wandered the galleries, I came upon what to me was an old friend: a collection of Rothko paintings hanging in a dedicated gallery known as "The Rothko Room." Since it was a weekday morning, the only other people in the gallery were a young British couple. I could overhear their conversation: the young woman—pretty, vivacious, with long dark hair and what was, to my American ear, a charming British accent—was trying to help her boyfriend acquire some culture. He was having none of it, however. His accent was decidedly more cockney Brit than hers, and he had definite opinions about what he saw in front of him.

"Dis is art? Lor' luv a duck! I could 'ave done dis. Sorted mate. Know what I mean? Blimey! Someone got paid apple pie fer dis? Boy, the museum sure got ripped off. Nuff said, yeah?" and so on and so on. His girlfriend tried to get him to open up to the art, but she couldn't find the right words to break through his defenses, not to mention the dynamics of British, stiff-upper-lip courtships. It was like a Monty Python sketch.

The young man had the air of a tradesman; I imagined him to be an auto mechanic, or a mason—someone who knew the value of a hard day's work creating utilitarian things with his own hands; he obviously couldn't fathom a person getting paid big bucks to paint colored squares on canvas. His girlfriend, on the other hand, wanted desperately for something more; you could tell that even though she didn't have "education," she yearned to be more cultured and wanted her young man to share her more sensitive urges.

I don't know what possessed me—perhaps it was the jet lag, perhaps the large quantity of British pub beer imbibed the night before. Perhaps I was just lonely traveling by myself and wanted someone to talk to, or perhaps I sensed that deep down the young man was ready for something more.

So I thought I'd attempt to do a good deed, saving this young couple's relationship before their different views of art hardened into irreconcilable world views. We were about the same age, and I'd already worked as a steelworker, auto mechanic and landscaper in my short career, so I felt a blue collar kinship with this young man and thought perhaps maybe, just maybe I could help open his eyes to the wonders and possibilities of modern art. I walked over and introduced myself and told them about Rothko, about how the deceptive simplicity of the canvas masked a far greater complexity of thought, how Rothko was trying to do what all painters did, which was to illustrate an idea, a feeling, through color and shape and form. I gave them a brief history of abstract expressionism and how Rothko was simply a modern extension of Turner, one of England's greatest artists, whose "Sunrise with Sea Monsters"—nothing more than swirls of yellow and ochre and white—hung in a nearby gallery.

Who knows what these two young Londoners really thought of this crazy American, this alien being who had suddenly intruded on their day telling them far-fetched stories about art history and theory? But the young man listened, asked a few questions and, turning back to the paintings, surveyed them with a fresh eye.

The young woman seemed relieved, and very thankful, and as I left them they were still contemplating the paintings. Perhaps it was the added time spent in front of the canvases, perhaps it was the hint of explanation opening up a new world for them, like the oyster shucker's knife prying open the shell to reveal a glimpse of the pearl within, but something about that simple, quiet room filled with the glow of deceptively unadorned oil paintings slowly worked its magic on them.

Rothko and Turner were both looking for ways to express spirituality through art. Rothko's nondenominational chapel in Houston, for which he painted fourteen paintings designed to aid in spiritual meditation, is one of the great marriages of modern art and mysticism. In my own history, I could see that I was trying to find that same fusion.

Why does the human memory work the way it does? Why, after my accident, could I remember long-ago moments in a London museum with such clarity, but couldn't remember what I had done the day before? I asked my doctors, and they had no ready explanation, saying only that the human memory is still one of the great mysteries of neurology. One theory is that our memory concentrates on items necessary for survival: where to find food, paying the rent, who is our enemy and who is our friend. But why would I remember something that happened twenty years before in a museum that seemingly had no bearing on my survival? I can only attribute my selective memory to an injured brain concentrating on the things that were really important to me, the pearl of wisdom embodied in an orange and gold Rothko painting, the pearl of art and spirituality, a pearl so precious that it was worth sharing with total strangers, so priceless that it was worth remembering.

White Mist

Jukai,
Exactly why?

~

I N LATE OCTOBER, 2009, THE manuscript for "Passage to Nirvana" was mostly finished, having gone through innumerable rewrites, additions and edits. I thought I was finished several times during the preceding months, but each time a new po would arrive unbidden, or I would think of additions to existing reflections. My still-healing brain was not yet ready to discharge itself from literary therapy. But at this point I was absolutely, positively, one-hundred-percent certain the book was finished. No more po. No more additions. I was done. Really. And then I attended a *zazenkai,* a day-long silent meditation retreat at the Ocean Zendo.

At 4:00 a.m. the alarm brought me out of a sound sleep, and I dressed slowly in the dark, not wanting to wake Meg or the dogs. Clothes were laid out from the night before on the table in the main saloon, although in typical dualistic Zen fashion, all attempts at starting the day with serious intentions were made comic by the challenge of putting on all-black clothing in the dark: pants went on backwards, arms ended up in neck holes, a black sweater disappeared under the table. Finally I gave sleeping Meg a kiss and drove the hour and a half from Nirvana's dock in Greenport to the Zendo.

There was ample time during the drive to ask, as I often did, why was I doing this? The rest of the world was sensibly asleep, snug and warm in their beds. Mine was one of few cars on the road. The early morning darkness was cold and damp and my body felt stiff; Nirvana had only a small space heater and even with thick blankets, my bones and joints were chilled.

But driving alone through the dark fields, along the narrow country roads while the world slept, there was a peace, a sense of purpose, a shadowy grace and calm that others were missing, curled up beneath their cozy comforters.

Other emotions manifested themselves, ghostlike, floating in and out of my half-awake consciousness. I had a vague sense of jealousy for those who lived only minutes from the Zendo, envious that their alarms probably went off at 5:00 or 5:30, since *zazenkai* began at 6:00. I also had a very real sense of unease and worry: shouldn't I be spending the day following up with literary agents? Or maybe taking the opposite tack: forget the whole dream of publishing a book and instead concentrate on finding a "real" job? I checked the odometer: 195,000 miles; the brakes felt rough. How much longer would the car last before a major repair bill? My bank account was down to a few thousand dollars; where was the next paycheck going to come from? Cash so I could visit my children? Wouldn't it be more responsible to spend the day figuring out how to make some money instead of sitting on my butt meditating on nothingness?

In Japanese *zendos* the day routinely begins at 4:00 a.m., so I had no real claim to hardship because of the early hour. If I was really a serious Zen student then getting up at 4:00 was par for the course. And work? This was my work. I had spent ten years studying, sitting, meditating, reading and immersing myself in Zen. If the Ocean Zendo had been a university and Matthiessen Roshi and Dai-en Sensei had been professors, I would have a Ph.D. by now. (Sensei is a Japanese honorific for teacher. Dai-en's English name is Dorothy Friedman; Dai-en is her dharma name, a spiritual moniker given to her by her own teacher when she took her Buddhist vows. Roshi Matthiessen's dharma name is Muryo, which translates as "No Boundaries.")

There was a symmetry to driving to the Zendo on this morning: it was almost ten years to the day since I had sent a letter to Peter Matthiessen asking to join his sangha and had received his welcoming reply. Along the way there had been deaths, divorce, brain-damaging accidents, pennilessness and pain. But there had also been life-affirming joy, clarity, wisdom and love, much of it brought about thanks to Zen teachers and daily meditation. As worried as I was, this was the path I had chosen. This path had resulted in giving up most of my worldly possessions and moving onto a boat. This path had resulted in a manuscript that I hoped would be of help to others. This path had led to an inner peace in spite of all the chaos that swirled throughout my life like blizzard whorls of swirling snow. There were moments when I wondered if the path was worth the struggle: maybe I should give up the fantasy of sharing what I had learned so that others could find peace. Maybe I should lead a "normal" life, get a nine-to-five job, settle down in a house. Maybe I should just turn the car around and go home.

But I had tried those other paths, and they hadn't worked, partly thanks to a brain injury that left me often forgetful, tired and confused. I had gotten a job in my previous field as a writer and been fired after one month. I had been hired as an estate manager and quit after six months because the stress had left me drained. I had tried real estate sales, but hadn't made much money thanks to a faulty memory that left me unable to remember clients and houses and prices and numbers of rooms. I worked as a part-time private yacht captain, but couldn't commit to the long, stressful hours a full-time captain's job would entail.

Yet throughout this journey my spiritual life had been a constant. I still believed in the Quaker proverb "Proceed As Way Opens" that I had adopted earlier, and new paths had always opened when things had seemed most hopeless. Have faith, I told myself. I had spent ten years getting to this point and it seemed wrong to turn back now. I was reminded of the René Descartes quote, "If you would be a real seeker after truth, it is necessary that at least once in your life you doubt, as far as possible, all things." It seemed to me that I doubted things more than just once in my life, but Descartes had said "at least once," leaving open the possibility for doubt again and again, the possibility to keep asking, "Why?"

There was time to stop at a 7–Eleven convenience store for a quick cup of tea to wake the brain and warm the body. I wondered what the

early morning collection of carpenters, farmers and Hispanic day laborers would think of the odd goings-on down the road, a cult of crazy
people all dressed in black, staring at blank walls, chanting strange
Japanese incantations. And yet somehow the tentacles of Eastern culture had wormed their way into even this icon of Western civilization;
packets of green tea were available next to the coffee, glazed donuts and
egg-and-sausage breakfast sandwiches.

At the Zendo the sky was an inky black, and the crisp cold air
reverberated with the reassuring "tok, tok, tok" of the *han*, a wooden
block hanging outside the Zendo door that a silent student struck with
a wooden mallet—Zen's version of a call to the faithful. In the morning stillness unseen crickets chirped in the fields. I settled onto a round
black *zafu*, fully expecting a day of peace. Arrayed around the Zendo
were a dozen or so other sangha members, all in black, all sitting facing
the blank white walls.

But the universe doesn't always work the way we desire. By the end
of the first half hour a burning, searing sensation had started in my legs.
During the first *kinhin*, or walking meditation, I felt a post-TBI stress
reaction setting in, a reaction to the pain. I felt body and brain go into
anxiety overdrive, or "want to scream" mode, a reaction I knew all too
well in the years since the brain injury, but hadn't felt in a long time. Why
now? In a place where I was supposed to be immune to such reactions? A
place of peace? A place that was supposed to be a refuge from the stresses
that were the usual flashpoint for such post-brain-injury stress reactions?

Perhaps the anxiety was a response to the pain, perhaps a response
to the very real worries about money, car, kids … life. Whatever it was,
the pain was real, the stress was real, the anxiety was real. Or was it?
Part of the Zen credo is that emotions, such as pain, are illusions. True
Buddhist adepts, such as the extremist Vietnamese monks who practiced self-immolation in the streets of Saigon during the Vietnam War
without flinching, have realized the illusory nature of pain, both physical and psychological.

But if pain is an illusion, that morning it was a very real, very strong
illusion, and it had its grip on body and brain. Having been through
this before, I sat down on the cushion for the second half-hour sitting
session, determined that the pain would not win, that I would control
it, instead of it controlling me.

After ten minutes, Roshi arose from his cushion at the far corner of the Zendo next to the altar. He moved quietly to the wooden altar table with its incense, flowers and small rustic statue of the Buddha. He stood quietly for some moments, preparing for his words. With eyes half-closed, all I could see was the wall a foot in front of my nose, yet I knew Roshi was standing there. In the early morning silence, awareness came through sounds, feelings and reverberations.

"This is a beautiful time of year," he began in his steady, sonorous voice. "On the ocean, all the animals are moving west. The anchovies, the striped bass, the bluefish are all moving out into the open sea for the winter. And the birds are following them: gulls, sea ducks—the big-bodied black and white eider ducks. But the most impressive bird," he continued, "is the gannet. Pure white, much bigger than the other birds, with a huge wingspan, black-tipped wings, it dives sideways into the water with a splash, one bird after the other. If there is a mist in the air, you don't even see the birds diving, you just see puffs of white, like smoke, where they dive. Splash... splash... splash.... Like Basho's haiku." Then he recited the famous three lines:

Ancient pond
frog jumps in
splash.

"That splash, that bird diving, is this very moment...." His slow words were a whisper now, barely audible:

splash...
splash...
splash....

By the end of the second half-hour the pain was so intense that sweat ran down my back, down armpits, soaking my black shirt. I practiced as I had been taught: breathing through the pain, breathing into the pain, embracing the pain. I silently repeated instructions from a biofeedback tape I had been given by my one of my doctors: "...take a deep breath, now let it go...." trying to calm a body and mind agitated from the pain.

I sat silently, waiting for the bell that would end the session, allowing me to arise and walk, easing the pain.

And yet, and yet....

In spite of the torment, there were moments when my mind and body would smile silently, happy, at peace. A paradox? Perhaps. Masochistic? I hope not. But glimpses of non-self allowed for no-pain. When there is no self, who is there to feel pain?

In the years since the accident, I have learned to live with chronic pain, both physical and psychological (although the two are not really separate). Pain has become a part of the daily fabric of life, like air currents playing across skin. It is most prevalent in my left hip and leg where the car hit, but the pain can also be in my shoulder, neck and skull where I hit the pavement. I have prescription painkillers, but rarely use them, preferring to deal with the pain naturally rather than becoming addicted to opiates. I can usually control the pain with meditation and biofeedback, although on occasions when the pain is so bad that I take painkillers, I am reminded of how good life feels when the pain is gone. Sometimes the pain will just disappear on its own, and my body relaxes with a large sigh of relief.

One of the stranger outcomes of the accident was that I felt very little pain when I awoke in the hospital. It was only weeks later that the pain grew and became more intense. When I asked Dr. Rubino about this, he explained that the pain was a good sign, it meant my brain was beginning to heal and could now feel pain. The pain had always been there, he said, I just couldn't feel it.

I wasn't sure whether to be thankful or not. I had read about people who suffered from leprosy, and how they had no feelings in their limbs, which would result in their cutting or burning their extremities without knowing it, thus developing infections which were often the cause of their losing fingers or toes. I had read accounts of leprosy sufferers who wished for pain, wished they could feel something, anything, rather than that dead numbness.

Pain for me had become simply an ever-present companion. Perhaps because of this I felt a special affinity for the Buddha's teaching that all life is suffering. But why was the pain suddenly so much worse now? Maybe it was from being fifty-one years old and sleeping in a cold, damp boat, waking stiff and creaky, and then driving in a car for an hour. Perhaps it was years of violent sports as a youth: football, ice hockey, lacrosse. Perhaps it was years of running on hard pavement, or playing tennis, or jumping off cliffs and pounding through icy moguls on skis. Perhaps it was hereditary: my mother had both knees replaced at the young age of sixty-three when degenerative arthritis made it nearly impossible for her to walk. Perhaps it was my own knee surgery to repair damaged cartilage several years ago, or perhaps it was the fact I had jogged yesterday, and had done some small injury to joints or bone. Perhaps it was an immune system reaction to the flu and tetanus shots I had received several days before. Perhaps it was because I'd gotten away from my daily yoga practice. Perhaps I needed to go back and reread one of my first po, "Water Wisdom," about the importance of soaking in a hot bath. Perhaps it was a combination of all these things.

Whatever it was, my body was teaching me once again the Buddhist truth that real unhappiness and pain comes from desire. I had been looking forward to a day of peaceful sitting. I had hungered for this *zazenkai* as a respite from the cares and concerns of daily life, and now my body was saying, "Tough luck sucker, you wanted a blissful, quiet, pain-free, peaceful day? Fuggedaboutit." And that chasm between want and reality was driving me crazy. Why was I doing this?

After the third sitting session, a morning service with chanting, bell ringing and bowing, I left the Zendo and drove to a nearby pharmacy to buy ibuprofen and pain-relieving gel. The Buddha famously taught the middle way; after years as a Hindu ascetic when he almost starved himself to death, he realized that such bodily abuse was not conducive to spiritual enlightenment. Right on, Buddha, I'm with you on that. Sitting in severe pain that causes post-traumatic-brain-damage-disorder-anxiety doesn't help anyone. Bring on the ibuprofen.

Even walking the aisles of the pharmacy was painful; I felt my back seize up as pain shot from my hip. I drove to the ocean beach near the Zendo, hoping that a walk would warm my joints and ease the pain, but also hoping for a glimpse of ducks, gulls, fish and perhaps even a flock of gannets diving in, white puffs of mist on the ocean waves... splash... splash... splash....

Wind blew hard from the North, grey clouds scudded low across the dark, jade-colored, foam-flecked ocean. Shafts of radiant golden sunlight broke through and sparkled on the water. Boots slipped in sand. Gulls and ducks bobbed in the waves, but no gannets were diving.

I drove back to the Zendo, parked the car, pulled out iPod and headphones and reclined the driver's seat. I began listening to a guided visualization biofeedback recording given me by one of my doctors. There was soft, healing music and a gentle male voice:

> As you exhale, allow the feeling of any pain that you may have to expand; yes, actually let it expand. Without resisting it, imagine the pain opening out and dissolving into space. As the sense of the pain expands, vividly imagine feeling an echo of healing energy pouring into you from the universe surrounding you. Feel this healing wave flowing into you, dissolving into the region of the pain. If you are experiencing a sense of burning, allow that feeling to expand, while simultaneously a cool, soothing energy is drawn back into you. If you are feeling agitated, allow that feeling to open ... expand ... and dissipate ... while at the same time you feel an infusion of deep peace and calm pouring into you, flooding you completely with well-being. Allow yourself to receive from the universe at large whatever you most need at this time. Allow your breath to naturally and effortlessly bathe your tissues in oxygen and light that dissolves tensions and pain.
>
> Exhaling, give yourself permission to release the fatigue that fogs your mind, and to let go of knots of tension that are locked in your body. Let everything within you move toward balance and toward harmony now. Allow the waves of your breath to fill you with the love, the courage and the strength that you need to let go of tension, to let go of fear, to release doubt, or anger, and come to rest in your wholeness.

Breathe in and receive the positive healing qualities that you need at this time. Release the old limitations that are now unnecessary. Rest in your wholeness, connected to, and belonging to the world....

Continue breathing effortlessly now, imagine that you are breathing in a pure crystalline mist of vibrant light, allow the waves of your breath to come and go with their own natural rhythm. Imagine that this vibrant light flows first to the center of your chest, and then pours forth throughout your whole body. Direct this powerful, purifying light to any region of your body that calls for more healing or harmonizing. Sense and feel that your whole being is now pure and clear like a crystal body flooded by rainbow light. Vividly imagine this luminous energy pouring through you and then out into the world. Imagine that as you mentally direct this vibrant light to others, that it helps to dissolve their tensions, to calm their minds and to open their hearts to a greater sense of relaxation, warmth and well-being. Vividly sense and affirm that this energy and light that pours through you brings greater harmony to the world in which you live....

At the Zendo it was *samu*, or work meditation time, when Ocean Zendo members silently clean the Zendo and the grounds, vacuuming cushions, sweeping the rock garden, picking up leaves and twigs shaken loose from trees by the autumn winds. I saw an old friend, George, one of the Ocean Zendo monks, picking up trash by the side of the road and felt guilty I wasn't helping. What would he think if he saw me sitting in the car with headphones on? Would he assume I was just hanging out, listening to music? But I knew I had to try calming my body and mind so I could sit through the rest of the day.

The similarity between ancient Zen meditation and modern bio-feedback always amazed me, and this morning I was again struck by the nuanced parallels: the emphasis on the breath, on letting go, the natural imagery—waves, light, mist—and finally the emphasis on helping others, bringing greater harmony to the world....

When the next sitting period began, the pain had receded, but I was fearful of its return. I tried sitting in one of the few chairs in the Zendo, facing the back wall. It was less painful, but I felt unmoored, about to topple over at the slightest breeze, a very different feeling from the solid feeling one gets when sitting cross-legged on a cushion on the ground. But I was able to concentrate on the breath, still my mind, and just be.

There is a curious background hum at moments like this. With the mind perfectly quiet, and the fields, trees, bushes and air around the Zendo perfectly still, I could hear a background hum, like white noise. It was not the deep hiss of the distant ocean, the waves crashing against the beach—I could hear that too, far, far away. No, this was a different sound, something that came from within, not from without. I remembered Rick McCawley, the cognitive therapist, asking if I heard a background noise when I meditated, and I told him that yes, I did, wondering if this would be further evidence of brain malfunction. In the months after my accident, I had suffered from fairly severe tinnitus, or ringing in the ears, but that had subsided by the time Rick asked about noise. Still, I worried that my admission of hearing this white noise when I meditated was proof of something "wrong."

But Rick just said, "You're lucky, not everyone can hear it; that's the sound of the electrical workings of your brain."

Now, years later, this morning at the Zendo was an allegory of life, working through the screaming pain to find the quiet hum of contentment, making the commitment to overcoming the daily pain of living. How many of us are too quick to give up? How many of us are too quick to file for divorce? Too quick to turn back when life turns painful? How many of us are not faithful to our commitments? Faithful to our ideals? Our principles? How many of us are unlucky enough to miss that background hum?

What does it mean to be faithful? To be filled with faith? To have faith? What is it that one has faith in? Does being faithful mean never asking "Why" at all? Does it mean only journeying forth when the sun is shining, the day warm and the waters calm? Or does it mean having the courage to set sail in spite of icy winds, grey skies and fierce waves, in spite of pain, in spite of the nagging, numbing, "Why?"

An hour later it was time for *dokusan*, the one-on-one meeting between teacher and student. I left the Zendo, made my way across a stone path to Peter's grey-shingled house and upstairs to a small room, where Dorothy sat in her dark monk's robes on a dark cushion, waiting. I bowed, entered the room, bowed again and settled cross-legged onto a cushion immediately in front of her, so close that I could have reached out and touched her robes. Light flooded the room from a single window behind her. A Japanese brushwork scroll hung on one wall. I told her about the agony I had experienced that morning.

"Do you ever go deeper into the pain?" she asked.

Yes, I assured her, I knew all the tricks.

"You live an interesting life, living on a boat, always moving."

"It's a lesson in impermanence. There is no solid ground, even when I am meditating in the morning and the boat rolls on the waves and I rock back and forth on my cushion." I should have said, "I'm not grounded, I'm oceaned." But I wasn't that quick on the mental draw.

"I think it's time for *jukai*," I said.

Jukai is the Japanese Zen Buddhist initiation ceremony where one formally becomes a Buddhist. It literally translates as "receiving the Precepts," and the ceremony revolves around vowing to live a moral, faithful life.

The Precepts are roughly analogous to the Ten Commandments in the Judeo-Christian tradition. The Buddhist Precepts were not handed down on stone tablets; like all Buddhist texts they were handed down orally for many generations, since there were no writing instruments in Northern India in the Buddha's time. So the English translations of the Precepts vary widely; however most English Zen translations take the form of a way of thinking and acting to be internalized, rather than a harsh external command from some stern patriarch. I rather like this gentler approach to moral teachings. The original Pali word used to describe the state of being prescribed by the Precepts is *sila*, which best translates as the unchanging state of being we are born with—our own true nature. For example, a small child does not know how to lie. The child learns to lie as he or she gets older to avoid punishment or get something it wants.

The Precepts are:

- Affirming Life *(ceasing from evil and killing)*
- Being Satisfied With What You Have *(non-stealing)*
- Honoring the Body *(not misusing sex)*
- Manifesting Truth *(non-lying)*
- Seeing Clearly *(not clouding the mind, especially with drugs)*
- Seeing The Perfection *(not speaking ill of others and situations)*
- Practicing Equality *(not raising oneself above others)*
- Practicing Generosity *(not being stingy)*
- Actualizing Harmony *(non-anger)*
- Honoring Ancestors, Teachings and Community *(Buddha, Dharma and Sangha)*

In the many years I had been a Buddhist, incredibly I had never had *jukai*. The first time I was scheduled to take the Precepts had been eight years earlier. I had been preparing for the event, taking Precepts classes, sewing my *rakusu*, the square cloth garment that Zen Buddhists wear around their necks like a giant bib when they are meditating. I had picked a date with several other Zendo members who were also going to take *jukai*, invited my parents and sisters to come from Buffalo for the ceremony. On the morning of September 28, 2001, I wrote the following haiku I planned to use in the service:

A long walk
circling seagulls cry
– waves crashing

I'm sure my mood when writing that haiku had been influenced by the deaths of thousands two weeks before only seventy miles away in Manhattan, but perhaps I also had intimations of things to come. That evening, my mother fell down the basement stairs, sustaining her brain injury, and the next day I raced to Buffalo. *Jukai* would have to wait.

Eight months later I again began preparing for *jukai*. My earlier *jukai* partners had gone ahead with their ceremony; I was now planning to do the ceremony with Joan, another friend from the Zendo. Then I was hit by a car.

"Why do you want to do *jukai?*" Dorothy asked me.

"I don't want to do *jukai*; it's just time."

I reminded her of the two previous times I had planned to do the ceremony and the intervening circumstances: my mother's accident, my own accident.

"I'm not sure I should try to do it again," I said, "after what happened the first two times. But I just feel that it's time. It isn't a matter of wanting. I'm not really sure why I want to do it; I just know it's time."

"That's the way I do things now," Dai-en said. "I just act and figure it out later. After all, I'm eighty-one years old."

"A while back—months, a year maybe, I had a dream," I tell her. "You were in it, and you said to me, 'Lee, you have a gift.'" As I talk to her, Dorothy's white unruly hair is luminous, glowing like a halo around her head. This moment is definitely not a dream. I'm reminded of one of our first meetings ten years ago in this same room when I was telling her how worn out I was from the business failure, my marriage falling apart, the constant fighting with my wife, my mother's crippling brain injury.

"Lee, you're stronger than you think you are," she had said at the time, and she was right.

Now she said, "Write me a letter telling me why you want to do *jukai*. I perform a lot of weddings, and that's something I always have both people do, write me a letter about why they want to get married. The results are always illuminating."

"I don't *want* to do *jukai*," I say again. "It's just time."

"Yes, time does not always move," she said. "Sometimes it just is. That's the way it was when I became a monk."

She pauses.

"You do have a gift, Lee."

"So do you."

We bow to each other, still sitting, bending at the waist, both knowing the interview is over. I stand and bow again before backing out the door.

"Why" indeed? Why would anyone want to subject themselves to something that causes such physical pain? Why subject themselves to getting up at four in the morning and driving more than an hour and "working" all day and not even getting paid for it? Why spend a whole day in ways that could be spent more "productively?" A day spent writing, getting caught up on work? Why make that commitment? Why *jukai?* Why have faith?

There were rational reasons, like the "Ticking Clock" reason: Daien was eighty-one, Roshi eighty-two, they wouldn't be around forever. They were my teachers; I should do *jukai* while there was still time. Then there was the "Moral Life" reason. It was important that I take the formal vow to follow the Precepts, to live a moral life every day. Even though in my own mind I had made that vow long ago, affirming it in a public ceremony would only deepen that commitment. There was the "Generosity" reason. My Zen teachers and the Buddhist teachings had given me so much; it was time to give something back. Time to affirm my faith and my belief in the teachings of the Buddha so that I could continue the work of my teachers. It was a gift I could give to them, to let them know that their work had borne fruit and would continue on, and it was a gift I could give others by carrying on the teachings.

But the real reason was a Zen reason, an illogical reason, a mysterious reason: It was time. To be totally aware means to just know. To just know the way something is. The real reason was just "because."

As a boy I had all sorts of books that gave rational, scientific answers to the question "why?" Books that answered questions such as, "Why is the sky blue? Where do clouds come from? What are stars made of? Do fish ever sleep?" And other questions that at the time seemed huge, mysterious, unknowable.

I was an inquisitive kid, always asking all sorts of questions, always wanting to know the answers. Like most kids at times I drove my parents crazy. Usually they'd give me good answers, but sometimes they'd drive me crazy. They'd just say, "Because," as in "because that's the way it is," or "because that's the way we've always done things," or the clincher, "because I'm your father, and I said so."

When I was twelve, I was in my best friend's kitchen, and I announced to his mother, who was a college history professor, that I was an agnostic.

"Oh Lee," she said, "you don't even know what that means."

"Yes I do," I said. "It means that I'm not really sure if God exists or not, because I can't see him or touch him. He might exist, but there's no scientific way to prove it."

She looked at me skeptically. "Hmmm, you do seem to know what it means." I had been asking if a Great Spirit really existed, and no one seemed to have a good answer.

Ten years later in college I was attracted to Zen because it promised a resolution to this huge question: Does a Great Spirit exist? Zen didn't promise to give me any rational answers, but only to let me experience, firsthand, the truth about existence. Maddening as it would be, Zen would not answer the why, but at least it would let me know and appreciate the "because." But that can be annoying, like being a kid and asking parents why you have to be home by eleven p.m. and they say, "Because we told you to."

So I felt a little sheepish answering Dai-en's question: "Why did I want to do *jukai?*" with a simple "Because." I could have written a letter giving all sorts of rational reasons, like the ticking time theory, or the value of commitment, or the importance of generosity. I could have given her a treatise on the importance of faith, of living a moral life, the importance of belief. I could have said that I hoped that my deepening peace would ripple out through the ether, giving comfort to those around me, like the day laborers at 7-Eleven—the butterfly effect. I could have told her that we are never finished, that our lives are a constant work-in-progress, that our life story is constantly being written. I could have said that we are all stronger than we think we are, that we need to be strong in building a devoted and noble life, and communal ceremony was part of tapping into that strength. All those were true. But the greater truth was, I could not give her a rational answer. I could only voice an enigmatic "Because … because it's time."

Time to take the plunge, time to have faith, time to have strength, time to dive in…

Ocean bird dives

splash…

white mist.

LIFE & DEATH

Life
(Elizabethan Version)

Thou fly,
ere thy die.

~

Life
(Victorian Version)

Oh fly!
Alone die.

~

Life
(Modern Version)

I Fly.
I Die.

~

Life
(Zen Version)

Fly!
Die.

~

I HAVE A SOFT SPOT FOR this little chronological Life series, which reminds me of jazz riffs on a theme. The Zen version is the shortest, truest "short poem," but the variations are, I think, somewhat fun and humorous, especially the Elizabethan and Victorian versions, with their element of over-the-top theatricality. No need to get too stuffy and somber about all this life and death stuff. The modern version reflects how modern life is all about ego, about "what's in it for me?" All about I.

Life and death are the great questions: How to live? How to die? To retreat from life, to fall into depression and despair from divorce, death and sickness? Or to voyage forth, to fly during this short time we have on earth? To me, the Zen version sums this question up in the typical succinct, direct Zen manner.

Coma

Buddha sleeps,
Family weeps.

~

THE PHONE CALL FROM MY FATHER is something I will never forget. He called me early on a Saturday morning. "Your mother took a serious fall last night and is not good," he said in a grave monotone that was scary in its flat delivery. My father was usually an optimistic, cheerful man, and over the years when he had called to deliver bad news, he usually did so with an upbeat note in his voice. There was none of that now.

"It looks like a long road ahead," he said.

It was such a matter-of-fact statement; I know he was just trying to make the best of things, to take the burden of responsibility on himself and not bother me with sharing that responsibility. I don't think he had fully realized what had happened; he was exhausted and still in a state of shock. He described her fall down a flight of basement stairs, the ambulance ride to the hospital, how she now lay unconscious in the intensive care unit. He told me there was no need to come home: I had a life of my own to take care of, he said. He knew that I was going through a rough time with my wife's failing business and marital problems. Even so, it was my mother, and it was my father too, and although I appreciated my father's solicitude, I thought they could both use any support I could give them. I quickly packed a bag and told my boys that their grandmother was sick and needed my help. I told Belinda what had happened. There was no "I'm sorry," or "tell your father and sisters my thoughts are with them," just a stony silence. It was sad, in many ways, because my mother and Belinda had been friends. My mother had come to Manhattan to help when Chas was born, because Belinda's own mother had died of cancer when Belinda was in college. When the boys were little, Belinda would take them to Naples in the winter and stay with my mother when I was too busy with work and couldn't go, and my father was still working in Buffalo, and the two of them would go to the beach, the pool, play with Chas and Niall and just hang out. But the marital problems had destroyed the relationship between my mother and Belinda as well.

I got in my car and drove the ten hours to Buffalo.

At the hospital, my father was right; there really wasn't anything I could do. My mother lay on her back in the bed, eyes closed, tubes and wires connecting her to various monitors and machines. She was in a deep coma and was outwardly unresponsive to any stimuli.

And yet, and yet….

I gently rubbed her arm and spoke softly to her, letting her know I was there, her only son, her baby boy, in the hopes that maybe, just maybe, some kernel of consciousness was aware of my presence and would help alleviate her pain, help her heal. I loved her, I was there for her, and I wanted her to get better.

Bernie Glassman, a well-known American Zen master who is Matthiessen Roshi's closest teacher, the one who gave Peter "transmission" or certification to teach as a Zen Roshi, is a proponent of what he calls "bearing witness." The belief behind bearing witness is that by letting go of fixed ideas, by bearing witness to whatever is taking place within us and right before our eyes, we can heal ourselves and others and bring peace to the world around us. I was at the hospital to bear witness.

As my father, sisters and I began our vigil at the hospital, there was nothing we could do but wait. The neurosurgeon met with us in the family meeting room down the hall and explained the facts: the MRI showed an area of severe damage in her frontal lobe, the images delineated an area of necrotic brain tissue, brain cells that had died from the impact of the fall. The dead brain tissue was in an area that controlled language and other higher functions. He could tell us that, if she lived, her speech would be severely impaired, and she would have other impairments as well, but he couldn't say exactly what. The next twenty-four hours would be crucial to her survival. The doctor had inserted a catheter to drain excess fluid from her brain to relieve pressure in the cranial cavity, but if her brain began to swell, much as an injured ankle balloons up, then she would be in serious trouble. When the brain swells, unlike an ankle, there is no place for the tissue to go; the resulting increased intracranial pressure kills the brain, crushing crucial tissue and restricting blood supply, which causes death in the patient. If the pressure in her cranium began to rise, the surgeon explained, we had two choices: let her die, or operate to remove the part of her brain that was already dead to provide enough space for her brain to swell.

There was no way to know what was going to happen, he said, and so no need to make a decision now. Some people's brains swelled more, some less. The nurses would keep monitoring the pressure inside my mother's skull—that was the function of one of the monitors behind her bed. However we should be thinking seriously about what decision we would make, he said, if the intracranial pressure rose, because he would need to get her quickly into surgery if we wanted her to live.

How does a family make a decision like that? My mother had a living will and health care proxy, stating she wanted no artificial life-sustaining measures in the event she became incapacitated with no chance of recovery, and giving my father the legal authority to make decisions about withholding artificial life support. But such decisions are rarely so cut and dried, especially with brain injury. How incapacitated would she be? What does "recovery" really mean? What level of disability would be acceptable to a person? And not just a hypothetical person, but my mother, the woman who had given birth to me, raised me, held me when I cried as a child? What level of disability would be acceptable to us as a family? What could we handle, emotionally, physically, financially? The neurosurgeon left us to our thoughts, and we hoped we would not be forced to make the decision he described.

I returned to my mother's room and sat by her bedside, watching her labored breathing, the bandages wrapped around her head, wondering what she would want, asking myself how so senseless an accident could have happened. She had always been an incredibly vibrant woman, full of life and laughter. She had many close friends, had always been an ardent sportswoman, had been active in the church and worked as a volunteer for a number of different charities. She had owned her own business and raised a family. Just the day before, Kristan told me, Kristan and Mom had played golf. The country was still reeling from the events of 9/11, so Kristan was not very busy with her real estate business. She called my mother that morning and suggested they play, since it was a gorgeous day. Afterward Kristan, Mom, Dad and Kristan's three-year-old daughter Elizabeth had walked to a favorite Greek restaurant near Kristan's house for a late lunch. How could a woman have such a carefree day and a day later be lying in a coma, unable to move, speak or smile?

On the night of the accident, my parents had been at a dinner party in an unfamiliar house. As people were finishing their meals, she leaned over to my father and told him she was going to the bathroom. It was an old, rambling house, and no one will ever know exactly what happened next, but she went through the kitchen and into a back hallway, where there were a number of doors. Apparently she had walked down the dimly lit back hall, opened what she thought was the bathroom door, probably looking for a light switch, and instead stepped into the void. Where she had expected her foot to find a solid bathroom floor in the dark, instead she found empty air, lost her balance and tumbled headfirst down the basement steps, smashing her skull on the concrete basement floor. A guest who was in the kitchen clearing her dishes heard a loud sound, went into the back hallway and found my mother unconscious at the foot of the basement stairs.

I grew up in old houses, and as I sat by her bedside I couldn't help but think that if the owners of that house had installed a simple dollar-fifty latch on the basement door, my mother wouldn't be lying unconscious in front of me. My mother was not a big drinker, usually having one glass of wine with dinner, so the fall couldn't be blamed on too much alcohol. She was relatively young, in good shape, no family history of heart attacks or dizziness or any number of other conditions that could cause a fall. It was a freak household accident, so senseless.

We took turns sitting by her bed and then retiring to the family waiting room for some rest. I wandered the halls of the hospital, finding a small chapel on the first floor where I could pray in silence for her recovery. Then I would come stand by her bed, hold her hand, or hold my sisters' hands, and we would cry, our tears falling silently on the crumpled sheets covering our mother's prostrate form.

Finally the thing we had dreaded happened. In the middle of the night the swelling became more pronounced, and the attending nurses called the neurosurgeon who rushed to the hospital and met with us in a private room at 4:00 a.m., where we could make the decision we had all hoped would never come. The doctor had a varnished box under his arm. It contained his operating glasses and instruments, he explained, and he never let anyone else keep them for him. He was ready.

The final decision was my father's, but we had always been a close family, and as much as possible this would be a family decision. "What would she be like?" we asked. "What would her quality of life be like? Would she be able to speak? To walk? To care for herself?" We peppered the surgeon with questions, and as before the doctor could give us no specific answers to those questions, only saying he believed she would always have impairments and disabilities, but with time and therapy she would be able to resume some activities of daily living. However, there were no guarantees. Even with all the advances in neurology and brain imaging and understanding how the brain worked, no one could say with certainty which parts of her brain had been damaged beyond repair and which hadn't. No one could say for sure what removing the part of her brain that had already died would do to her. It was a part of the brain that controlled language, memory and cognition, that much was certain, but the brain worked in interconnected ways that still weren't fully understood, and parts of her brain that survived might take over functions that had been previously controlled by the now-dead tissue. It was a relatively new area of neurology known as neuroplasticity.

My mother loved life; we all felt certain she would want to live, given the chance, but what kind of life would she want to live? She had been an expert skier, sailor and tennis player, but degenerative arthritis had forced her to have both knees replaced seven years before and prevented her from ever skiing or playing tennis again, so she had taken up golf. She had been diagnosed with a rare sinus cancer in 1999 and had suffered through chemo, radiation and a brutal operation to remove a tumor that left her face partly disfigured, even with reconstructive plastic surgery. Told she only had a forty percent chance of surviving, she had beaten the odds, and even though she had her days of tears, mostly she kept smiling and laughing throughout the entire ordeal.

As we stood there with the neurosurgeon I finally asked the one question that I thought would be most important to her: "Will she know her grandchildren? Will they be able to sit on her knee and hug their grandma and have her hug them back? Will she be able to play games with them, however basic those games might be? Read to them, even if it's with impaired speech?" The neurosurgeon said, yes, he believed that she would still be herself, would still have her own personality, would still recognize people and be able to take part in the joys of daily living, albeit with disabilities. So we said all right, do the operation, we can't just let her die. She loved life. She would want to live.

In the months that followed I made the trip back and forth to Buffalo many times, spending a week at my mother's side as she still lay in a coma after the operation, then returning to my own family and work. I would meditate silently by the side of her bed, praying for her recovery. I would go down to the chapel and pray some more. I went to our family church, Westminster Presbyterian, where my parents had been married, where both my sisters and I had been married, where my aunt and uncle were married, where my grandparents' funerals had been held. I was amazed to discover that this bastion of WASP conservatism was holding weekly Zen meditation sessions in the basement meeting room, and I would sometimes join them. The minister, Tom Yorty, a friend of my mother, frequently stopped by her bed in the hospital.

As I silently sat with her for days on end in the intensive care unit, watching her hover in a state somewhere between life and death, connected to all the life support tubes and machines, I would meditate in a chair, back straight, hands in my lap, concentrating on my breath, and I began to get a sense of how precious my mother's life was, how precious she was. At times I almost felt guilty, because instead of feeling the immense grief I usually felt, I would feel a simple joy just being in her presence, being in the presence of a sleeping buddha, and tears of joy would mix with the tears of sorrow staining my mother's sheets.

Time

Just now,
Wow...

~

WHEN I FIRST REGAINED CONSCIOUSNESS in the hospital I felt an incredible sense of euphoria. Even though I was lying in a hospital bed, unable to get up and walk on my own, with tubes stuck in holes in my body, I felt like I was ready to get up and fly. I joked with the nurses and doctors, laughed with my sister who sat by my bedside, and generally felt right at home.

When I was transferred from the hospital to Florida for rehab, this strange euphoric feeling continued. At first I didn't question the sensation, I just went with it and enjoyed it. Cognitively I wasn't functioning well enough to question such things as my emotional state. But after a few weeks, as my brain began to function more normally and I became aware that this constant state of unbridled happiness was not "normal," I asked one of my doctors, Dr. Earl Rectanus, the psychologist who had been assigned to help me deal with the psychological minefields resulting from Traumatic Brain Injury, why I might be feeling this way. Earl was like a gentle bear, with his salt-and-pepper beard, serene demeanor and soothing voice.

"It's because you've gotten away from your wife," he half-joked, since he was well aware of my home life, or lack thereof. A large part of his job was understanding my living situation and helping me deal with the difficult problems most TBI patients have dealing with a suddenly upended family life. But as we talked, I realized that it wasn't just my wife I had gotten away from, but almost any sense of my past, or even my future. Partly this was because of my memory problems. I had been diagnosed with retrograde amnesia, which meant that I had very little memory of the several months before my accident, and other memories were scrambled as well. As Dr. Rubino described it to me, my brain was like a computer, and I hadn't damaged the hard drive, the place where memories were saved, but only the operating system that knew where the memories were stored and could retrieve them. I had a sort of adult version of shaken baby syndrome, he said; my brain cells were all still intact, but many of the wires connecting them—the neurons—had been severed by the rapid shaking of my brain in the skull as it hit the pavement. In medical terms this is known as axonal shearing. So the memories were there, I just couldn't access them. But with time and treatment the healing process would help those neurons regenerate. And he was right, my memory has improved over time, enough to write a book, although my memory will never be what it once was.

My brain had, thankfully, lost its ability to worry about things that weren't immediately apparent, moment by moment. Bills that needed to be paid? No problem—I didn't remember them. Client deadlines? A thing of the past, and since I had no past, no worry there. An angry, critical soon-to-be-ex-wife? What wife? She was a thousand miles away and out of the daily picture.

In fact, the daily picture was all that my brain could handle. Time became a very different commodity. I lived very much in the moment— no past, no future, only the blissful, blessed present.

One of the really strange things about this state of bliss was that living in the present moment is one of the holy grails of Zen, and intellectually I had been trying to achieve the goal of living in the present moment for several years through meditation, reading Buddhist texts and attending talks by well-known Buddhist teachers. But to suddenly experience this state in all its wonder and fullness, all because of a blow to the head, was, well, weird. As much as I enjoyed the feeling of happiness, it was also somewhat unsettling. It was as if the solid ground I had been walking on for forty-four years had suddenly started shifting below me, a seismic mind-quake registering a nearly perfect 9.9 on the Richter scale.

This state was at once both so delightful and so disconcerting that it worried me. And what about Zen? Did this mean that the state I had been striving for was the same as being a brain-damaged, blithering idiot? Or had I become a kind of Buddhist idiot-savant? Knowing something without having the intellectual capacity to really understand it?

I looked for a local Zen group in southwest Florida, and was pleased to find the Naples Community of Mindfulness, whose teacher, Fred Eppsteiner, had lived with and studied extensively under Thich Nhat Hanh, one of the great Zen teachers of the modern age. A small, slight, sweet-tempered man, Fred led meditation sessions every Tuesday night from 7:00 to 9:00 p.m. for about twenty to thirty people in the yoga studio where I had begun to take my restorative yoga classes. There would be sitting meditation, walking meditation, more sitting meditation and then a brief talk by Fred on some aspect of Buddhist teachings. Some people sat on meditation cushions on the polished wood floor, some people sat in chairs. It was all very relaxed and informal: there were no black-robed monks, no requirement to wear black clothing, long sleeves and long pants like I was used to in the Ocean Zendo. This being Florida, the opposite aesthetic prevailed: brightly colored Hawaiian shirts, tank tops, shorts and generally colorful clothing was the norm. But I couldn't totally leave my black Zen behind. I found a black Hawaiian shirt with a white leaf pattern on sale; I was good to go.

One evening after the official session was over I talked to Fred about this state of timelessness I was living in, and about my concerns, and he just laughed and with a twinkle in his eye said, "Just enjoy it; you're experiencing what the rest of us spend a lifetime trying to achieve."

The idea of time, the experience of time and how it relates to life is one of the great philosophical, spiritual and scientific puzzles. Great thinkers, both Western and Eastern, have wrestled with the concept of time and how it relates to our very existence: from ancient Greeks such as Parmenides who philosophized that existence is timeless, to the great Japanese Zen master Dogen who described "beingtime," to Einstein who described "spacetime," time has been one of life's great enigmas.

So to be experiencing time in a totally different way, if not totally understanding it, was a very heady experience.

And yet time does move in a linear fashion. Every day I had to get out of bed, check my therapy schedule, keep my eye on the clock, make sure I was in the right doctor's office at the right time. There was a duality to time: it both moved forward and stood still, both at the same, well … time. And as much as we'd like to believe in H.G. Wells and time travel, so far as I know we cannot turn back the clock, we cannot reclaim "lost" time. As euphoric as I was, I also missed my children; I was not at home to read bedtime stories to them, or coach their soccer games, or share all the other little moments we had together, and I knew from talking with them on the phone they missed me as well. Time with my children was slipping away, and could not be regained. Living in the moment had its advantages, but missing precious time with children, family and friends thousands of miles away was bittersweet.

As my brain healed, and as I came back to our regular time-world with memory, with past and future, as if I were an astronaut reentering the earth's atmosphere, that feeling of euphoria gradually faded. But I can still remember that sensation of living completely in the moment, of living in a timeless world, and say simply, purely…

Wow…

Recovery

Abandon hope,
Cope.

~

IN "THE INFERNO," DANTE FAMOUSLY wrote that the words "Abandon All Hope, Ye Who Enter Here" were inscribed above the entrance to the gates of hell. Yet is that really true? If we leave hope behind, will we find ourselves living in a hellacious world, a world of demons, doubt and despair? The phrase "Abandon All Hope, Ye Who Enter Here" has become such an iconic cornerstone of Western thought that we take its truth for granted. We accept without questioning that the abandonment of hope is tantamount to entering the realm of fire, brimstone and suffering. But what if the opposite were true? What if by abandoning hope we instead found an earthly paradise? What if instead we found nirvana? It is true there were many times during the dark years after my mother's accident and my accident that hope kept me moving forward: hope that my mother would improve, hope that I would improve, hope that my children would be with me more, hope that all the death and dysfunction and divorce wasn't scarring them too badly. But it was a frenetic, anxiety producing hope; there was no peace in it.

One of the hardest ordeals was to give up hope, to accept what had happened, to find joy in the way things were, instead of looking for joy in the way I hoped things would be. While all of my doctors, therapists and spiritual teachers tried to teach me this lesson in one way or another, the biggest proponent of this world view was Dr. Rectanus, which only made sense, since my psychological outlook on life was his domain, and I saw him twice weekly, more than my other doctors. "You may need to accept that you're not going to be the same person you were before the accident," he would often tell me, "and develop coping strategies to deal with the changes. Who knows? In some ways you may even end up being better than you were before."

There were two distinctly different categories of coping strategies that we would work on. One was learning to cope with the psychological changes wrought by TBI, emotions such as stress and anxiety. Into the psychological coping category fell such activities as meditation, biofeedback, breathing exercises and something as simple and yet as daunting as changing one's world view. We even talked about how denial was a viable coping strategy for some people, although I couldn't see that working for me; I had always been the type of person who wanted to get to the truth of matters, not deny them.

Then there were the behavioral coping strategies. Dr. Rectanus suggested such simple devices as keeping a notebook with me at all times to write down the details of my daily routine as a way to cope with memory loss problems. I bought a notebook and titled it "Lee Carlson's Recovery Management Notebook." On the cover I put "If found please return to: Lee Carlson," along with my address and phone number, like writing a child's name in magic marker on their clothes before sending them off to camp. Inside I wrote to-do lists, diet lists, medication lists, addresses of doctors' and therapists' offices, a daily diary and a wide collection of other information related to my recovery.

I bought a PalmPilot and struggled with learning how to use it to keep track of all my various medical appointments and therapy sessions. Before the accident I had been the guy that everyone else came to with computer problems. At Skiing magazine coworkers would come to me before calling the IT department. But now I could barely figure out how to use this simple handheld computer. It was frustrating, but I told myself it was part of my cognitive therapy, teaching my brain to think again. I struggled with the directions, words swimming on the page, but finally after days of headache-inducing effort I figured out how to get appointments and phone numbers into the little bugger and get them to sync with my laptop. I liked the PalmPilot. It was smaller, less conspicuous than a notebook when dealing with people. It fit right into my pocket, as opposed to my notebook, which I clutched in my hand like the teddy bear I had as a child. During my next appointment with Dr. Rubino, he asked how things were going, how I was doing with all my various therapies and with Dr. Rectanus.

"Great, we're working on coping strategies," I said, showing him my notebook.

"That's good; that will really help."

"But this is what I'm most proud of," I said, pulling out the PalmPilot. "My new surrogate brain."

He laughed.

At first, I would write down my daily schedule every morning in the notebook, and then write the same appointments and tasks in the PalmPilot. The more times I wrote these things down, the better chance I had of remembering them. Also, I didn't really trust the PalmPilot, or more precisely, I didn't trust my ability to remember to charge it, or not lose the stylus, or not leave the PalmPilot somewhere. The notebook was bigger, bulkier, harder to lose. I would consult both the PalmPilot and the notebook throughout the day, trying to remind myself what I was supposed to be doing, and when and where I was supposed to be doing it. All this organizing was incredibly time-consuming, but without it, I would have been lost.

I made lists and posted them everywhere, such as "Lee's Get Well Lifestyle Changes," which listed a number of different items, such as:

#5: Avoid Loud, Noisy Rooms: arouses body's fight-or-flight response, increasing anxiety."

Or:

#7: Exercise the Mind: crossword puzzles, mind games and challenging reading all help make brain agile and strong.

I wrote entire treatises on subjects, such as "Lee's Get Well Stress Primer," a ten-page document I typed on my laptop in which I detailed all that my doctors had taught me about stress: how to avoid it, cope with it and mitigate it. By writing this information out I figured I would do a better job of learning, internalizing and remembering what my doctors were drilling into me. The document covered such topics as "Common Stress Factors," "Controlling Fatigue," "Taking Responsibility for Your Own Well-Being" and even "Blood Sugar."

There were the now ubiquitous lists that I taped up on the refrigerator, on the bedroom mirror, and kept copies in my notebook, such as this list I made of things that could alleviate stress, which I prefaced with a quote from the great Greek physician Hippocrates:

> "It is the job of the physician to help the patient find the healing power within himself":

> Massage
> Acupuncture
> Exercise
> Henry!
> Soothing music
> Long walks on the beach
> Reading a good book
> No loud noises
> Prayer

Under the heading "Fatigue" I wrote:

> Many people with vestibular disorders deal with a chronic illness and must adapt to a slower pace. Their medical condition is not always visible, so others may not understand their condition or their fatigue.
>
> If you have a chronic vestibular disorder, you probably struggle with fatigue. It may rob you of your spontaneity. When you're feeling good, you may tend to overdo and pay for it later.

It's important to learn to deal with fatigue and get needed rest. Doing so may require making tough but necessary decisions to cut back. This is a big change for many people.

Particularly critical is to recognize early indicators of fatigue so you know when to pull back. Learn to do a self-check. Then do what you must to regenerate yourself. You need to do what is best for you.

I most likely copied this out of a book, or from a web site or from some printed material that Meredyth, my vestibular therapist had given me, but I don't remember.

I look back on these simple lists and writings now and laugh—they seem so childlike—but that is how my mind was working in the months following the accident. In many ways I was childlike and naive; my mental functioning had been greatly reduced.

One of the written reminders I put in the notebook was a biofeedback spreadsheet I made to chart my progress. There were two types of biofeedback I could do at home. The first type, with results that could be tracked on a spreadsheet, consisted of a simple thermometer that measured the surface temperature of my fingertips. A low measurement meant I was highly stressed while a high number meant I was relaxed. Even in warm, sunny Florida, my fingertip temperature was often in the low 70's, showing that I was stressed out and anxious. But by listening to biofeedback tapes while concentrating on relaxing and raising my hand temperature, eventually I learned to raise the temperature into the low or mid-nineties over the course of twenty to thirty minutes, a change of twenty to twenty-five degrees! On the spreadsheet I religiously filled in the columns for date, time of day, symptoms before starting, beginning temperature, ending temperature, elapsed time and ending symptoms.

The other type of biofeedback was harder to track; there were no numbers—like temperature—that I could write down. But I still wrote down symptoms before and afterwards. In this biofeedback there was a small device into which I inserted the first two fingers of my right hand. The device measured galvanic skin response and translated it into a high-pitched whine. By calming my body, over the course of ten or twenty minutes I could reduce the annoying whine to a low-pitched, soothing drone.

I started keeping a diary, partly to help me remember, but also because Dr. Rectanus had told me about research showing that people who kept diaries were better able to manage their stress. "Don't just keep a list of dates and times," he advised, "but write down how you're dealing with things as well as what actually happened. Write down how things make you feel."

Some sample diary entries approximately three months after the accident:

> Sat., Sept. 7, 8:30 am
> Tried to do word puzzles/exercises given to me by Rick [the cognitive therapist], thinking that morning when I'm fresh would be great time, put stereo on for background noise to help learn multitasking, but headaches, sweating, words swimming on page—took me forever.

> Sunday, Sept. 8, 9 am
> Went for short walk before it got hot, maybe 20 minutes. Caused incredible headache, so bad it hurt just to chew on cereal. Checked to make sure I hadn't skipped any medications, but I hadn't.

I kept at the diary and five months later my symptoms continued to improve, but a simple thing like getting sick could seemingly set my recovery back months, as recorded in this entry:

> Jan. 21
> Having a lot of severe leg and body jerking in my sleep, lying down. Haven't had this for at least several months. Also just feel like shit from the bronchitis— much worse than would normally feel from being sick. Rectanus says it is the lack of oxygen flow to my brain from being sick, and that since brain is already damaged and not functioning at high level, lack of oxygen causes much more problems.

One of the more humorous coping mechanisms I used was one that I developed on my own, without any input from my doctors. I call it the "Supermarket Checkout Coping Strategy." As I would stand in line at the grocery store, I would find myself inevitably drawn to the trashy celebrity magazines that are always displayed by the cash register, magazines that chronicle the foibles, faults and freakish behavior of famous entertainers, athletes, politicians and Wall Street financiers. As I scanned the headlines that trumpeted every celebrity sex tape, every extramarital affair, every car crash, every drug- and alcohol-fueled behavioral meltdown, every financial fraud, I would feel immensely better: if all these supposedly bright, successful people who had "normal" brains could be doing so many incredibly dumb things, what did I have to worry about? I wasn't doing anything even *remotely* as stupid as they were! My brain was functioning at least as well as theirs! I fit right in! I was normal!

That idea of where I fit in now that I was no longer the same person was one of my main concerns, and figuring out how to cope with the changes the accident had wrought continued to be a major theme. I brought up the same idea, although a bit more subtly than using gossip magazines, one day with Fred Eppsteiner, my Buddhist teacher and friend. We were sitting in the kitchen at his house, having a cup of tea while his beautiful collection of finches twittered and flew about in a huge floor-to-ceiling cage on his outdoor patio that was connected to the kitchen by open sliding glass doors.

"You know Fred, when I was a kid I thought that when I grew up things would be different, that adults would act like adults and be responsible, high-functioning individuals. I'm always amazed at the dumb things that seemingly intelligent adult people do."

"Yes, the adult world is just like one giant romper room," he said with a chuckle, referring to the classic children's television show featuring four and five year olds.

"That's it! The world is really just like one giant romper room!" I exclaimed. My childlike mind fit right in!

I did have a momentary pang of guilt. One of the Buddhist vows is not to elevate oneself above others; was I doing that? But I wasn't elevating myself above all these crazy people; I wasn't feeling superior to them, I was just feeling as if I was raising myself to their level. I was in the romper room! I was one of them and it felt great! I could be as crazy and brain-addled as I wanted and just be part of the normal world.

When I returned from Florida, I thought one coping strategy that would be beneficial would be to join a brain injury support group. In Florida, my support group had been my network of doctors and therapists; now I was mostly on my own. I went to the nearest support group meeting I could find, which was more than an hour's drive from the house I had rented. The people were nice, but the meeting was at night, I was exhausted driving home afterward and the whole meeting had just seemed like a giant bitch session, an opportunity for people to complain about their doctors, their families, their friends and people they met who didn't understand about dealing with brain-injured people. Perhaps it was just the vibe on that particular night—whatever it was I didn't go to another meeting. There was also a part of me that felt the best coping strategy was not to reinforce my status as a TBI survivor, but to leave it behind.

Several years later, however, I discovered that a woman I knew had recently been in a bad car accident, had sustained a Traumatic Brain Injury and had decided to start a local support group. Jenny and her husband owned a local deli where I sometimes ate, and the meetings were held at night at the deli after closing. I went to the third-ever meeting of the support group and found a dozen people sitting around two tables pulled together in the small eating area of the deli. Four of the participants, including me, were TBI survivors. The rest were family members, caregivers and medical professionals. We broke out into two different groups: survivors in one group and caregivers/professionals in the other group. I joined the survivor's group and we shared our stories, problems and coping mechanisms. After a few minutes of sharing the usual medically endorsed coping mechanisms, I leaned forward across the table and in a low voice said, "I've got one coping strategy that no doctor will tell you about," and proceeded to talk about my grocery checkout coping strategy. Everyone laughed, and the other man at the table, David, said, "Yes! I do the same thing! And do you know about _____" and he proceeded to detail the latest gossip about a certain female celebrity and her marital problems.

Several days later I received an e-mail from Jenny:

> Hi Lee,
>
> I must confess my sins. Today I bought two 'trash/gossip' magazines & laughed. All I could think about is you saying how it makes you feel normal. It makes me feel normal too!! And who is on the cover, _____ and 'Why She's Staying'!
>
> Have a great week,
> Jenny

I was glad to have helped someone else to laugh, to feel normal, and also glad that I wasn't the only out-to-lunch, brain-damaged person who felt "normal" after reading trashy gossip magazines.

But of all these coping strategies, the one that was hardest to learn was the coping strategy of giving up hope.

What is hope, really, but a kind of wanting? A desire for our life to be different, to be "better?" One of the most famous teachings of the Buddha is what's known as the Four Noble Truths: 1) the human condition is suffering; 2) the origin of suffering is desire; 3) there is a way out of suffering, a way to find nirvana; 4) that way is the Eightfold Path: right view, right intention, right speech, right action, right livelihood, right effort, right mindfulness and right concentration.

So a huge part of the Buddha's teaching is that finding nirvana takes a lot of hard work—the Eightfold Path—which fits right in with my Protestant work ethic, and may be part of why I find the Buddha's teachings so appealing. Finding nirvana involves changes in how we think, speak, act, work and live. One of the hardest tasks is learning to live in the moment—right mindfulness and right concentration—instead of hoping for, desiring, something different in the future.

A large part of that work ethic and world view had come from my mother (as well as my father). Her German heritage came with a strong belief in the importance of hard work. Part of the family mythos was the story of how my grandfather had started his construction company with a borrowed pickup truck, wheelbarrow and shovel on the day my mother was born, and had built his company into a large regional powerhouse. That mythos came with the belief that with hard work and a positive mental attitude, a hopeful attitude, almost anything was possible. So one of the hardest lessons for me was learning that no matter how hard we worked on her recovery, no matter how much we hoped, my mother was not going to get better. One of the hardest shifts was to accept my mother's disabilities, instead of hoping for improvement. Would I be letting my mother down? Would I be somehow violating those values of hard work and positive thinking that she had taught me? What was doubly hard was learning to accept things as they were while still working hard every moment, every breath, to improve her lot, her life, while not being attached to the outcome. It was difficult not to just collapse into despair after giving up hope.

My mother was confined to a wheelchair, and yet with help she could stand and take a few faltering steps. Part of her daily therapy was to get her up out of the wheelchair and help her walk. The part of her brain that controlled those motor skills had been damaged, but our hope was that with enough daily training eventually other parts of her brain would learn to take over that function—neural plasticity. Several times a week we would take her to physical therapy, where the therapists would, among other things, help her to stand and, with a therapist on either side holding her up, try to teach her to walk again. My mother and I both went to the same physical therapy clinic, and I would watch from across the large, open room as the therapists struggled with my mother while I did my own therapy. I could walk, but my balance had been severely damaged and I often stumbled, so I was learning to regain my equilibrium by balancing on small round wobbly disks while the therapist helped me keep from falling over.

After several months, when I had reached a point in my therapy where I knew I would not fall over, I would emulate my mother's therapists at home with the help of my mother's caregivers. I would lock the wheels on her wheelchair, put one arm around her waist and one hand under her armpit and half-lift, half-coax her into a standing position with me on one side and her caregiver on the other side. My mother's muscles had atrophied from the months in a hospital bed and it was hard to get her to stand. To see and feel the lack of strength and motor control in this woman who had been so athletic, so vigorous, was always heartbreaking. By holding her up I could get her to take a few steps, perhaps turn and take a few steps more, and then the caregiver would have to position the wheelchair behind my mother so I could gently lower her down before my own strength gave out.

My hope was that some day she would walk again on her own. She would never again walk a golf course, or take long walks on the beach with her grandchildren, but still, we all hoped that she might at least improve to the point of being able to negotiate a path from the living room to the kitchen with minimal help, or walk to her own bedroom. After many months it became clear that those dreams were probably never going to happen. Abandoning that hope and just appreciating that she was alive, that she could smile when I picked her up out of the wheelchair, that she could take a few steps with my help on the patio—that was one of the hardest things I've ever done. And yet it liberated me to just live in the moment, to be grateful that she was in my life and I in hers.

As someone who had been a business person, I used an example from the business world to help me focus on the difficult task of staying in the moment. There was a Ritz Carlton hotel in Naples, and I drove by it every day on my way to therapy appointments. I remembered a management seminar I had attended when I was researching an article on the top skiing hotels in the world. A senior manager from the Ritz Carlton chain had given a talk about how Ritz Carlton focuses on the little things, the processes, such as knowing guests by name, listening to guests' wants, bringing them a Coke instead of telling them where the bar is. By focusing on those in-the-moment processes, the customer felt safe, comfortable and even loved, and the Ritz Carlton's goals such as reaching sales targets would just naturally flow. It was a kind of "build it and they will come" approach.

So I focused on process-oriented living, instead of goal-oriented living. While such a shift sounds simple, for me it was incredibly hard after years of being conditioned to work toward goals: getting better grades, handing in a story on time, hitting a quarterly sales target. But as I drove to my next appointment, I thought of that management style, that way of achieving excellence, and understood that the same process-oriented approach could be applied to every aspect of life, including recovering from brain injury and managing my mother's daily life. I might not make her "better," but by being there for her, holding her, helping her walk, lifting a spoon to her mouth, I could make her feel safe, comfortable and unconditionally loved.

I learned to give up hope for my mother, and eventually her death made hope a moot point anyway, but I can't say I've ever completely totally given up hope for my own recovery, even after eight years. Meg says she thinks it's more of a rearranging of priorities to target small, tangible changes, like hoping for a daysailer instead of a megayacht, and perhaps she's right. On occasion I do still hope for some small, incremental improvement in my memory, or a temporary relief from pain. Maybe if I could learn to completely, totally abandon hope I'd be better off. But I do know I've learned not to cling to that hope. Hey, if my memory improves somewhat, great. If it doesn't, well that's okay too. I haven't given up optimism. In fact, letting go of hope for things to be "better" has made me more optimistic. I see that things are already optimal, already wonderful just as they are. There is no stress from worrying about—hoping for—smoother seas ahead.

Some people may view the idea of abandoning hope as a sort of pessimistic fatalism, as a giving up, but the opposite is really true. Spending all one's psychic energy on hoping for something better in the future is draining, anxiety-provoking. But letting go of that wanting, not clinging to that desire, can be liberating, freeing up one's energy to concentrate on helping your invalid mother walk, or loving your children, loving your partner, helping others laugh or helping yourself to heal. Letting go of hope for something better in the future can help you focus on this very moment, on what is happening right in front of you, on seeing the completeness of the world as it truly is. For me, letting go of hope ended up being the most effective coping mechanism of all.

Contemporary
Conundrum

Life or pills,
cure ills?

~

BEFORE I EVEN LEFT THE hospital, I was prescribed a veritable cornucopia of drugs to control everything from pain to anxiety. At one point or another in the months after the accident I took sixteen different prescription medications; early on in my recovery I would be taking five or six drugs at the same time. There was Lortab, Vicodin and prescription-strength ibuprofen for pain; Ativan, Xanax, buspirone and Valium for anxiety; Prozac, Lexapro, Celexa, trazadone and Wellbutrin for depression; Midrin for headaches; Provigil for alertness; Strattera and Adderal for focus and concentration; Viagra and Levitra for sexual dysfunction and probably a few I've forgotten. I would not be taking all these at once, only one or two from each class of medication, for a total of five of six drugs. For example the anti-anxiety medications were all tried by themselves at various times, with varying degrees of success, and sometimes prescribed by different doctors. One might work, but have side effects, so another would be substituted. Or one might not work well at all, so another was tried.

This extreme reliance on pharmacology to control our brain and body chemistry is a relatively contemporary phenomena as modern science discovers the thousands of different chemicals that control us and drug makers rush to synthesize those compounds, spending millions of dollars to convince us of their efficacy. Where just a few years ago doctors might have prescribed one or two pills, now they have no qualms about prescribing a veritable drug ratatouille: one of the red ones, two of the blue ones, half of this white one, etc., etc. I had to type up a spreadsheet of all my medications—which ones I took with breakfast, which at lunchtime, dinnertime, before bed—along with dosages and tape the list to the refrigerator door.

As someone who had tried to live a fairly healthy lifestyle before the accident, with regular exercise, proper eating habits, moderate alcohol use, no smoking, etc., I wasn't wild about all the different drugs going into my system. After a couple months, I laid out my concerns to Dr. Rubino and asked him if there weren't more natural ways I could control some of the effects from the brain injury. It just seemed like this pharmacological soup had possibilities for side effects and unforeseen drug interactions that couldn't be good.

We had already discussed my Zen meditation and how it could be beneficial, but now I wanted to go further; could I go off my meds? Perhaps, I thought, my regular meditation could at least eliminate the anti-anxiety and anti-depression medications. Anxiety and depression are both common problems for brain injury patients, and medications had been prescribed before I even left the hospital to ward off this probability.

"How have you been feeling?" Dr. Rubino asked. "Your psychological testing still shows some depression and anxiety, although what shows up on the tests as depression is likely a head injury symptom, not a psychological depression."

"I feel okay," I told him. "I don't really feel depressed, although I do feel a bit anxious at times, but nothing out of the ordinary, considering everything that has happened to me."

"I'd rather you stay on the meds for a while, they're likely what's keeping you feeling okay. Let's give them some time."

And the truth was that I was probably more anxious than I was willing to admit. It's hard to explain to other people how badly chronic anxiety can affect one's life. We've all had varying degrees of anxiety and we think we know what it feels like. Going on a date, for example, or taking a test, or going to a job interview, or speaking in public— these are all common life events that can be anxiety-provoking, and I thought I knew what anxiety was.

But the kind of anxiety I experienced after the accident was hundreds of times worse, and could come on without warning. One afternoon a few weeks after my conversation with Dr. Rubino I was driving back to my parents' house after therapy and stopped at the grocery store to pick up a few items. I parked the car, grabbed a cart and started walking the aisles, looking for my usual items: pasta for dinner, cereal and milk for breakfast, etc. I had been in this supermarket before, so it was not an unfamiliar place. And yet something about that store at that time of day, with all the strange people in it, began to affect me, and I began to feel more and more anxious as I pushed the cart through the aisles. I stopped in front of the cereal boxes stacked on the shelves, looking for my usual orange-colored box of granola. My brain must have been exhausted from the difficult therapies, and it was having trouble concentrating. I was having trouble seeing the different boxes, differentiating the words, thinking clearly enough to do a simple task most people take for granted: choosing and pulling a cereal box off the shelf. I started to feel increasingly agitated as my brain refused to work, as strangers swirled around me and the boxes began to swim before my eyes. The boxes became menacing, frightening. I felt like the whole store was closing in around me, boxes coming to get me, almost screaming at me, about to topple over on top of me, and I left the cart and walked as quickly as I could toward the exit, half-running, trying with every fiber of my being to hold onto myself, to keep from screaming and breaking into a mad dash for the store's exit, trying not to make a scene.

I somehow held it together and made it to my car, locked myself in and sat there, panting, heart pounding, sweaty hands gripping the steering wheel, for what seemed like an eternity. It felt as if a giant fist had wrapped itself around my chest and was squeezing tight. I had never experienced anything even remotely like this before. Finally I gained enough control to drive home, where I lay down to calm my exhausted, anxious body and brain.

Incidents like this brought home how much I needed medication: If I thought I could exist without my meds, the combination of my brain shutting down—lack of cognition—and the flight response—anxiety—taught me otherwise. Dr. Rubino was right: I wasn't ready to go off my medications. But still, I felt there must be natural ways I could use to at least assist the healing process.

So when I next met with Dr. Rubino, I asked him about other natural therapies and remedies, and told him my concern about all the medications. I was even concerned that some unknown drug interaction could be exacerbating my anxiety, not helping it. Since he had already encouraged my meditation, I thought he might be similarly open-minded about other ways to get me off my meds. Could I do more with diet, exercise, natural herbs and medicines?

"Look," he said, "every pill I give you just mimics a natural chemical already in the brain. You can produce every one of those compounds naturally through exercise, meditation, diet, getting out in the sun and performing the regular activities of daily living. My problem as a doctor is that most people won't follow that prescription; it's too hard, too time-consuming, and most Americans just want to take a little pill and have everything be fixed. I'm a big advocate of natural healing, but most patients just won't do it. They might follow it for a time, but then they start tapering off and their recovery suffers. If you're willing to commit to a regular, daily program of natural healing, that's great, and then we can get you off some of these meds, but the medications can also help you jump start the healing process, especially in the beginning, so I still want you taking them, for now."

Those were, for me, the most liberating words I could have heard. Where before I had been hesitant to even broach the subject, now I had been given the green light to throw myself headlong into a course of more natural healing. I meditated longer every day. I exercised and took long power walks with Henry (I tried jogging but the motion gave me headaches); at the urging of the occupational therapist I enrolled in my first-ever yoga classes—restorative yoga—at a nearby yoga studio. I consulted with a nutritionist at the hospital, who told me to eat more eggs for breakfast and worry less about granola.

"You're trying to repair your brain, not bring down your cholesterol," she said.

There were also a number of over-the-counter natural remedies recommended by various doctors or therapists: omega-3 capsules for cognitive functioning, phosphatidylserine DMAE complex for memory, turmeric capsules for cognition (people in India have a much lower rate of Alzheimer's, dementia and brain-related disorders, which some people attribute to their widespread use of the spice turmeric, an anti-inflammatory), multivitamins, ashwagandha (also known as Indian ginseng) for memory and cognition, and a few others.

I typed up and taped two new lists to the refrigerator, "Lee's Get-Well Quick Daily Routine" and "Brain-Improving Diet Changes." The first had my entire day mapped out, beginning with my alarm going off at 5:30 a.m., bathroom and light stretching from 5:30 to 6:00, then sitting meditation from 6:00 to 6:30, breakfast from 6:30 to 7:00. At 7:00 there was a big "PILLS!" in bold letters, reminding me to take my medications. From 7:00 to 8:00 was "walking meditation" with Henry, on the local quiet streets or on the beach. Eight to 8:30 was shower and dress. At 8:30 every Monday through Friday I'd leave the house for therapy. From 8:30 a.m. to 7:00 p.m. every day was taken up with therapy and exercise, with a break for lunch. Dinner was from 7:00 to 8:00, then call the boys at 8:00, which was both joyful and anxiety-provoking at the same time. Finally I got some relaxation time from 8:30 to 10:00, although the list admonished me that this was reading time, no television.

The diet sheet covered such things as no caffeine, no alcohol; instead drink plenty of water, herbal iced tea and natural fruit juices without sugar. It reminded me to eat regular portions at regular times to alleviate stress, to start my day with a high-protein breakfast such as eggs, to eat foods rich in vitamins C & E, such as beans, oatmeal, citrus fruits and wheat germ. It prompted me to use ginger and turmeric as spices, and to avoid MSG and other chemicals, such as preservatives.

I also embarked on a regular program of biofeedback with Dr. Rectanus to control the anxiety. In one of the more humorous moments during my recovery, he hooked me up to the biofeedback machine in his office for the first time to show me how biofeedback worked.

"How are you feeling?" he asked. "Comfortable? Relaxed?"

"Yes," I said, "I'm feeling pretty good today."

He had put electrodes on my fingers and my forehead, with wires running to a computer monitor. The monitor was facing away from me, where only he could see the screen.

"Okay," he said, "I'm going to ask you some questions."

He proceeded to ask me innocuous questions about the weather, my day, etc., and then he said, "How is your divorce going?"

"I'm fine with it," I said. "When the whole process first began I was very upset, but I've dealt with it, I'm reconciled to it and being down here in Florida away from my wife, concentrating on my recovery, I really don't worry about it. I'm fine with it, really."

He stopped his questions and turned the monitor to show me. The line had started out relatively flat, and then practically gone off the chart. "See, you think you're fine and that your divorce isn't causing you stress and hurting your recovery, but right here," he pointed to where the line started to rocket upwards, "is where I asked you about your divorce. Your subconscious mind is much different from your conscious mind. You're under a tremendous amount of stress from the divorce, and stress is the enemy as far as healing your brain. Stress chemicals such as cortisol are extremely harmful and will hurt your recovery. Biofeedback will definitely help you bring that under control."

We talked about my feelings of anxiety, what caused them and what could help cure them.

"Do I have Post-Traumatic Stress Disorder?" I wanted to know.

"The symptoms are the same, but the cause is different. We don't use a PTSD template, we use the TBI template. You've had an actual physical injury to your brain, which is different from being exposed to a psychological trauma."

In the weeks that followed I didn't stop taking my meds right away; after all, as my doctors kept reminding me, I had suffered a very serious injury. As Dr. Rubino had said, "You've been diagnosed with mild TBI, but there's nothing mild about Traumatic Brain Injury."

The meds were helping me heal. But I did buy several biofeedback devices for home use, worked hard on my diet, exercise, yoga and meditation. I also on my own nickel went to see an acupuncturist, which seemed to help with the pain and anxiety. I even tried visiting a reiki healer and a craniosacral therapist, although neither of those had any effect that I could discern. A month or so later during one of my daily cognitive rehab sessions with Rick McCawley, I announced that I had gone off all my meds. "Does Dr. Rubino know about this?" he said.

"No, but we talked about the possibility the last time I saw him."

"So you've thrown away your crutches, then?"

"I guess so."

"And how's it going?"

"Good, I feel good." And I did feel good, liberated in a way. He was right—I had thrown away my crutches.

In the months that followed, sticking to the natural healing regimen was, as Dr. Rubino predicted, extremely difficult. Finding time every day to meditate, exercise, eat right, do biofeedback and go to yoga or my Zen group, in addition to my regular therapy schedule, was hard, and exhausting. There were many times I felt like just saying "the hell with it" and taking a handful of little pills instead.

Even now, seven years later, one of the hardest parts of being a TBI survivor has been keeping up that routine. If I stop exercising or meditating I immediately feel my brain shutting down: I have trouble remembering close friends' names, or concentrating on my work. There just isn't enough time in the day to exercise, mediate, do yoga, biofeedback, eat carefully and still have time to work, be a father, a lover and a friend, but I try. I still believe that natural, ancient, time-tested remedies are the best way to cure life's modern ills: accidents, divorces or the thousands of other daily life stresses that affect us all.

Suicide

Why
Die?

AFTER MEDITATION AT THE OCEAN ZENDO one Monday evening during our discussion period, one of the Zendo members, Allen Planz, a wonderful poet, was despondent because a friend of his had taken his life. We all felt his despair. The big question at a moment like this is, "What drives someone to commit suicide?" Allen said he could almost understand the urge to kill oneself and nearly felt like killing himself because of the loss of his friend.

"Allen," I said," if you ever seriously feel that way, make sure you call me first."

Perhaps it was arrogant to think I might talk someone out of killing themselves if they were depressed and determined, but I'd certainly try. Allen has a special place in my heart; he was one of the few friends who found time to visit me in the hospital after my accident. I don't remember much from that time, but I do remember him sitting by my bedside, and how much it meant to me. He was in his early sixties when we first met and was a fixture around the Zendo, with a shock of unruly white hair, a white beard and a wheezing, rambling way of speaking. He would pull into the Zendo's parking field in his beat-up old Suzuki jeep, with a surf fishing rod on the roof, having just come from the beach, and shamble down the path to the Zendo mumbling to himself, punching people he met on the arm and making silly jokes. His dharma name given him by Roshi Matthiessen was Kanzan, "crazy wisdom," and Allen played the part of the Zen fool very well. But his seemingly loopy demeanor masked one of the most compassionate souls I have ever met. We also had a shared love of the sea: over the years Allen had supported himself as a writer by working as a private yacht captain.

After my mother died her funeral in Buffalo was attended by hundreds of people. Westminster Presbyterian Church was packed. I was asked to give the eulogy and I spoke of her life, her love for family and friends, her generosity and selfless charity work, her accident, her eventual awakening from her coma and her struggles to speak, to walk, to recognize those around her. I talked about how she was a severely diminished version of her previous self, yet her eyes would light up at the sight of a friend or grandchild. There was still a spark, a life inside her crippled body and brain. I spoke of these things and included this line I had written: "Mom taught us all something very special in her final year: we cannot judge the quality of a human life. A human life is a human life, a precious thing, in whatever form it takes."

Years after my accident, my mother's death and that night at the Ocean Zendo, the hardscrabble life of a poet and a lifelong smoking habit took their toll on Allen. He hadn't been trying to kill himself, but his lifestyle caught up with him. He developed pneumonia during the winter and ended up in the hospital, then came home where he needed nursing care. I wanted to show him the manuscript for "Passage to Nirvana" and ask his thoughts, but feared he was too frail. Even so he would still show up at the Zendo, driven by one of the members, joking and coughing and laughing and punching people in the arm. He reminded me of my mother; as sick as he was, he still had that spark. Then unexpectedly, at age seventy-three, he died.

Sometimes there is no why to death, sometimes it just happens too soon. If Allen had ever called me feeling suicidal, I would have told him what I learned from my mother's death: A life is a precious thing, no matter what form it takes. But I think Allen already knew that.

Death

I

Cry.

I FOUND THIS PO IN MY handwriting on the back of a printed program for a friend's *shuso hossen* ceremony at the Ocean Zendo. *Shuso hossen* is a formal ceremony when a senior Zen monk is verbally tested in their knowledge of the dharma (teachings of the Buddha) by the roshi and other senior Zen monks and students. Informally it is known as "dharma combat" for its freewheeling, back and forth verbal parrying. The monk sits on a cushion in the middle of the Zendo while other monks and the roshi fling questions at them in rapid-fire succession, and just as quickly the monk fires back pithy, iconoclastic Zen answers, while the other members of the sangha sit in a circle around the monk. The woman who was tested at this ceremony, Katri Kepponen, was at the time fighting breast cancer, and died several years later. Did I write this po at Katri's ceremony? Sometime later? And whose death was I crying for? My friend Katri? My mother? My brother-in-law? A college friend who suddenly died of a stroke at age forty-six? I have no memory at all....

Sickness

Be Well,
No hell.

~

IN LATE DECEMBER 2008, MEG and I left Nirvana tied to a dock in
Georgetown, South Carolina, in the hands of a diesel mechanic,
since the engine was feeling a bit ill. We drove to Buffalo a couple days after Christmas, where we planned to stay at my sister
Kristan's house. Chas and Niall had spent Christmas week with my
ex-wife at her sister's house in Buffalo and were spending the week after
Christmas with me. In the four years since her husband Kevin's death,
Kristan had met a new man, Robin, who was wonderfully loving to
my sister and great with her kids. She and Robin had married the year
before. And in November Meg and I had gotten engaged. We were all
looking forward to a relaxing, fun, drama-free holiday where the family bonds of cousins, aunts, uncles, sisters, brothers, nieces, nephews,
spouses and fiancés would reign supreme.

At four in the afternoon the day after we arrived, my oldest son
Chas was laughing, eating chicken wings and watching a Buffalo Bills
football game with everyone in the family room. By six o'clock he said

he wasn't feeling well and went up to the bedroom on the third floor to lie down. At 8:00 p.m. he sent me a text message to my phone saying, "Help me!" I thought he was being melodramatic and slowly made my way upstairs, thinking he was just trying to get me to bring him something to eat or drink, but when I got there I was shocked to see him clutching his body, contorted with pain, his teeth clenched, his face an agonized grimace. He had sent the message because he couldn't get up off the couch to walk downstairs.

Chas was fifteen years old, and not normally a complainer; it was clear something very bad was happening. I took his temperature, and he had a dangerously high fever, 104.5 degrees. I stood him up and he leaned on my shoulder as I helped him down the stairs and into the car. Meg came with us as we raced to the emergency room at Children's Hospital which, as luck would have it, was only a few blocks away. At Children's the ER doctor admitted Chas into an isolation room, clearly dismayed by his condition. Not knowing what might be wrong the doctor didn't want him to infect other people. The room was small and dark, with a bed and monitors and a chair in the corner. There was a single door that was kept tightly closed.

Shortly after Chas was admitted to the isolation room, he looked up from his fetal position, his teeth clenched, and asked, "Did you call mom?"

I hadn't called her yet, there hadn't been time, and I was hoping the doctors would have some word for me, some inkling of what was causing Chas' distress so I could tell Belinda what was happening. Also, cell phone use was not allowed in the ER, and I hadn't wanted to leave Chas' side.

"No buddy, I haven't called her yet."

"Please call her, I want Mom," he moaned. I wasn't insulted. He was only fifteen. He was sick; he wanted his mommy. I could remember that feeling from my childhood. And there had been times over the past five years when I wished my own mother was still alive so I could call her, talk to her, hear her soothing voice. Chas' mother was also still in Buffalo, still visiting her sisters for the holidays, so I knew she could come to the hospital.

"I promise, I'll call her as soon as I can, I just didn't want to leave you."

"I want mom."

"Okay, buddy, okay," I said, stroking his side. "You're going to be alright, everything is going to be fine."

"Call mom, dad. Tell her I'm here."

According to the divorce agreement, we have joint custody, and no medical decisions or treatments are to be done without the informed consent of the other parent. Each parent is supposed to notify the other of any medical emergencies. Belinda regularly violated this agreement. Boys being boys there had been trips to the doctor or the emergency room while in her care, since they lived with her the majority of the time, and usually I only found out about these episodes days or weeks later. There was certainly a part of me that wanted to say, "Screw her—she never calls me when there is a problem. Chas is in my care now and I'll take good care of him." But there was a much bigger part of me that didn't want to sink to that level of an eye for an eye, that wanted to respect her as a mother, and more than anything wanted Chas to feel safe and comfortable.

In the nearly seven years since my accident, she had not relented in her coldness toward me, my sisters, my father, my friends. When my mother died Belinda had allowed the boys to attend the memorial service but then tried to stop them from attending the reception afterwards, telling them they were having an ice cream party at her sister's house instead. When Kevin died and we were at Kristan's house getting dressed for his memorial service at Westminster, Belinda had called to talk to Chas and Niall. Kristan answered and Belinda didn't say hello, didn't tell Kristan how sorry she was about Kevin's death. Instead in a curt tone she had just said, "I want to speak to Chas or Niall." There was no chance of mistaken identity; Kristan had said "Hello Belinda, it's Kristan." There had been hundreds of calls from other people to express condolences; this was the first time someone had not said a word of comfort. Even in the midst of her grief, Kristan was speechless.

In her e-mails Belinda would refer to my accident with the word "accident" in quotes, as if the accident was all a fiction. Then she would berate me for not taking responsibility for my life, saying I should get a job at McDonald's or the post office, telling me that I would never do that because I was a narcissist and felt such work was beneath me. There was no acknowledgement or appreciation of the brain injury; of all the hard work to regain my mental faculties; of how I had found other jobs since the accident: writer, estate manager, yacht captain, real estate agent; no understanding of how none of these jobs had worked out thanks to continuing problems with memory and cognition. Nothing had changed since those first days in the hospital after my accident. Any chance at reconciliation, any chance that we could have at least been friendly and cordial to each other and work as a team in the best interests of the children had long ago been squashed by my brain injury. To her I looked fine, sounded fine … what was my problem? Why wasn't I paying more in child support? Why wasn't I taking more responsibility for the children's lives?

My situation was unique, thanks to the accident, and one therapist had warned me of just that: "You'll hear lots of stories," she said, "but remember that your story is uniquely your own."But in another way my story was also universal; many TBI survivors have problems with family members, bosses, friends and other people who want to know why we aren't behaving "normally." Family members get angry, or frustrated or annoyed at our actions—or seeming lack of action. In my case my ex-wife's anger toward me was palpable. When we were in the same physical space, such as when I picked up the boys, Belinda would just ignore me and walk right by without a word. I had never understood what passive-aggressive behavior was, but now I comprehended it all too well. I vastly preferred the cold shoulder treatment to angry outbursts; as an adult I figured I could handle anything she threw my way, but I always felt deep sorrow for the boys. The animosity created a tension in the air you would need a machete to cut through—forget using a knife—and I would watch the boys' faces, their body language, and just want to cry out, "Belinda, do you realize what we are doing to these children?" But I had never figured out how to get through to her. Maybe I just wasn't smart enough, or maybe her own issues just ran too deep. Either way, the result wasn't good.

All of this was going through my head as Chas asked me to call his mother. The isolation room was small, with barely room to move around the bed. I was not leaving his side, which meant that Belinda and I would be in closer proximity than was good for me, provoking post-TBI stress reactions. But more importantly, would Chas be better off with his mother here? Would he feel safer, more protected? Or would the tension between his mother and me create such bad vibes that he would feel less secure?

The painkillers they had given Chas seemed to have an effect, and he drifted off to sleep momentarily.

"Can you watch Chas while I go outside and call Belinda?" I asked Meg.

"Of course, I'll come get you if they need you."

I knew I could trust Meg. We had been together now for five years and the boys trusted her, liked her. She had children of her own. She had wonderful maternal instincts. She was a great mother, a great step-mother. She also knew that Chas was not her child, and didn't overstep her boundaries and try to act like his mother. I made my way through the maze of rooms and hallways until I found the doors leading out into the cold, snowy Buffalo night.

"Chas is in the hospital. We're at Children's."

"What happened? What's the matter?"

"They don't know. He was fine around dinner time and then he just got really sick. He's got a high fever and stomach pains. I think it might be food poisoning or something. He really wants you here."

"Have they done tests?"

"They've taken blood and cultures and examined him, but nothing has come back yet. He's in a lot of pain but they've given him painkill-ers. He seems to be a little better."

"Call me when you know more. I'm at my friend's house."

"He's asking for you; he wants you here."

"I'm leaving soon to go to my sister's house, you can reach me there."

Back in the room Chas was awake again. "Did you call mom?"

"Yes, I got hold of her."

"Where is she? When's she going to get here?"

"I told her I'd call when we know more."

"Call her dad!" He was writhing in pain again. "Please! Call her!"

I rubbed his arm. "She'll be here buddy, she'll be here."

Meg looked at me and said nothing.

A few hours later after several more calls, Belinda arrived at the hospital. She walked briskly into the room, ignoring me, glanced over at Meg sitting in the darkened corner and said, "Oh, I didn't know *you* were here." Then she turned to Chas laying on the bed and asked him how he was feeling.

Chas' blood pressure kept dropping, in spite of the administration of blood pressure medications and huge amounts of intravenous fluids.

At one point the doctor asked us to leave the room while the ER staff worked on Chas, and not until the next day did the doctor tell me how seriously they had thought they might lose him, how they had to resuscitate him, which is why they asked us all to leave.

The diagnosis was septic shock, which I had never heard of. Septic shock is a severe immune system reaction to an infection, usually bacterial, that can quickly result in organ failure. The doctors took blood samples and cultures and tested for everything but chicken wing poisoning, but never did find the source of the infection.

The next day, after Chas was stable and hopefully out of danger, I was trying to find something to relieve the seriousness of the situation, and joked with the nurses and Chas that it had all been a reaction to the Bills game (as usual, they lost badly). In Buffalo, everyone knows how the Bills do, and there was general joking agreement among nurses and doctors that "Bills poisoning" could be the diagnosis. We spent the next five days in the hospital, with either Belinda or myself in the room with him round-the-clock, especially the first few nights. We would exchange perfunctory information about his condition when we relieved each other, but I knew the only way to get reliable information was to talk to the nurses or doctors directly. He was one sick boy, and although he recovered quickly, they still kept him in the intensive care unit for several days until he was out of the woods.

It is not easy for a parent to watch their child in so much pain and to realize how close you came to losing a child. You want the best for your offspring. I wanted him to be healthy, I wanted him to have a home life where he felt loved, protected and safe. I wanted him to have a "normal" father. I wanted him to be laughing and playing outside in the snow with his cousins, not lying in a hospital bed hooked up to IV's and vital sign monitors, sedated to alleviate the pain, with parents who barely spoke. The whole episode brought back vivid memories of my own time in the hospital, of my mother's accident and my brother-in-law's slow wasting away from cancer, of the bitter dissolution of a family. I just kept praying, "Be well, be well," and wanted him out of this hellish state he was in, especially the first twenty-four hours when his body was wracked with pain. These words, were a chant I could keep repeating over and over, a cry for the innocent heaven of childhood, an incantation to ward off the adult hell of sickness, death and divorce.

Atonement

Old friends,
Make amends.

~

HOW THE CREATIVE MIND WORKS is a mystery. We were anchored off Shroud Cay in the Bahamas with the wind blowing hard out of the east, just Meg and me and the dogs, so that we couldn't go anywhere for days and had been forced to deal with our inner selves: no phone, no Internet, no TV, just nature and thoughts.

In the middle of the night this po welled up from my dreams, and I awoke and wrote it down in the journal I keep by our bunk. I had been working on a short story that had brought up issues from my long-ago past, issues of betrayal by close friends and the unfaithfulness of lovers. I believe this is an admonishment from my subconscious to make peace with the past. There have been a number of old friends over the years I have had unsettled relations with, for one reason or another: my best childhood friend and my college sweetheart who married each other; my mountaineering partner who wasn't in my wedding because of my ex-wife's insistence, even though I had been an usher in his wedding;

my close friend and coworker who had to fire me after my accident because I couldn't perform at the level I should have, and a few others.

It was always easier in those cases to walk away, to go on with life than to do the hard work of mending those tattered friendships. In some ways they can never be the same; the relationship has changed and you cannot put the genie back in the bottle. But most people are good, and mean well, and there was a reason you were friends with them in the first place. And the "mistake," if there was one, wasn't always theirs. Realizing, accepting and making amends for one's own role in such breakups is the hard part.

In Zen there is a chant called the "Gatha of Atonement":

> All evil Karma ever committed by me since of old,
> on account of my greed, anger and ignorance,
> born of my body, mouth and thought,
> now I atone for it all.

Chanting this, one realizes how our own actions, speech and even thoughts can create unpleasant, unhappy situations. We can want something too much, we can be angry or we can just be unaware of what is happening around us; there are a million ways to screw things up. Realizing, admitting and taking responsibility for this isn't easy, but it is still not as hard as figuring out how to fix the problems we've created. How to atone? That is the truly hard part.

After my accident, when I was still undergoing rehab in Florida, but towards the end when I could once again think and act relatively clearly, I went to a correctional facility to visit with an inmate who had requested a Buddhist spiritual teacher. The man had already been part of a meditation group that was run by a Zen friend of mine, Mitch Cantor, in another correctional institute, but this inmate had been transferred and needed some spiritual guidance at his new facility, where there was no organized group.

This man was a convicted child molester who had done such awful things—having sex with girls as young as seven years old—that he was found guilty on eighty-two child sex abuse cases and sentenced to ten concurrent life sentences, plus additional sentences for the other seventy-two cases. He would be in prison for life, with no chance of parole. Any study he did with me would have no bearing on the physical aspects of his life; it would not get him a shorter sentence, or a better shot at parole, or better food, etc. And yet for several years he had been faithfully getting up early every morning and sitting and meditating on his bunk while his cell mate slept. This work had finally given him an awareness of how much pain and suffering he had caused others, and how much damage he had done to himself. There was nothing he could do that would undo what had already been done, but I suggested that he chant the Gatha of Atonement every day, softly to himself after meditating, to bring some element of peace to himself, his world, and by extension to the world around him. Perhaps, just perhaps, his newfound peace would ripple out into the ether, like widening circles from a small pebble dropped in a large pond, helping to make a more peaceful world in his own sphere of influence. It was his only way to make amends; he could not change what he had done.

While I certainly have never done anything even remotely as egregious as this man, I know I too cannot alter my past. I will never have the same relationships with friends I had conflicts with. I will certainly never have the same relationship with my ex-wife. My mother used to say that time heals all wounds, and I think there is great wisdom in that reliance on patience, but I prefer a more proactive approach: I can sit, meditate, chant the Gatha of Atonement, rid myself of the anger, greed and ignorance that caused the problem in the first place, and pray for the best.

Alone

Sad day,
Be okay.

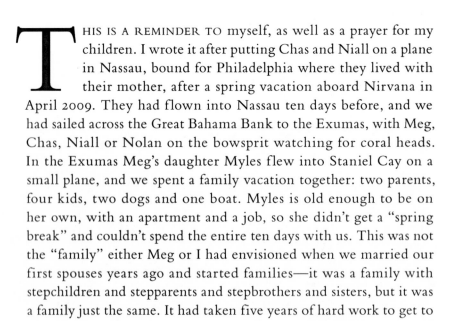

THIS IS A REMINDER TO myself, as well as a prayer for my children. I wrote it after putting Chas and Niall on a plane in Nassau, bound for Philadelphia where they lived with their mother, after a spring vacation aboard Nirvana in April 2009. They had flown into Nassau ten days before, and we had sailed across the Great Bahama Bank to the Exumas, with Meg, Chas, Niall or Nolan on the bowsprit watching for coral heads. In the Exumas Meg's daughter Myles flew into Staniel Cay on a small plane, and we spent a family vacation together: two parents, four kids, two dogs and one boat. Myles is old enough to be on her own, with an apartment and a job, so she didn't get a "spring break" and couldn't spend the entire ten days with us. This was not the "family" either Meg or I had envisioned when we married our first spouses years ago and started families—it was a family with stepchildren and stepparents and stepbrothers and sisters, but it was a family just the same. It had taken five years of hard work to get to this point. Real life blended families are not nearly as easy as "The Brady Bunch" would make it seem.

It was great having a family vacation; we snorkeled together among brightly colored fish and coral on the reefs; we explored caves and searched out iguanas and played games in the cockpit. We had family meals together onboard and in small island restaurants, where meals were served "family style," everyone in the restaurant seated at the same time. We just generally hung out and had a great time.

When our time was up, we sailed back to Nassau. The next morning Nolan and Myles got in a cab for their trip to the airport and then back to the States, while Chas, Niall and I spent the morning exploring the classic old stone buildings of downtown Nassau, the bustling straw market, Fort Fincastle with its commanding view of the harbor where we could see Nirvana at her dock, dwarfed by giant cruise ships, and The Queen's Staircase, with its sixty-six treads cut into the solid rock by slaves in the 1700's. Then it was time for them to go. We got a cab to the airport, where I watched them go through security, then disappear through a doorway leading to their flight's departure gate. I stayed in the terminal for more than an hour, alone in the crowds, watching the doorway, wishing they would walk back through. Afterwards I went back to Nirvana, where I finally broke down, as I often did when they left. Meg silently wrapped her arms around me and held me while my body shook with sobs of sadness.

I wrote this as an admonishment to remember that life goes on, that everything will be okay, in spite of the distance that separates my boys and me as a result of an acrimonious divorce and a terrible accident, in spite of the overwhelming sadness I always feel watching them go, in spite of the heartbreak they tell me they feel at not having their father in their lives every day. I was reminded of the Zen master who cried over his daughter's death and was confronted by one of his longtime students, who accused the master of being a charlatan, someone who had not really achieved the ideal of detachment that he professed to teach. The master looked at his pupil and said simply, "I cry because I can."

We do not check our basic humanity at the door when we become a Zen adept. We can still feel the very real and true emotions of sadness and grief. But we can also know that somehow, someway, this is part of the heavenliness of life and in the end everything will be okay.

LOVE & HAPPINESS

Love

Wellspring
Of all things.

~

WHAT IS LOVE? AS A word, love has been corrupted by overuse; you can love just about anything, from your car to a vacation at Disney World. The word love has almost become a worthless commodity, so banal as to have nearly lost its profound meaning. And yet, and yet.... What about true love? Real, absolute, unconditional love? The concept of love? A feeling so pure it transcends rational thought? The love that permeates all things at every moment, like a whispered background hum, if only we could open our senses to it? An energy so powerful it causes grown men and women to fall on their knees and shed tears of joy when they experience it? Is there any better word in the English language than just plain "love"? Love is more than compassion, more than intimacy, more than affection or adoration or kindness or a thousand other words that come close, but don't quite hit the bull's-eye. Love is love, plain and simple; there is nothing deeper, more profound, more basic and elemental than love.

Happiness I

You.
Me.
We.

L YING IN BED WITH MEG, after we had moved in together, the first time in our relationship that we had spent almost two weeks sleeping together every night, it all felt so right, and I compared it to how I felt when she wasn't there, when there was no "we." Why does it feel so good when we find someone we can share our bed with, in a way that is not just sexual, but intimate, loving and close? Does it address a need born out of anxiety, a fear of being alone? Does the togetherness act like a balm to soothe the anxiety? Or does the feeling come from a kind of closure, a connecting with our other half that has somehow been separated from us?

The feeling can be a result of either, or both, but the healthier of the two reasons is one not born from angst or fear, but from love, from acceptance, from letting go of anxiety and just being open to this union with another human being that can complete the circle, like the two interlocking waves of yin and yang.

Happiness II

You,
Me,
Wheeee!!!

~

AFTER I TOLD MEG MY happiness po that ended up being "Happiness I," she asked, "Is it 'You/Me/We'—double-u, eee? Or is it 'You/Me/Wwwwhhheeeee!!!'" Meg had never heard the Muhammad Ali poem "Whee!/Me" (see "Ancestor Wordship" in Part III, Bricolage), so she wasn't making a reference to his poem that is one of the world's shortest poems; in one sense she was just asking about the spelling, being the writer and English composition teacher that she is.

But in another sense she was also asking my thoughts behind the words. I like the fact that even without knowing the Ali poem, her mind worked the same way as mine, or as Ali's, showing the universality of we/wwhheee! But more importantly, more subtly, "Happiness I" and "Happiness II" are illustrative of the two sides of an intimate relationship: the deep, contemplative, loving side of "We" and the fun, joyful side of "Wheeee!!!"

Unhappy Hour

Shrink,
Think.

LIKE MANY MODERN AMERICANS, I have been through psychotherapy. First during the dissolution of my marriage, as I tried to save my family and find some answer to what was happening as my world came crashing down, then after my accident when I had to struggle with post-TBI symptoms and the difficult realization that my brain no longer worked in the ways I had come to expect during forty-four years of living.

As wonderful and helpful as those therapists were, and as cathartic as the therapeutic process was in the long run, the actual weekly fifty-minute-long sessions were, as most people can attest who have been through them, not a boatload of fun. The therapist forces you to recall painful memories and think through your patterns of behavior, how you've dealt with life's difficulties in the past and how you might do things differently (and hopefully better) in the future. The entire exercise can be very, very emotionally draining, especially when doing it twice a week, as I was required to do after the accident.

The whole process is about change, either making changes in your life, or dealing with changes that have been thrust upon you, and most of us don't deal with change very well.

Why is "Unhappy Hour" in the Love & Happiness section? Because one therapist told me that probably eighty percent of his practice was dealing with relationship issues (the Love part) and because, as painful as it was, the process did lead to a new understanding, a new enjoyment of who I am and the world around me (the Happiness part).

Modern therapy is very different in many ways from a mystical, Zen perspective, in which you try to stop all rational, active thought so that you can intuit the underlying truth of the world. In therapy you talk about yourself and talk some more; it is very much about ego, about "I." In Zen meditation you are absolutely silent, stopping all egocentric thought to become more aware of the world around you, letting go of "I." But these two approaches are really complementary, two sides to the same coin: talk therapy and no-talk therapy. One of the greatest Zen masters was a Japanese man named Eihei Dogen, who lived in Japan 800 years ago. One of his more famous sayings is, "To study Buddhism is to study the self. To study the self is to forget the self. To forget the self is to be enlightened by all things. To be enlightened by all things is to be free from attachment to the body and mind of one's self and of others." Modern therapy is all about studying the self.

For nearly 400 years in the West we have been caught up in the Cartesian Duality, Descartes' idea that mind and matter are separate, distinct entities. But to truly understand human behavior, both in yourself and in others, one cannot separate the two—body and mind. Indeed, one must synthesize them, which is a large part of Eastern thought. To sit and meditate and be truly aware of your mind and body, as well as the spiritual and physical world around you and how they all work as one—that is a wonderful gift.

So I would dutifully see my therapist on a twice-weekly basis, talk and listen and learn and squirm, then go to my own meditation cushion on my father's dock, or in a corner of my own house, or at the Zendo, and sit and meditate on what had transpired in the therapist's office, synthesizing the two approaches, allowing understanding to ripen slowly like a luscious golden apple on a gnarled but sun-kissed bough.

Lover's Lament

Go?

No!

~

ANOTHER PO I FOUND SCRIBBLED on a piece of paper. As usual with my memory-challenged brain, I have no idea when I wrote it, why I wrote it or where it came from. There were no reflections to go with it; I had obviously hastily written it down, thinking I would get to writing the basic notes about time, place, etc., later, as I would have done easily before the accident. I still have trouble understanding that I am not the same person I once was, a person who could remember and recall without the aide of scrawled reminders. Is this po the lament of the leaver? Or the one being left behind? Or both?

Lovers' Dance I

Hello?

I go.

~

HOW SAD THAT LOVERS OFTEN miscommunicate as they dance around each other, figuratively speaking, each trying to discern the true feelings and intentions of the other. They tentatively come together, greeting one another, eager yet wary, questioning: does the other person feel the same way about me as I do about them? Am I giving myself too freely? Will I be hurt? We tentatively say hello and when we don't get the response we think we should, we pull back from the relationship, often with a hint of anger that the other person's reaction isn't what we wanted or expected. The blank space on the page between "Hello" and "I go" represents that large unfilled, blank moment, so full of promise, and yet, and yet....

So often that blank moment ends in a parting, instead of a coming together, often because our egos get in the way: I didn't get what I

179

wanted? What I deserved? What I needed? I might get hurt? The other person didn't react the way they were "supposed to" toward me? Then I'm going.

These issues are hard enough when you're a "normal" person, but try being forty-four, jobless, brain-damaged, almost-divorced and living on your parents' couch.

One day about six months into my rehab Dr. Rectanus broached a question:

"Are you doing any dating?" he asked.

"Nooooo…." I hesitatingly replied. Re-entering the dating scene would be hard enough after being married for fifteen years, but the obstacles now seemed almost insurmountable.

"You should try it," he said. "I've seen too many head injury patients just retreat into their own worlds, and you have to guard against that."

"How am I going to meet anyone? I can't just hang out at the bars by myself, that seems kind of sad, and I can't hear what people are saying anyway. I don't really have any friends here, and a health club is out because I'm always in some sort of therapy all day. And I don't have any money for going out on dates anyway."

"This is Naples, you should be able to find some rich divorcée," he joked.

"Yeah, just my style—TBI gigolo," I joked back.

There were no easy answers, but the conversation did get me thinking. Maybe I could start dating. And so I tentatively looked for a way to say, "Hello?"

There was a yoga teacher at the studio I was attending who seemed very nice. Her name was Cheri and she was a bit younger than me, but not overly so. She was cute, vivacious, and I thought a yoga teacher would have some of the same Eastern-leaning interests I had. We had chatted after class a few times. But a date? That was too much. So I asked her if she liked to go to the beach. She did, and we made plans to take my fishing skiff, the Rascal, and head south from Naples to Keewaydin Island, which had a beautiful, natural Gulf of Mexico beach that could only be reached by boat: no high-rises, no condos, no multimillion dollar mansions on the beach. I picked her up in my car and brought her back to my parents' house where my boat was tied to the small dock behind the house. As we walked through the house and onto the back porch my mother was sitting in her wheelchair, watching whatever it was she saw. Nobody ever knew for sure what she was really aware of. Her caregiver sat nearby. I stopped and made introductions.

"Mom, this is Cheri; Cheri, this is my mother."

My mother turned her head and her eyes lit up briefly and she tried to raise a trembling arm off her armrest, then let it fall back. Unintelligible sounds came out of her mouth. Her usual odor of hospital antiseptic and diaper urine wafted across the patio. Cheri obviously didn't know what to say or how to respond. None of us ever did, really. Even after more than a year of caring for her we all just did the best we could.

"I'll see you later Mom, we're going to the beach," I said and patted her on the arm and kissed her on the head. This was me, the guy who at age forty-four didn't even have his own place, who lived with his invalid mother. I must have seemed like a real catch. Before her accident, Mom would have greeted Cheri warmly and made her feel welcome, made small talk, but now their was only an undercurrent of anxiety and stress.

We had a seemingly nice afternoon at the beach. I don't remember the exact conversation, but it probably went something like this:

"So, tell me about yourself," I say (noticing that she looks great in her bikini, thinking that my brain must be working okay after all, thankful that my sunglasses hide my eyes so she can't see where I'm looking, thinking that January in Florida is so much better than January up north).

"Well, I've lived in Naples for a few years. I moved here from Pennsylvania, where I grew up; I was raised a good Catholic girl. I like it a lot better here, the winters are a lot nicer, and it's a lot more fun. "

"Yeah, I was raised up north too, in Buffalo, a good Presbyterian. Western New York is a lot like Pennsylvania: good solid values and cold, long winters. We seem to have a lot in common. I also much prefer the beaches of Florida in the winter." (And the bikinis, I'm thinking, although what am I supposed to say about the fun part? I'm not fun. I'm depressing. I never go out, never do anything except take my dog for walks on the beach, go to therapy, have conversations with my invalid mother who can't talk back. What do I talk about with this beautiful, pleasant person who's looking for fun? My accident? My mother's accident? How I miss my kids? My nasty divorce? How I spend my days in doctors' and therapists' offices? Yikes!)

"Soooo … tell me about yourself," I say. (Uh-oh, already tried that.)

And so we walk on the beach, go for a swim, lie on our towels. Finally I take her home, drive her to her apartment. She invites me up. She lives alone, has a nice place, tastefully decorated, has a life of her own, has belongings of her own, pictures on the wall, knick-knacks on the coffee table. Plants.

I live with my father, invalid mother and a passel of caregivers, all in a house not much larger than her apartment. All my possessions are in a storage unit up north. My books, my pictures of family and friends, my clothes, my mementos from all my travels: Noh masks and raku tea bowls from Japan, Indian handicrafts from Argentina, watercolors from the streets of Paris, a hat given me by a French ski instructor in Val d'Isère in the French Alps. I arrived in Naples with nothing but the clothes on my back. I've bought a few shirts, shorts and bathing suits when I've found things on sale. Thankfully I don't need much here: no winter coats, boots, gloves. No work suits, no ties, no dress shoes.

It's a first date, but not really a first date, and she's invited me up to her apartment. What am I supposed to do? Hello? There is what seems like a giant blank page. Am I supposed to sit down on the couch? Is it possible that we could, should kiss? It's a first date, but it's not really a first date. Or is it? Or are we just friends? And it's only late afternoon. We didn't go out for drinks or dinner or anything. Yet we've known each other around the studio for several months. She did invite me up, but… but….

I decide to go.

"You've got a nice place."

"Thanks." (Here is where she could say, "You've got a nice place too," but naturally she can't, since I don't have a place.)

"Maybe we could go out for drinks sometime."

"That would be fun."

"Okay, I'll call you."

"Okay, thanks for a nice day at the beach."

So I called her and we went out for drinks a few days later at the only bar in Naples that is on the beach where you can watch the sunset. We met some people she knew. Everyone was drinking and having a good time and laughing. Except for me. I was having trouble being fun. I was tired from a day of therapy, and because of my aphasia I couldn't hear very well what anyone was saying. Aphasia is a relatively common result of Traumatic Brain Injury, and there are many different types. Technically aphasia is defined as an acquired language disorder in which there is difficulty producing or comprehending spoken or written language. In my case I could comprehend other people as long as I was in a quiet room, but put me in a room of talking people, or a restaurant, or even outdoors where there was any type of ambient noise, such as wind and waves, and I had difficulty separating people's speech from the background noise. This would also somehow trigger dysnomia, which is difficulty or inability to retrieve the correct word from memory. So if I was put in a noisy social setting, especially a beach bar, I would have difficulty hearing and speaking, which meant I couldn't join in normal conversation with people I met.

We were standing close to each other when one guy, younger than me, closer to her age, asked, "So, are you two married?" She sidled away from me ever-so-imperceptibly.

We really never hit it off. She goes.

A month or so later I tried again. I had finished my vestibular therapy a couple months before, and my vestibular therapist, Meredyth, had been pretty, intelligent, fun and full of laughter. After months of having her tilt me up, tilt me down, spin me around, make me dizzy, make me un-dizzy, looking into my eyes for signs of vertigo and talking to each other about life while I lay on her therapy table, I felt like we knew each other fairly well, and I liked her. She had met and treated my mother; she knew about my injury, my divorce, my living situation. None of that seemed to phase her. She was compassionate and kind. I was no longer a patient, so ethically I didn't see any problems. I called her.

We met for dinner at a nice-but-not-too-expensive restaurant. She was smiling and bouncy and happy. It felt good. We were friends, even though that friendship had only come about because I was her patient. She was younger than I was, probably by at least fifteen years, although as a perfect gentleman I never asked her age. I knew from our conversations that her dad had been a career Navy man (my father had been the lieutenant commander of a destroyer) and she liked boats. She lived alone, liked to cook, was athletic (she had been a gymnast when she was younger). We seemed to have a lot in common, except our age.

"I told some of the girls at work about our date, and a few of them gave me kind of hard time about it; you could tell they didn't think it was right considering our age difference. But the others were okay with it."

"What do you think?" I asked, although I was already pretty sure I knew. She was here, she had a big smile on her face, but I wasn't really sure of anything in my life anymore. Everything I thought I knew about women, about trust, about life, had been turned upside down.

"I'm having a good time."

It was a fun dinner. We were friends, no pressure. If it went somewhere, great, if it didn't, great. It was just nice to be out with a beautiful woman who didn't seem to judge me, who knew me, knew my situation, and didn't seem bothered by any of it.

She had driven herself to the restaurant, had a cute little sports car. I walked her to her car after dinner.

"Let's do this again."

"I would like that; it would be great."

"Okay, I'll call you."

And then a few days later I flew to Wisconsin to see my children for Niall's birthday and to see where they were living, and realized that in a few months I would be released from therapy and would have to make a choice about where I would start a new life. Naples? Wisconsin? When I returned to Naples I talked to my doctors. They said I would need a support network: friends, doctors, therapists, work, money. I knew no one in Wisconsin. I couldn't keep living on my parents' couch. I flew to the North Fork to look for a house to rent. Then my mother died.

Emotionally, it was a release, but it was also draining. My sisters flew down from Buffalo and we made arrangements for a small service in Naples, then a much larger service in Buffalo a few months later. They left and then Chas and Niall and my sister Kristan and her kids came to visit for Easter, and then it was time to fly to Buffalo for my mother's service, and then it was only a month until I would leave Florida.

I never did call Meredyth. She probably wondered what had happened to me. Life had happened to me. Death had happened to me. I go.

In the meantime on a trip to Long Island to look for a house I reconnected with a woman I knew in Brooklyn, Rachel. She was in the media business as I had been, but was thirteen years younger than me. We had talked about my doing some writing for her web design company before my accident, and then all that had been put on hold. We admitted a mutual attraction for each other, saw each other a few times that spring when I was back on Long Island looking for a place to rent, reconnecting with clients so I could start working again when I returned (so I thought). She was attractive, sexy, funny, smart, self-assured with her own career. But even more than that we were from the same tribe; she was also from Buffalo, had gone to the same high school, we had mutual friends. Things were looking up.

One Friday night we left Manhattan in her Mercedes coupe to head up to her friend's house outside the city. It was dark, raining.

"Why don't you drive?" she suggested.

I'm a man, I'm older, I'm in charge, I'll drive. It doesn't matter that I'm a little slow, still get a bit confused sometimes. We're fine. I'm fine. You can't tell your date that you're not fine. I have to be a man, be manly, be in charge, be the alpha male. That's what women want, right? They want virile, strong men, not damaged goods.

We made it halfway there with no problem, then we had to get off the highway. At the top of the off ramp I couldn't see very well in the dark countryside. I'd never been on this road before, had no idea where I was, which way to turn. Suddenly my brain shut down, like a circuit breaker had tripped. Too much information for my damaged brain. I ran over the median, started going the wrong way into oncoming traffic. My brain switched back on. I swerved back onto my side of the road.

"Are you alright?" She had no idea what had just happened.

"I'm fine, really, just got a bit confused in the dark." I drove on.

We had a nice weekend; I returned to Naples. A few months went by and the time for my move back to the North Fork came closer. I flew to Long Island to supervise the movers delivering my things from storage. I went to see Barbara Seifert, the clinical social worker I had been seeing before the accident to help me with the emotional upheaval surrounding my divorce. She had been the couples therapist I hoped would help save our marriage, but when that didn't work I had continued seeing her, thinking that at the very least I could learn what had gone wrong so that nothing like that would ever happen again. She was a normal, nice, calm, grounded woman who was willing to listen, have intelligent conversations and not be judgmental. After years of living with a woman who was the opposite, dealing with a woman like Barbara was a welcome change.

She knew about the accident, my rehab. I had talked with her on the phone several times from Florida. I told her about my impending return, the house I had rented; told her about the kids living in

Wisconsin but coming back to live with me for the summer. I told her my doctors had said I'd need professional help to deal with the challenges of starting life over again on my own. Was she the right therapist for the job? She'd be delighted to help, she said.

Then I told her about Rachel.

"You can't see her this summer, you know," she said.

"Why not?" The thought had never crossed my mind. Rachel was sweet, kind, good with kids. She'd like them, they'd like her. I was sure of it. She wasn't exactly the wicked stepmother type. And I wanted my kids to see what a good, loving adult relationship could be like, to set a good example for them. What they had seen between their mother and myself was anything but.

"Your kids need you all to themselves right now," she said. "They won't want to share you with anyone. You've been out of their life on a daily basis for more than a year. They need to know that you're still there for them. They need some continuity, some safety. A new woman in your life, especially one who lives in Brooklyn and would have to come out and stay over, just would be too much for them right now. They've had way too much uncertainty in their life between your accident, the divorce, their grandmother's accident and death. They need you." She was right—I hadn't thought in those terms. I called Rachel.

She was disappointed, but incredibly understanding. She'd already been planning what she would cook for them, how we would be one happy family over the summer. The kids arrived and they got my full attention, although I would often call Rachel at night after the boys had gone to bed, or send her an e-mail, trying to keep things going with her. Fall came, and we reconnected. I drove back and forth to Brooklyn, she drove out to Southold. I tried to get back to work, to keep focusing on my health, seeing neurologists and therapists, doing my daily therapy routines: yoga, biofeedback, meditation, exercise, reading, writing. I looked for work, contacted old clients. I called my boys every night. It would have been exhausting for anyone, but for a TBI survivor with continuing problems with cognition, stamina, aphasia and other issues, it was doubly hard. I was standing in my kitchen one evening and felt my brain going blank, felt everything spinning, the vertigo coming back. I almost blacked out. I was supposed to drive into Brooklyn a few days later for a Friday night out with Rachel. I cancelled.

It wasn't the first time. I had cancelled a whole summer, I had cancelled other dates. Several days later I sent her an e-mail, apologizing that I had stood her up on a Friday night, apologizing for being a tired, brain-damaged boyfriend, apologizing for not giving her what she deserved: someone who was there for her physically, emotionally, cognitively. I go. Maybe our age and other differences would have ultimately separated us, but if I hadn't had the accident and divorce and kids, hadn't felt so drained emotionally and physically, perhaps I would have had the strength to stay in the relationship, instead of saying "I go."

But I wasn't about to give up. Several months later I met a woman who lived in the same town. She owned the local health food store, taught yoga; her husband had died several years before from cancer. We seemed to have much in common—interest in health and Eastern spirituality, our recent tragedies. Perhaps we would understand each other and aid each other's healing. She lived only a couple miles away. No long drives. But we didn't last long, only a couple months. "Being around you is so dark," she said. I was trying, but death, divorce, brain injury, losing my kids, not being able to get back to work. Things were dark. And all we seemed to do was talk about each other's tragic pasts, instead of moving on. That was no fun. We went.

Most of us have trouble finding a comfortable lover; very few of us marry our childhood sweethearts and stay happily married for fifty years. There are endless dates, getting to know someone, figuring out someone else's wants and desires, figuring out our own wants and desires, finding that special chemistry—the lovers' dance.

So much of the lovers' dance is about letting go of our ego so that we can see more deeply into the hearts of others. I'm sure that my own "I" got in the way of the dance. How could it not? I was still healing, still trying to figure out who "I" was, still trying to rebuild a new "I" that integrated the old one. Still trying to figure out who this new "I" was, what it wanted and needed. Still trying to figure out how much of the old "I" would heal and return.

When we let go of our own wants, fears and past hurts, we can see the wants, insecurities and fears of others and reach out to them, stay present in their lives and give them love and reassurance, instead of saying, "I've had it, this isn't for me, I'm going."

When there is no "I" there can be no "I go."

Lovers' Dance II

Hi,

Bye?

∼

THIS IS VERY SIMILAR TO "Lovers' Dance I" except the lovers are more willing to wade right in, to be open to what the other person is feeling. Just that simple moving of a question mark can change the whole mood. The lovers in "Lovers' Dance I" are insecure, questioning, but are afraid to show it, and cover up their insecurity with a bold statement: "I go." These lovers are more honest, willing to admit their frailties, to live with uncertainty. Both are honest, in their own way, but these lovers are more respectful of the other person: "Do you want me to stay or go?" There is no forcing the situation, just a simple, honest question, "Bye?" that leaves the brave person asking the question open to the possibility of rejection, but also the possibility the other person will say, "Don't go, stay."

I had known Meg before my accident, although not well. She lived in the next town; we had mutual friends but hadn't been friends ourselves, except to run into each other at parties. It was now more than two years since my accident and I was stronger, braver; I had healed more. The previous attempts at dating were now months or years in the past. I wasn't really looking to date, instead concentrating on getting back to work and spending a second wonderful summer with my boys.

Friends had always told me I would be a great teacher; I loved kids, had coached my boys' summer soccer teams, was a good communicator, but I had no training, no teaching degree. Perhaps my brain had healed enough that I could go back to school and get a master's degree. I could teach writing or English. My friend Nancy said, "You should call Meg, you remember her. Since you last saw her she's been through a tough divorce but she went back to school and got not one, but two master's degrees, one in creative writing and one in teaching. She could tell you what it's like to change careers and go back to school in midlife."

I remembered Meg as being sexy, smart, compassionate, quick to laugh and a great mother. That first time we had met when she had been dressed as an Indian maiden fortune teller—surrounded by wide-eyed children sitting cross-legged on the teepee floor—I had no idea she'd wanted to be a writer, but I could tell from her bewitched audience that she was a natural-born storyteller. I called her and suggested we meet for lunch at our local diner. We had a good lunch, she told me about school, gave me some ideas, professors to call. We seemed to have a lot in common; maybe I should follow up by asking her out for dinner. However I was leaving shortly for Buffalo to help my sister Kristan; her husband Kevin was in the hospital now and didn't have much time left. Dates, school—all that would have to wait.

My brother-in-law died, my kids arrived for the summer. Chas and Niall and I fished, swam at the beach, played miniature golf, swung on the swing I hung from the thick branches of the spreading oak tree in the back yard. My sister came to visit to get away from Buffalo and the memories of a dying husband. The boys got new kittens. There was no time for romance.

Fall came, the kids left. I invited Meg to a party at my house. She was going away for the weekend and couldn't come. I called her again a few weeks later and we had lunch again to talk about writing, work, kids. I suggested dinner next time. It had been four months since our first lunch.

What were we doing? Were we just friends? Two middle-aged divorced writers getting together to talk about writing? Or was there something more? Yes, dinner would be nice, she said. We had been dancing around now for months; where, if anywhere, was this going?

That first dinner led to others. She cooked at her house, I at mine. Dinner led to romance; romance was leading to...? In one of the more humorous moments Meg asked me after we'd been dating for a short time, "So, are we just seeing each other?"

"Well ... I'm not exactly sure what you mean," I said warily. I mean, it had only been a few weeks, and what more would we be doing? Pledging undying love to each other forever and ever? I mean, I liked her, but I wasn't about to run off to a Las Vegas wedding chapel yet either. What did she mean, "... just seeing each other?" Did she want something more so soon in a relationship?

"I mean, are we, like, um...." You could tell I had embarrassed her. She had gotten up the courage to ask what to her was an important and intimate question, and I had thrown it back in her face. "... are we dating other people, too?"

"Oh!" I said, relieved. "You mean are we seeing just each other!" The thought that I (or she) might also be dating other people at the same time had never crossed my mind. We had a good laugh about how the transposition of two simple words can entirely change a sentence's meaning: "... seeing just ..." versus "... just seeing...." It's a story she often uses when teaching freshman writing students at Stony Brook University where she teaches, and being at the age where they understand the complexities of the lovers' dance the students usually get a good laugh out of the mix-up.

"Yes," I assured her. I, at least, was seeing only her, with no plans to be dating other women. It wasn't my style, and my brain had enough trouble dealing with one lovers' dance. I was willing to see where things went with her, with no preconceived notion of where I wanted it to go. If she wanted to try the same thing, I was willing. Was she?

Hi? ... or ... bye?

To be truly willing to love someone without any attachment to the outcome is the most courageous act there is. Just simple, true love. This po fits that ideal, just two simple words, two people, with no notion of how the dance will end.

Summer Night Nirvana

Sweaty breasts,
Penis erect.

~

ANCHORED ON NIRVANA, ON A muggy summer night with barely any breeze, the air heavy with humidity so that everything—sheets, pillows, books—seem to ooze moisture, and our bodies sweat tenderly in the dark. I reach out to touch Meg and find her skin deliciously dewy under my caressing fingertips. She reaches over and rubs her hand over my chest, my groin. Our sweat is like massage lotion, letting skin slide across skin in a gently, loving touch, allowing us both to fondle and explore the other's willing body.

Some people may find this po a bit too vivid, graphic or even shocking, but sexual intimacy between two people who truly love and care for each other is one of the greatest gifts of our species. Sex may not be something one talks about in polite company, and I feel some embarrassment writing about it, but sexual dysfunction is often one of the byproducts of Traumatic Brain Injury. Some months after my accident, it became apparent to me that my sexuality had also been impaired. Without going into graphic detail, let's just say things didn't work the way they once had. I was devastated, and when I asked Dr. Rubino about this, he said, "Most people think our sexual organs are between our legs, but our biggest sexual organ is between our ears, and you've injured yours."

Thanks to drugs, therapy, time and a loving partner, I healed, although, as with most impairments from brain injury, I will never be completely the same. Things will not always work completely "right," but at the same time the experience gave me a new gratitude for the sexual nature of our bodies, a feeling of honoring not only my own body's sexuality but of wanting to honor my partner's body as well.

The third Zen Precept is honoring the body, or not misusing sex (see "White Splash"). At its most basic, this precept means such things as not using sex to hurt, dominate or humiliate another person or oneself. But this precept goes beyond these basic prohibitions. I was raised a Northeastern WASP, and while sex was not taboo or even frowned upon in my family, like most families it was not celebrated either. It was hinted at, and alluded to in bawdy titilating jokes, but honored and celebrated? That might have been a bit too embarrassing for all involved.

My eyes were opened to this possibility of celebration by my American History professor in college, James Kettlewell, who was an expert on Puritan architecture and furnishings. In a dusty corner of a little antique store in New England Kettlewell had discovered one of the few Puritan marital beds known to still exist, and had bought it for a song because the store owner didn't realize what it was. Apparently the Puritans, for all their self-righteous ways, revered and worshiped the sexual union between a married man and woman so much that when a couple were married they were given a specially carved bed, with a headboard covered with abstract symbols. The reason so few of these headboards survived is that they were considered personal and individual to each couple and were destroyed upon their deaths.

According to Kettlewell:

This headboard was part of a bed made for a Puritan, probably by a Puritan, probably shortly after the most famous of all Puritan works of art was created, John Milton's "Paradise Lost."... In "Paradise Lost"

Milton wrote of the first marriage. The bed to which this headboard belonged would have been made on the occasion of a Puritan marriage. These Puritans believed that, in a true marriage, the lives of Adam and Eve are replicated, the events of Genesis relived. However, there is one significant difference. The current of the old story is now reversed. Through the rituals of a Christian marriage, played out through a lifetime, Paradise could be regained. That is what the symbols on this headboard say. ... When the Puritan husband and wife slept together and made love they were "imparadised;" that is, returned to Paradise through the medium of sexual love.

There is a school of thought that believes that sexual orgasm is a glimpse of the divine, that at that moment of letting go of all thought, at that moment of total abandonment, we can feel the overwhelming truth and beauty of the universe. I believe that to be true. I believe that sexual ecstasy is similar to the joy one feels when one realizes the paradise of the world around us. So I told Meg that our bed together on Nirvana can be paradise regained, especially since neither of us found paradise in our first attempt at marriage. How fitting that nirvana is often translated as paradise. A naked paradise, a dewy paradise, a sexual paradise: nirvana.

Anger

Shout!
Stomp about.

~

HAT IS ANGER? IN MANY ways anger is the flip side of love and happiness. Instead of feeling a calm, joyful peace, one feels agitated and irritated. Anger can have many levels, from an underlying hum, to "seeing red," to yelling, screaming, stomping one's feet and throwing things, to its most extreme and frightening manifestation where a person feels such uncontrolled rage that they will harm another living creature, including people they love. Many people confuse passion with anger, excusing their angry behavior as just part of their passionate nature.

One of the scarier repercussions of Traumatic Brain Injury can be the effect on a person's ability to control their emotions, to filter what is happening between brain and body, to control urges and passions, especially when it comes to anger. Injuries to the brain often mean an injury to the part of you that knows how to say "no." All of us feel anger at various times; it is a normal human emotion. But most of us can control that anger when we feel it welling up inside of us; our brain is able to contain it, or deflect it, or even transform it into a more positive human emotion such as compassion. But a brain injury can injure the cognitive function we call restraint.

One of the tests I was given when I first arrived in Florida was something called the Stroop Test. The Stroop Test is a neuropsychological test that can measure a number of cognitive functions, including mental processing speed, concentration and memory. The doctors explained to me that these brain activities all fell under the rubric of "Executive Function," brain processes that are responsible for planning, cognitive flexibility, abstract thinking, initiating appropriate actions and inhibiting inappropriate actions. For some reason I got a kick out of this terminology, since half the executives I knew couldn't think their way out of a paper bag. I told Dr. Rubino I thought they should rename it "Housewife Function" or "Waiter/Waitress Function," since in my experience those people had a better grip on cognitive flexibility and quickly taking appropriate actions than any executive I knew.

In my case the Stroop Test was also used to measure my "impulsivity." I had never thought of impulsivity as something that could be tested, but there it was. It was a very simple test: I was given a list of words—blue, red, yellow, orange, green, blue, purple, red, purple, yellow, red—and asked to read them back in a certain amount of time, which basically meant I had to read them quickly—no time to slowly reason out each word. However, each word was in a different color than its name. That is, the word "blue" would be printed in green, or the word "red" would be printed in yellow. I was told to read the words, not the color of the words. Then I was given the same test but asked to do the opposite: tell the tester the color of the word, not the word itself. I was tested on how many answers I got right, and how long it took me.

Most healthy people would have little trouble with this simple test, but for a Traumatic Brain Injury patient the test can be extremely difficult. Your impulse is to blurt out the word, not the color the word is printed in, and controlling that impulse is very, very difficult (especially for a writer whose first impulse is always to see the word; if I had been a painter, perhaps my impulse would have been to see the color). The part of my brain that controls inhibition had been damaged, and in my first testing sessions I was unable to stop myself from giving the "wrong" answer. Over the next several months I would be able to give the "right" answer as my brain healed, but even then it took prodigious amounts of concentration, holding onto myself with everything I had, and my response time would be very slow.

I was already aware I was having problems with impulsivity. At meals I would shovel food into my mouth with an almost manic compulsion, clearing an entire plate in less than a minute. It would have been considered rude behavior in a normal person, but I couldn't control myself and had no idea why my finely tuned manners had suddenly abandoned me.

Several months after the accident I had an appointment for an EKG test on the far side of town. I had been experiencing a racing, irregular heartbeat, and while it was probably a byproduct of anxiety caused by TBI, my neurologist wanted to see if there was anything more serious going on. I was now able to drive myself, although I still had huge problems remembering and following directions, so I allowed plenty of extra time (I thought) to reach the cardiology center.

It had been hard to find a time that fit with all my other therapy sessions, and the appointment was for late in the afternoon. As was typical in South Florida in the summer, large storm clouds were forming as I pulled out of my parents' driveway. Sure enough I got lost thanks to my trouble remembering directions, then it started to pour cats and dogs, which caused the late-afternoon traffic to pile up. I inched along toward my destination, straining to see through the windshield, one eye on the dashboard clock, feeling more and more anxious, partly from the driving conditions, partly as I realized I would be late for the appointment, and partly from my post-traumatic-brain-injury disorder.

When I got there I raced up to the waiting room, where I was told to, naturally, wait. I was only fifteen minutes late, since I had left a lot of extra time, knowing that I usually got lost. I figured that, as with most doctors' offices, they were running behind and when they finished with the patient before me they would usher me in for the test. I sat down and picked up a magazine, but my brain couldn't focus on the words. After a few minutes the receptionist called me to the window and informed me that I had arrived too late; the technician had already gone home for the day and I would have to reschedule.

I don't remember exactly what happened next, but I exploded. I was holding the magazine in my hand and I threw it on the floor, screaming and stomping around the waiting room, yelling about how I had driven all the way in the rain, and how difficult it had been, and didn't they know it was raining and the rain would cause traffic jams and cause patients to show up late!!?? Couldn't the technician have waited a few minutes to see if I showed up!!??

Fortunately the anger receded as quickly as it had come, but it scared the hell out of me. So I would have to reschedule? What was the big deal? And it certainly wasn't this woman's fault. She seemed to take it all in stride. I apologized, told her I was a head injury patient and quickly left the office.

When I met with Dr. Rectanus and described what had happened, he explained that this was fairly typical for head injury patients, and that I shouldn't obsess over it or worry about it, which would only make the anxiety that caused it worse, and that it would subside over time.

He was right, I never had another reaction like it again. There were a few other times when I came close, but I would recognize the onset, quickly use breathing exercises I had learned from my Zen meditation to calm my mind, and the anger urge would pass.

It was not as if I had never felt a high level of anger before. Several years earlier, as the business was failing and my marriage was disintegrating, I had come home one night at around 9 p.m., after a sixteen-hour day dealing with creditors looking for money, customers looking for orders, employees looking for guidance, and the other stresses of running a failing business. I walked in the door and Belinda immediately started in on me, goading me, yelling at me, pushing all my buttons: I didn't care about the children, the business failing was all my fault, I was lazy, stupid, uncaring, selfish, etc. etc. etc. I asked her to stop—I'd had a long, bad day. She wouldn't drop it. I walked away into the kitchen to make myself some dinner. She followed me, continuing her harangue. I kept saying, "Please stop," but she wouldn't. I took a pot out of the cupboard, went to the sink and started to fill the pot with water for pasta. She followed me, shouting her imprecations. I could feel myself getting angrier and angrier. I asked her to stop once more and when she wouldn't, I took the pot of water and threw it on the floor at my feet and screamed, "STOP! PLEASE JUST STOP!"

Well, that did it. My outburst had the desired effect. She stopped. I picked up the pan and tried to make dinner, but I was enraged and shaking and scared all at the same time. It took me hours to calm down. Unfortunately that episode scared her too, but even more unfortunate, it gave her an opening. She used that incident to claim that I was abusive, that she feared for her personal safety, even though I had never in our lives together threatened her, abused her, attacked her or hurt her in any way. I knew it was an isolated incident, and I knew I had not thrown anything at her. I could never imagine myself doing anything like that. I had thrown something on the floor to show how angry I was, and to release some of the anger, and to just get her to stop her personal verbal attacks.

The kind of anger I experienced that night had taken weeks, probably months, to build to that point, and it took weeks to subside; the couples therapist got me to admit how inappropriate my response had been, and to apologize for it, but it took an entire session. The therapist tried to get Belinda to see her role, to apologize for it, but she wouldn't; my angry outburst had scared her and overshadowed everything, and her own anger wouldn't allow her to admit she was also wrong. If I had known how to walk away that night, how to practice non-anger, I doubt it would have saved our marriage, but it wouldn't have allowed her to seize on that one incident and make it the cornerstone of her case for what an awful human being I was. And what would have happened if I'd been able to see past my own ego, my own hurt, my own anger, to see that her own hurt was fueling her anger? What would have happened if, in spite of her verbal attacks, I'd simply given her a hug and said, "I love you"?

I'll never know.

My anger had scared me, too. It was one of the things that had made me seek out a meditation group, because I didn't want a scene like that to happen again. How different the anger that night in our kitchen had been from what I experienced in that waiting room. That anger before my accident came on slowly, like a slow burn, fueled by Belinda's constant goading and criticism. That anger lasted for weeks, and took months of meditation to calm. The anger in the waiting room came on suddenly, seemingly out of nowhere, and soared to new heights and exploded, like a Roman candle, then flamed out and fell back to earth as quickly as it came.

Yet they were both scary, both life-changing, and both manifested themselves in "Shout!/Stomp about."

Non-Anger

Smile,
Laugh awhile.

~

WHAT IS THE OPPOSITE OF anger? What is non-anger? Harmony, peace, love, happiness, tranquility, calm, serenity—they all fit. Smiling and laughing definitely fit. Many translations of the Precepts refer to this state of being as "non-anger." I usually prefer a more positive way of describing things, preferring to describe something by what it is, instead of what it isn't. Thich Nhat Hanh, the Vietnamese Zen master who has written extensively on anger and non-anger, calls it "being peace."

But how does one achieve this state of being filled with peace? Meditation definitely works. Psychotherapy can work for some people. Going for a long walk on the beach or in the woods can do the trick. For some people gardening or playing a musical instrument works. Going for a sail certainly works for me. But one of the simplest, easiest ways to be happy and peaceful, a way that can be used anywhere, any time, is to smile and laugh. Thich Nhat Hanh in his book "Being Peace" writes about an experience he had:

Recently I was sitting with a group of children, and a boy named Tim was smiling beautifully. I said, "Tim, you have a very beautiful smile," and he said, "Thank you." I told him, "You don't have to thank me, I have to thank you. Because of your smile, you make life more beautiful. Instead of saying, 'Thank you,' you should say 'You're welcome.'"

If a child smiles, if an adult smiles, that is very important. If in our daily life we can smile, if we can be peaceful and happy, not only we, but everyone will profit from it. This is the most basic kind of peace world. When I see Tim smiling, I am so happy. If he is aware that he is making other people happy, he can say, "You are welcome."

When I was a child we would sometimes go on vacation with several different families. These families always had kids our own age, so both parents and kids had peers they could enjoy the trip with. This usually made for a large group of four to six adults and seven to ten kids, which led to a kind of festive, circus atmosphere, but could also lead to disagreements and resentment with so many competing needs and wants: "I want to go here!" "No, I want to go there!"

One of the games my parents liked to play with us to diffuse such family travel trauma was called "Ha Ha." In "Ha Ha," everyone lies down together on their backs on the floor or the grass, with one person resting his or her head on the stomach of the person behind them, so that everyone is connected in a Scrabble/domino-like pattern. A kind of mock-serious tone is affected, with the "goal" of the game being to not laugh, and to see how far the "Ha Ha" chain can go without being broken. The first person begins by saying, "Ha!" The bouncing of their stomach is felt by the next person in line, who then says, usually louder, "HA! HA!" and then the third person says, "HA! HA! HA!" and so on through the group. Invariably someone starts to giggle, then others can't hold back the rising tide of lighthearted laughter, and the whole exercise turns into a writhing, giggling mass of human mirth rolling on the ground.

Finally the laughter would subside and we would lie there, spent, exhausted and thoroughly happy, not a shred of anger in the bunch. We would do this anywhere. One time when we were kids at Disney World we were all tired and cranky from a long day of standing in line in the heat, and my mother walked over to an open grassy area and lay down, telling us to come play Ha! Ha!, as park-goers swirled around us. We got a lot of strange looks, but invariably passersby would stop, smile and chuckle to themselves; the good feelings were infectious.

Roshi Matthiessen had several Zen masters as teachers, including some of the first great Japanese teachers to come to the United States in the 1970s. These men were stern, Zen taskmasters. His most immediate teacher, Bernie Glassman, also studied under the same masters. Roshi Glassman is one of the proponents of what is known as "socially engaged Buddhism." In 1982, while in his forties, he founded the Greystone Bakery in a part of Yonkers, New York, that was plagued by poverty, violence and drugs. Greystone now employs 175 people and serves at least 1,200 men, women and children annually. In 1994, on the occasion of his fifty-fifth birthday, Bernie created the Zen Peacemaker Order, a confederation of Buddhist teachers focused on socially engaged Buddhism. In 1997 he opened the Maitri Center, a medical center serving 180 people with AIDS-related illnesses. As you can see Bernie is a very committed, very intense, very serious Zen master, like his teachers.

But in 1999, now in his sixties, he also decided to start clowning around, and founded the Order of DisOrder, a spiritually based order of clowns, in which he literally began wearing clown noses, doing clown routines and teaching others how to do the same. He did not give up his serious commitment to social engagement and Zen, but developed the Order of Disorder as a parallel path. Bernie has said the world "needs more honoring of the clown part of ourselves. Everybody has some clown in them and [to empower] people to let their clown part speak is good." Bernie has taken his clowning to such places as an Auschwitz Bearing Witness Retreat and a refugee camp in Chiapas, Mexico. Bernie is a very silly Zen master.

One of my favorite Zen icons is a small figurine of a jolly, fat, smiling monk that most people refer to as the "Fat Buddha" or the "Laughing Buddha," a tchotchke that can be found in almost any novelty store in any mall, or on any street vendor's table in Chinatown or

SoHo. In reality this is not a statue of the Buddha at all, but of Hotei, a wandering Zen monk who lived in China around 900 A.D. Most representations of Hotei depict him carrying a sack, and tradition holds that his sack is filled with candy, fruit and donuts that he hands out to children who gather around him on his travels, causing squeals of delight. He is said to have started laughing when he attained enlightenment, and was thereafter always laughing. People would surround him in the village square, smiling and laughing, infected by his good humor. He's a sort of Zen Santa Claus, handing out gifts and always saying "ho, ho, ho."

There is a Zen koan regarding Hotei. In the koan another monk walks up to Hotei one day and asks, "What is the meaning of Zen?"

Hotei just drops his bag and looks at the monk, most likely with a bemused smile and a twinkle in his eye.

Not receiving a spoken answer, the other monk presses on, "How does one realize Zen?"

Hotei then simply picks up his bag and walks away. And being Hotei, the laughing one, he most likely chucks to himself as he strolls down the road.

I find that often when I meditate, a small, almost imperceptible smile comes to my face as I let go of the cares of the world, and I feel my whole body and soul sitting and smiling contentedly. Sometimes if I'm meditating at the Zendo I have to stifle an urge to laugh out loud so as not to startle others who are meditating silently. My life has not necessarily gotten that much better; I still struggle with the cognitive aftereffects of TBI, I still have a lot of pain in my body from the accident, I still miss my children terribly, I still have no health insurance to pay for medical costs, and I still live with the daily terror of having no money and not knowing where cash will come from to buy food, pay the boat mortgage, buy gas for the car, etc.

And yet, and yet…. I have learned how to smile at life, pick up my bag and continue walking.

I love these two po together: "Anger" and "Non-Anger." They illustrate one of the most basic elements of a passage to nirvana, how to go from angry stomping to joyful smiling and laughing. What could be more loving, more happy, more peaceful, more compassionate, more non-angry, than to clown around, to smile, laugh and say, "Ha, HA!"?

Henry

Crazy wild
Golden Child.

~

BOOK ABOUT SURVIVING AND RECOVERING from Traumatic Brain Injury would be incomplete without paying tribute to one of my best therapists, my golden retriever Henry, who I sometimes call, only half-jokingly, my Golden Child. Henry came into our lives two years before my accident, when our beagle, Lucy, who we had adopted from the local animal shelter a couple years before, passed away of old age. While we all loved Lucy, and she had been a great dog, she was with us only a short time and I wanted to get a true family dog for our boys, a dog who would grow up with them, who would go through its own doggy childhood at the same time the boys were going through their childhoods.

About six months after Lucy died the woman at our local pet store told me about an elderly couple with a nine-month old golden retriever they couldn't control, and they were looking for a good home for him. I called them up, and they interviewed me extensively over the phone. They asked if I had kids, and when I told them I had two boys, ages three and seven, they said no, we weren't the right home for Henry, since he was too crazy and rambunctious for a three-year-old child and would just run the poor boy over and leave him crying.

What they didn't know was that my three year old was a rambunctious hellion himself; Henry was about to meet his match. I pleaded with them on the phone to at least let us come visit and see what happened. They finally relented, and we drove over immediately. When we arrived, Niall and Chas tumbled out of the car, ran straight to the dog and in minutes Henry and Chas and Niall were all running around in the backyard, chasing and tumbling over one another, and the owners looked at me with tears in their eyes and said, "He's yours."

The boys were still too young to properly care for Henry, so I became his new alpha male, feeding him, running him, and most importantly teaching him some discipline and manners. He was as crazy and unmanageable as advertised when we first adopted him, but it was an exuberant craziness, born of a golden love of life, a boyish doggy enthusiasm that one couldn't help but love.

With patience, daily training and a lot of exercise to release his energy, he was, if not a perfectly behaved canine, at least somewhat manageable, and he was my constant companion, accompanying me to work, to pick up the boys at school, on my daily runs, and at the end of a long day, lying by my feet at night as I read on the couch.

When I had my accident, I suddenly disappeared from his life; one day I was there, and the next day I was gone: in a hospital, then shipped off to rehab in Florida. Who knows what he thought, but it must have been confusing and upsetting to him to lose his master and friend, especially since he had lost his previous masters only two years before.

After several months I made my first trip back to my house to visit my boys, and when Henry saw me I thought he was going to knock me over and cause another head injury; he was so excited he couldn't stop jumping up on me, licking my face, running around in circles—I wish everyone I knew was so unabashedly happy to see me. Several months after that I got word through a friend that Belinda was looking to get rid of him and was going to give him away without telling me. How she could contemplate giving away her children's dog was beyond me, but I was not about to let it happen. I got on a plane, flew up to Long Island and rescued him before he could be exiled from our family forever.

In Florida Henry became my therapy dog. I would take him for long walks in the morning before the day became too hot; I would sneak him onto the Gulf beaches in the early morning hours before the beach patrol began their rounds (no dogs were allowed on the beach). He wouldn't let me out of his sight if he had any say in the matter; after losing me once, he wasn't about to lose me again. I had very little social life; I was too exhausted after therapy each day to do much of anything and my mild aphasia and dysnomia made it difficult to communicate effectively with humans. Before the accident I had been a very outgoing person, enjoying people's company, but now I felt cut off, different, unable to communicate in normal social situations: a cocktail party, a restaurant, a health club, or a bar—like on my date with Cheri. Even noise from a television in the background made it difficult for me to hear, understand and speak. When I did find myself in conversation with others where environmental noise made it impossible for me to comprehend what was being said, I became very adept at nodding my head and saying "mmm" and faking it, pretending that I understood.

But Henry didn't care. He didn't speak English. We had always communicated on a different level anyway. I would come home from therapy and he would wag his tail and give me a big lick and let me know that I was okay with him, language problems or no language problems. I spoke dog just fine. A nod of the head, a look in the eyes, a woof from him or me, and we understood each other. He didn't give a damn if I sometimes got confused, or forgot things, or acted a little spacey; just the fact that I was there in his life was good enough for him.

When I moved back to Southold the house that I rented had an attic room on the second floor that I turned into an office. It was the perfect room for both Henry and me: big enough for a desk, bookshelves, a table to hold my printer and files, and space in the corner large enough to fashion a small Zen altar and meditation space. Perhaps the best feature from Henry's point of view was that the window was only a foot or two off the floor, and so he could easily gaze out over the farmer's fields surrounding the house, watching the birds, rabbits and deer that populated the grassy meadows and would emerge out of the tall waving grass onto our lawn.

I would sit at my desk for hours, staring at the computer screen, sobbing because the words just wouldn't come. Even though my dysnomia was improving over time, and even though I had surrounded myself with every dictionary, reverse dictionary, thesaurus, flip dictionary, style manual and writer's reference book known to mankind, I still had great difficulty doing what I had always done best: writing.

But just when I would be feeling the most down, wondering how I had ended up all alone in this house, with no social life, my children gone, my ability to write gone, Henry would get up off the floor and nudge my elbow with his snout, knocking my ineffectual fingers from the keyboard, telling me to just forget the whole thing and take him for a walk. I would put on my boots and coat and walk through the muddy fields, surrounded by waving grass and blowing clouds and flocks of birds wheeling in the trees in the distance and Henry running and jumping and chasing his ball, and everything would be all right. He was the best therapist I could ever have, my Golden Child, worth more than all the gold in the world.

FUN & GAMES

Bodysurfing

Fave

wave.

~

THERE IS NOTHING SO SIMPLY pleasurable and elemental as wading out into the surf, turning toward shore and throwing yourself down the face of an onrushing wave. I did it as a kid and was wild about it, and as an adult I've done it with my own sons who are wild about it too. My son Niall is especially fond of anything having to do with being in the water; I sometimes think he is part fish. He loves bodysurfing; it is something we can do as father and son that strengthens the bond between us. We have been thrown onto the beach in the breaking surf on the ocean beaches on Long Island; we have run shouting into the waves on a windblown day on the shores of Lake Erie, and we somehow managed to find waves big enough along the calm Gulf beaches of Southwest Florida. One of our favorite places after we got Nirvana was the beach at Watch Hill in Rhode Island. We could anchor overnight in the sheltered waters behind the barrier island and take the dinghy and ashore and walk the fifty yards across the dunes to the ocean side, where cold surf rolled in from the Atlantic, with waves just the right height for bodysurfing.

But before Nirvana, before Watch Hill, even when Niall was only a young child he was fearless, charging out into the surf, calling to me to follow him: "Come on, Dad! Hurry up! Let's see who can catch the biggest wave!" He would spend so much time in the water that his lips would turn blue and he'd be shivering and I'd still have to force him to come out of the water and warm up on the beach.

As a parent I find myself saying "no" so often, trying to protect my children and be a responsible adult, that my first instinct is to say, "No! You can't go in the water, the waves are too big," or "No, you're too small," or "No, you just ate lunch," or "No, you're already too cold."

And then, as always in my life, there is the head injury factor. Although I've continued to improve, in the first few years after the accident I'd worry that because of my problems concentrating and my trouble hearing in noisy situations like waves, I might miss something bad happening to Niall, like being pulled out by an undertow. I'd worry that I'd slam my head on the bottom and become disoriented. I still had a lot of pain in my left leg and hip where the car hit me, which sometimes made it hard to move easily.

I'd find myself saying, "No, I can't bodysurf with you: I have to sit on the beach and watch you and your brother and be the lifeguard," or "My leg hurts too much," or "I'm too tired." (Exhaustion and lack of stamina can be a big problem for Traumatic Brain Injury patients.) But Niall's youthful enthusiasm was always infectious and I'd find I just couldn't say no; I'd feel the stiffness leaving my joints, I'd feel my energy level surge, and I'd run in after him, splashing and yelling and whooping and seeing who could catch the biggest wave and surf the furthest toward the shore, perhaps even landing up on the beach, laughing, wiping saltwater from my eyes and sand from inside my bathing suit.

Bodysurfing can teach you to say yes instead of no; it can be a wonderful affirmation of the joy of living. The delight of bodysurfing with my sons always brings out the child in me and fills me with a cheerful contentment when I finally flop down on my towel, exhausted and exhilarated. No boards, no sails, no boats, no paddles—nothing but our own bodies and nature. What could be simpler? What could be more joyful? What could be more healing?

Halloween

Who?
Boo!

~

SOMETIMES A LITTLE LIGHTHEARTED VERSE is a good thing, an antidote to all the seriousness, the comedic yin to the tragic yang. I think of this po as being in the same tradition as Ali's "Whee! Me!", his personal paean in the face of such a deadly, brain-damaging occupation as heavyweight boxing. This is my own elfin word talisman to ward off the evil spirits that seemed to be surrounding me, determined to punch my lights out.

After all the tragedies of my life, I tried to maintain some of the family traditions I had enjoyed with my children before my accident and divorce. I had always been the one who took them out on Halloween night, going door to door in the part of town with old Victorian houses where owners put out fake tombstones in front yards and hang ghosts on front porches. There was even a miniature railroad—rescued from a defunct amusement park—that a the local volunteer fire department turned into a haunted train ride through the woods every year, and which was always the traditional grand finale of our Halloween night.

The real monsters and fears of a small child—losing a parent, being abandoned, not having a safe home—can be allayed by imaginary horrors: ghosts, goblins and things that go bump in the night, and by maintaining some sense of continuity in their lives. A year after I had finished rehab and moved back to the North Fork and rented a house and started to create a new life, Chas and Niall came to visit for Halloween. We went to the local farm stands and bought gourds and Indian corn and apple cider, then we searched out special pumpkins in a farmer's field, finding just the right shape and size among all the thousands of other dirt-encrusted pumpkins still on the vines. We wandered through a farmer's corn maze, happily playing hide and seek, getting lost in the green and gold stalks that towered over us, hiding us, protecting us. When we got home we spread newspaper on the table and carved the pumpkins we had bought; I can still see Niall standing on our porch, leaning against a pumpkin he had carved that was almost as big as he was, with a big grin on his face matching the pumpkin's gap-toothed smile.

For trick or treating Niall dressed up as Harry Potter and Chas as the Grim Reaper and I as a green-faced ghoul of indeterminate origin. We did our traditional trick or treat route through the Victorian houses, going door to door on a coal-black, cold, windswept night, the three of us holding hands, protected against the darkness that had engulfed our lives for the past three years. Our trek culminated with a ride on the miniature railroad. The railroad starts in a backyard before winding its way through the woods. There is a miniature train station, crossings, engine house, switches and side tracks and several different locomotives and assorted cars that you sit in, adult knees scrunched up to adult chest. The man who owned the railroad and his friends and members of the volunteer fire department had decorated the woods and lawn with white-sheet ghosts hanging from the trees, severed heads spinning on old record turntables, and assorted other wickedly wonderful Halloween kitsch. Ever since the boys were small children, barely big enough to hold their plastic pumpkins filled with candy, riding through the scary woods on the miniature railroad had been our Halloween ritual, and it was reassuring to be together again, clack-clacking through the darkness, goblins popping out from behind the gray trees. Who goes there? Who indeed? Who? Boo!

Travel

Go
slow.

~

FOR MOST OF MY ADULT life I made my living as a travel editor and travel writer. I journeyed all over the globe, in as many
ways as you can imagine: jet plane, bush plane, helicopter, car,
jeep, truck, bus, train, foot, horse, sailboat, motorboat, ferry,
canoe, skis, snowcat; alone, with a few friends or as part of a tour; staying in luxury hotels, charming inns or third-world hovels; spending
money extravagantly on corporate expense account or scraping by on
my own nickel. One thing I learned: every place can be wonderful if
you give it time; unfamiliar locales usually give up their most precious
secrets slowly.

A year and a half before my accident I had been assigned by Outside
Magazine to write a story about sailing and diving in Belize, using a
chartered catamaran to dive some of least accessible and still pristine reefs
on the planet that lay off the Belize coast. It would have been easy to fly
in, spend a week sailing the mangrove coast, venturing to the offshore
atolls, diving the reefs, taking notes and then flying home to my desk to

write the story, but the country's lush tropical interior called to me. I had recruited my friends Neil O'Keeffe and Scott and Connie Hambley as dive models for the professional photographer who accompanied us, and we decided to stay a few extra days, rent a four-wheel-drive Jeep and travel inland to San Ignacio, deep in the mountains near the Guatemalan border. We had no reservations, no set itinerary; we just went, far off the beaten tourist path. The first night we spent in a fleabag hotel with concrete walls and beds that sagged almost to the floor. We wandered into a corner bar and drank cold beer with some locals, then roamed the streets, but there was nothing memorable or exciting. We asked around, however, and found that a small lodge with a handful of cabins had recently been built in the jungle, down a long, tortuous dirt road that at one point passed under a waterfall that came off an overhanging cliff. The Black Rock Lodge was situated on a mountainside overlooking a deep gorge, on a plateau that had been home to Mayan Indians thousands of years before. We were the only guests, and that first evening, sitting quietly on a wooden deck cantilevered out over the mountainside, looking into the deep river gorge below us, it seemed I could feel the ancient spirits inhabiting the mountain valley.

The next day we contracted with a local guide to take us on pack-horses into the mountains. The animals had been used to carry heavy loads through the mountains: building materials, food, agricultural supplies—and now were living out their golden years doing easy work, carrying gringo tourists. We rode for hours, first through small plantations hacked out of the jungle by local farmers, then up steep rocky trails into the upper elevations. We visited huge Mayan pyramids that had never been excavated, still covered with jungle growth. We found narrow shafts where grave robbers had dug deep into the pyramids. We explored deep caves still filled with shards of ancient pottery. The horses slipped and swayed on the muddy, tree-lined jungle trails. One of our group who grew up riding horses in the mountains in the U.S. said she had never seen horses negotiate such steep, rocky, dangerous trails.

If we had simply flown home after diving, or hurried through San Ignacio because it seemed a stale town, all these wonders would have been lost to us. Most of us tend to rush through somewhere on our way to the next stop, not taking the time to savor where we are. Travel can be a metaphor for life.

Colors

No use
for puce.

~

MEG AND I WERE VISITING Meg's friends Jenny and Carole at Carole's apartment in New York City; somehow the idea of colors came up. Meg and I had been talking for several weeks about how many interesting different words exist in the English language to describe colors, words like periwinkle and cobalt and vermilion. One of the words that fascinated us all that afternoon was "puce" and how it came into being in the late eighteenth century from the French word for flea, because puce is supposedly the color of a flea, or of a flea's belly, or the blood in a flea that is has sucked out of a host and is released when the flea is squashed. How do these things get started? What kind of mind names a color after something with such negative psychological associations as monstrous little biting machines that leave red welts on the skin and carry diseases such as the plague? Puce isn't named after a beautiful flower, like periwinkle, or a luscious fruit, like persimmon, or a beautiful natural mineral, like cobalt. Not only that, "puce" doesn't really rhyme with anything (except another color, chartreuse, or a math term—obtuse, so it's nearly useless for rhyming poetry).

I do have to grudgingly admit that fleas have a positive place in popular culture totally out of proportion to their size, for some reason capturing the public's imagination not only in poetry but in flea circuses (featured in films as diverse as Charlie Chaplin's "Limelight" and the counterculture classic "Easy Rider") and as animated characters in movies such as "A Bug's Life." And then of course there is the big favorite of many people on a weekend, or when traveling in foreign city—the flea market. The original flea market, and likely the most famous, may be the *Marché aux puces* ("market with fleas") of Saint-Ouen in the northern suburbs of Paris.

So, fleas are an integral part of Western culture. But still, naming a color after the little buggers?

The flea circus featured in "Easy Rider" was the famous Heckler's Flea Circus that for years was located in Manhattan's Times Square, so perhaps we felt a nostalgic New York connection with fleas, or perhaps just a New York creepy crawly connection in general, but in any event we all had a good laugh ruminating on puce, fleas and flea blood, and trying to figure out what kind of person named a color after something so loathsome. In the end, we all decided we had little use for puce.

What we did have use for, although we couldn't have elucidated it at the time, was the company of old friends, the excitement of new friends, and the joy of laughter and shared wordplay, brains working together in fun and games.

I like that this po comes full circle with the idea of the world's shortest poems, since it has to do with fleas, and relates back to the very first world's shortest poem, written in 1927: "Adam/had' em."

Numbers

Three!
Wheee!

~

THERE IS SOMETHING MAGICAL ABOUT the number three that seems to reverberate throughout our collective human consciousness. In religion, Christianity has the Holy Trinity of Father, Son and Holy Ghost; in Buddhism there are many examples of three being sacred, perhaps the most well-known being The Three Jewels of the Buddha (the teacher), the Dharma (the teachings) and the Sangha (the congregation, or learners); in Judaism, adherents traditionally pray three times daily. There were three main Greek gods, Zeus, Poseidon and Hades (air, water and earth) mirrored in the three Roman gods, Jupiter, Neptune and Pluto. In Muslim devotional rites, many formulas are repeated three times.

In the arts, most plays are in three acts; the most basic chords have three notes; there are the Three Little Pigs, Three Blind Mice, Three Musketeers, Goldilocks and the Three Bears, the Three Stooges, and our most modern threesome, Charlie's Angels. In writing there is the rule of three, which posits that whether writing slogans, books, movies, plays or even jokes, three is the best structure. James Joyce envisioned three aesthetic stages: arrest (by wholeness), fascination (by harmony) and enchantment (by radiance). In psychology Freud proposed that the psyche was divided into three parts: ego, superego and id. Plato split the soul into three parts: desire, spirit and reason. Three has strength: a triangle is the most durable shape possible, the only "perfect" figure which if all endpoints have hinges will never change its shape unless the sides themselves are bent.

Three has an ethereal lightness of being. When drawing clouds, the simplest way is to draw a nice white, fluffy cumulous cloud with three humps, the middle being higher than the sides. We rarely draw dark, angry storm clouds with many lobes, or straight cirrus clouds, or cumulous clouds with only two humps. Three's a cloud.

One possibility for our fascination with the number three is that it is basically strange to humans. Most of our obvious body parts come in twos: two eyes, two ears, two nostrils, two arms, two legs, two hands and two feet. We also have ones: one head, one torso, one nose and one belly button (I hope). We have fours: four limbs, four extremities. And we certainly have fives: five fingers and toes on each hand and foot. But we don't have three of anything, unless we tie one leg to a partner to join a three-legged race at the family picnic.

In primitive counting systems there are usually only three numbers: one, two and "many." Once cultures developed more sophisticated counting systems, the number three is usually the last one that is represented by a direct visual device. One is represented by one mark, two by two marks, three by three marks, but four is represented by a more abstract symbol, such as IV, or 4; our own 3 is basically three horizontal lines that over time grew together to form the symbol 3.

And why are many of our best-known acronyms composed of three letters? CIA, FBI, UPS, IBM, NBC, CBS, ABC, CNN—even TBI?

On the downside, people always say that "bad things happen in threes." Barbara Seifert told me that most people can handle one stressful life event, have a more difficult time with two stressful life events, but that three stressful life events can create profound problems with anxiety, depression and cognition. She later told me that when I first came to see her I was "off the charts" thanks to the triple whammy of divorce, business failure and my mother's accident. Then before I had the chance to recover, I was hit with the next threesome: my own accident, my children being taken away and my mother's death. Then, to top it all off, the final three, my aunt's death, my brother-in-law's death and the death of a college friend. I had been hit by the perfect, perfect, perfect storm.

So how does one not only survive such tempests, but in the end learn to overcome them, to thrive? How does one make the passage to nirvana in spite of so many stressful life events? How does one learn to say, "Three! Wheee!"? There is no one answer; every human being is different, every situation is different. In my case I believe it was a combination of factors: psychotherapy, meditation, medication, spiritual practice, good doctors, good friends, exercise, diet, and parents and teachers who instilled in me a lifelong positive mental attitude. If I had to boil it down to a list of three I'd say: ancient wisdom, modern medicine and of-the-moment peer support.

There is one other, more profound possibility: perhaps such Sisyphean obstacles are an important part of the journey. While I certainly am not advocating anyone running out and throwing themselves in front of a car, I do believe there is credence to the idea that learning to overcome great difficulties is an important element in any passage to nirvana. It's easy to laugh at the Three Stooges, or to appreciate the Holy Trinity, but learning to say "Three! Wheee!" in the face of death and despair, learning to see that three's a cloud, not a crowd—that is the challenge.

I learned to still like the number three, so I chose a tripartite organization to "Passage to Nirvana": Book I, the Prologue; Book II, The Book of Po, Book III, Bricolage. Most of the po themselves are composed of three lines: the title and two lines of verse.

And this po, with its "Wheee!" is another homage and allusion to the champ of short poetry, Muhammad Ali, a man who overcame many great hurdles himself, from racism to people wanting to punch his lights out. I feel a special affinity with Ali, because his biggest hurdle, Parkinson's Syndrome, is a debilitating form of brain disease brought on by the severe head trauma he suffered, although in his case he was hit by human fists, not by motorized metal.

New England Nirvana

Skiing,
Spirit soaring,
Being.

~

SKIING WAS ONE OF THE benchmarks in my recovery, a watershed moment, a sign of rebirth and rejuvenation. I was at Stratton Mountain with my two boys, as well as my friend David and his family—his son Henry who was eight and his daughter Jane, who was only six, and David's girlfriend Kate. Chas was thirteen at the time and Niall was nine. David had been there from the beginning of this whole crazy ride, from the day I was on my way to meet him in New York and got hit by a car. He had a condo at Stratton, and just as he had been the first person to the hospital after my accident, he had been a good friend throughout my recovery, offering assistance, friendship, and now a place to reconnect with one of the touchstones of my life, skiing.

To be on skis again after five years of rehab, healing and recovery was like manna from heaven. Skiing has always had a special significance for me: my parents were both skiers, and my mother taught me to ski as a child by taking me to a local toboggan hill after school and holding me between her legs as we snowplowed down the slope together. As we got older my parents would pile my two sisters and me into the family station wagon every Saturday and Sunday and drive us to the local ski area, where we were given the freedom to explore the hills and forests, play with friends and ride the T-bar by ourselves. It was the first real taste of independence for a young boy, the first step toward finding out who I really was.

I remember vividly the smells, sights and textures: black leather ski boots, colorful wool sweaters, tan wicker lunch backpacks, the invigorating cold, the black and white landscape of leafless trees and snow-covered ground, scratchy wool ski hats, wet leather gloves, the perfume of melted ski wax, the symphonic scrape of metal edges on ice and rock and snow, the hoary silence of the woods when you snuck away from the main hill.

As I grew up I became a ski racer, then a ski instructor, then a ski shop employee and finally a ski shop manager. I saved money and took trips to bigger and bigger mountains, where I learned how to jump off cliffs into the mountain's soft white powdery embrace. I learned how to overcome fear and trembling knees by jumping into a chute so steep that if you fell you risked serious injury or even death. Skiing taught me commitment: hang back and you lose your balance and fall on your ass or worse; reach forward and you will fly down the mountain having sprouted imaginary wings.

Eventually I blended three of my passions—skiing, writing and travel; I became the senior travel editor for Skiing magazine, at the time one of the largest and most successful special interest sports magazines in the world. Throughout all the permutations that skiing took in my life, including the sometime drudgery of skiing as work, it never stopped being fun. Skiing could always bring a smile to my face, erase the cares of the world, send my spirit soaring.

As an adult, skiing became something I could do with my own children. I first took Chas skiing at age two in Sun Valley, Idaho, favorite haunt, ski mountain and final resting place of Hemingway. I remember the pure joy of holding Chas between my legs just as my mother held me. I taught Niall to ski between my legs when he was only three at Smuggler's Notch in Vermont. When Chas was seven he and I went alone on a father/son weekend to Windham Mountain in New York's Catskill Mountains. It was a cold winter day, and he kept falling down on the icy moguls. As I was leaning over to help him up for the hundredth time I could see the tears in his eyes. "I can't do this dad," he said, disconsolately.

I helped him down the mountain and hustled him into the base lodge, where I warmed and nourished him with hot chocolate and words of encouragement. "You can do it Chas. Just keep telling yourself that. Keep saying to yourself, 'I can do it, I can do it.'"

He was ready to give up, but I coaxed him back out onto the chairlift. At the top of the mountain he fell again, and again, but he picked himself up and as he started down the mountain I could hear him saying under his breath, "I can do it, I can do it, I can do it." There were a couple more falls, but within minutes he was skiing down the mountain, turning in beautiful rhythmic arcs, repeating his new mantra over and over: "I can do it, I can do it." He finally fell toward the bottom of the mountain and I skied up to his side. He looked up at me and said with a huge smile on his face, "Dad, you're the best dad in the whole wide world." It was my turn to have tears in my eyes.

So skiing had always been an integral part of my being, something that defined who I was: father, husband, writer, skier and sailor. And then one day I could no longer ski, and didn't know if I would ever ski again. Skiing was one more thing that had been taken away by a careless car wash attendant, a two-ton motorized hunk of metal and a concrete parking lot.

To be skiing with my children, my old friend David and his children, brought me incomparable joy. I kept saying to myself, in spite of a Traumatic Brain Injury and a left leg/hip that was extremely painful and didn't work the way it once did, in spite of continuing balance problems, "I can do it, I can do it."

And I did do it. I skied. At first tentatively, but with each turn I grew bolder, and stronger, and before long I was flying down the mountain. I could do it. I had regained my wings. I reached the bottom laughing, gasping for breath, and laughing some more at the sheer wonder of it all.

And to be at Stratton, where another of my skier/writer heroes, Robert Penn Warren had lived, was a bonus. Warren, onetime U.S.

Poet Laureate, wrote what is probably the quintessential skiing poem, "Skiers," which includes these lines: "With the motion of angels, out of / Snow-spume and swirl of gold mist, they / Emerge to the positive sun."

Standing there at the base of Stratton, having just swooped and whooped my way down the mountain, I definitely felt as if I had finally emerged into a positive, bright place. Skiing that day reminded me of a talk I'd had with my son Chas a few months before, when I told him all the adult, responsible reasons we were going to move from a house onto a boat: learning teamwork, respect for others, respect for the environment, how to live simply, how to be creative (finding things to do instead of sitting around watching TV or playing video games). After I'd given my spiel, he said to me with a big grin on his face: "Dad, you forgot the most important reason."

"What's that?" I said, wracking my brain; I'd gone over the entire list.

"C'mon Dad, you know!"

"What? What did I forget?"

"To have fun, Dad! To have fun!"

It was Chas' turn to give me my own personal mantra: "Have fun, Have fun, Have fun." Children can be wonderful teachers.

Balance

Moon snow,
Skis flow.

~

THIS IS AN HOMAGE TO a different kind of skiing: cross-country skiing, where the point is not to go fast or swoop down the hillside but to glide silently along, at one with the woods and the fields. Most people tend to be proponents of one or the other type of skiing, but I enjoy both and appreciate them for their own merits. I've also cross-country skied since I was a kid. Growing up in the country outside of Buffalo I would sometimes ski through the farmers' fields to my best friend Bill's house to play Stratego on his family room floor. Or sometimes I would just go for a long ski with my dog, Bonnie, a big lumbering Newfoundland who was my other best friend. When Bonnie finally got too tired because her weight made her paws punch deep into the snow, while my skis allowed me to glide on top, she would throw herself on the back of my skis to stop me, her way of telling me that it was time to turn around and go home.

Now, thirty years later, two years after my accident, I was cross-country skiing through the crisp, fresh snow on a moonlit night behind my new rental house in Southold, with ice crystals crunching underneath, my new best friend, Henry, following in my tracks. The skis glided across a silvery landscape devoid of color but still glowing with a soft sparkling light that seemed to come from within the snow itself. Coming out of the woods by a small inlet, a house on the opposite shore cast a warming yellow glow from its windows, smoke curling from the chimney. It was a midwinter night, bone-chilling cold, enough to numb the cheeks, and I had a choice: I could focus on the discomfort, how damn cold it was, how nice and warm it surely was in that house, or I could keep moving, working hard to ski through the woods and fields, generating body heat to keep warm, marveling at the beauty that everyone else was missing, snug in their homes, restaurants or bars.

How often do we wish we were somewhere else? Thinking anywhere must be better than here: warmer, more fun, less stressful. The people would be nicer, the food better, the work less taxing, the money more plentiful, the bills smaller. How often had I wished I hadn't been hit by a car, that my mother was still alive, that my children lived with me, that my mind and body worked the way I once expected them to work?

There would be plenty of time for warmth and gaiety later. I could even dream of a hot buttered rum by a roaring fire, surrounded by laughing friends, but for now, this moment, right here, right now, there was not a more beautiful place than standing alone on skis in these cold, snowy woods. I could learn to appreciate this moment, this new Lee.

When I first woke in the hospital and tried to get out of bed, I fell over. I had injured the part of my brain that controls the body's vestibular system. I had never heard of the vestibular system, which controls our balance. Like most people I had been taught that our inner ear controls balance, but the reality is much more complex. There is a part of our brain that takes the input from inner ear and eyes, the feeling of air on skin, and does millions of calculations, sending out signals to our muscles to keep us upright. As I recovered in the hospital, at first I could only walk with someone holding me upright, then by leaning against a wall. In Florida I went through months of vestibular therapy, learning to balance on inflatable pods and other strange devices.

Now to be balancing on these skinny skis without tipping over, to have found balance in my life—these were both things I could appreciate, things that cured any desire to be someplace else.

225

Fishing

Might
Bite.

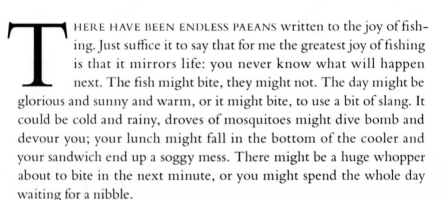

THERE HAVE BEEN ENDLESS PAEANS written to the joy of fishing. Just suffice it to say that for me the greatest joy of fishing is that it mirrors life: you never know what will happen next. The fish might bite, they might not. The day might be glorious and sunny and warm, or it might bite, to use a bit of slang. It could be cold and rainy, droves of mosquitoes might dive bomb and devour you; your lunch might fall in the bottom of the cooler and your sandwich end up a soggy mess. There might be a huge whopper about to bite in the next minute, or you might spend the whole day waiting for a nibble.

Fishing has been a huge part of my life; both my grandfathers took me fishing when I was a young boy, and the pleasant memories have stayed with me for forty years. A thoughtful, taciturn Scandinavian, my grandfather on my father's side was a fly-fisherman who enjoyed the solitude of standing in one of the many small trout streams south of Buffalo—fabled blue-ribbon waters such as the Wiscoy and the

East Koy. But I was too young to fly-fish, so he was content to take me to a stocked trout pond, where he would rent a rowboat, put a worm on my hook, attach a bobber to my line and lean back in the stern with his hat pulled over his face, happily napping while I rowed around the pond and caught beautifully hued rainbow trout, their shining, glistening green, gold and red the most spectacular thing my young eyes had ever seen.

My mother's father was a different animal entirely. A tough construction magnate of German heritage, he was more gregarious and boisterous. He lived in Southwest Florida and his fishing vehicle was a small yellow houseboat he kept in an old wooden boathouse. When I visited we would cast shrimp in among the mangrove roots, where the wily snook lay in wait. It was a different kind of fishing, as suited to his temperament as fly-fishing for trout was to my paternal grandfather. Where the trout were delicate and graceful, caught on a worm hanging placidly beneath a bobber from a rowboat, snook were big and brawny saltwater fish, slashing at the darting shrimp, pulling thick line off the casting reels. I loved them both: my grandfathers and their different ways of interacting with the natural world.

As a parent, I wanted to make sure I gave my own children the same wondrous experiences my grandfathers gave me and instill in my boys a reverence for the miracles of nature. When they were only four and eight we fished for small porgies using bobbers from our seventeen-foot fishing boat on Peconic Bay. When the boys gained a few years and could handle a spinning reel, we cast from the sandy banks of tidal inlets, reeling in feisty snapper blues. We've pulled red snappers from the mangrove roots of Florida, fishing from a small nineteen-foot flats boat. We've had days where we caught nothing at all, except for the joy of being together. As they got older we tackled bigger quarry: bluefish and flounder and stripers from a slightly larger twenty-two-foot bay boat.

The flats boat was something acquired during my recovery from my accident, a gift to myself for being alive. My doctors had asked me what I liked to do best, and I told them boating: fishing, sailing, working on boats, just being on the water. They told me one of the best things for my recovery would be to get a boat, something to engage my mind and my body and my interest, something to help me heal. Rick McCawley told me the story of one of his patients who was into cars and had bought an old car and fixed it up, and how therapeutic that process had been for that man. So I found an old boat for sale and worked on fixing her up in my father's driveway, and when both the boat and my brain were ready I put her in the water and spent hours exploring the mangrove channels south of Naples, casting for snook, redfish and snapper. I named her "Rascal" in honor of my boys, my little rascals. Those days I spent on the water during my recovery were some of the most joyous of my life, just being alive, immersed in sun and water, wind and calm.

I took Roshi Matthiessen fishing once. He had come to Naples to give a talk to a nature conservancy group. There was much interest at the time in his Watson trilogy set in Southwest Florida, a story that would eventually win him the National Book Award. Fortuitously, I was still in Naples, finishing my rehab, and was well enough at that point to handle Rascal in the currents and eddies that swirled around the mangroves in the rivers that emptied out of the Everglades. Roshi was in his mid-seventies then, and had spent his life traveling, climbing mountains, exploring jungles and savannas and indigenous people and the great spiritual unknown. He was an avid fisherman who had fished all over the world. That day he hooked a small juvenile snook using a rod I rigged up for him, and as he reeled it into the boat, he gave a small sigh and said softly, "Oh, no," then gently coaxed the hook from the fish's mouth and let it swim away. It was one of the gentlest expressions of kindness I had ever seen and it endeared him to me more than ever, this big, craggy, man's man who was also the very embodiment of compassion.

Another of the biggest fishing moments after the accident came when I had just started dating Meg and took her fishing for her first time. We were on the newest Rascal. (I had traded in the nineteen-foot flats boat for the slightly bigger, safer, more seaworthy twenty-two-footer that could handle the open ocean waters off Long Island's East End.) We were working a long tidal rip off the southern end of Cartwright Island, a small, half-moon-shaped sandy islet in Napeague Bay off the South Fork of Long Island, close to the Atlantic, where the bluefish grow large and voracious. The island is a bird refuge, and the gulls and terns were crying and wheeling overhead. The day had been hot and sunny, but it was getting late and most of the other boats had long gone home and we had the rip to ourselves. Meg cast a large blue wooden popper into the rip just where I pointed and sure enough a huge bluefish hit with a vengeance. I will never forget the squeals of delight from Meg as she reeled in the first fish of her life. She pulled the fish to the side of the boat and asked me to remove the hook and let it swim away, an act of tenderness totally in character with her loving nature, an act that made me love her even more.

There are stories of Zen masters who spent hours in a rowboat or on a riverbank, with a bamboo pole, a line, a hook and no bait, knowing they would never catch anything, that the real answer was just in the sitting. I love those stories, and as I get older, wiser and more compassionate myself I have less and less desire to actually catch and kill a fish; I much prefer to catch and release, or just watch the fish swimming in their natural environment. But I'm not sure I'll ever sit with no bait on my hook at all; with no bait, there is the certainty of not catching. While most of us have trouble with change in our lives, true happiness comes from embracing uncertainty, from embracing this elemental law of nature: even with all the best preparations and intentions, even with the best bait, they might bite, they might not.

Middle Age

Aye, glasses,
mind molasses.

~

MY DICTIONARY DEFINES MIDDLE AGE as being from ages forty-five to sixty-five, and for that I am very thankful, since that means at age fifty-two I am not even to the middle of middle age. Even so, I have had to admit that I have arrived at that time in life when my eyes need glasses for reading, and my mind is not as sharp as it once was, especially when I awake in the morning. For several years I totally denied that I might need glasses, in spite of all evidence to the contrary, and would borrow Meg's glasses on a "temporary" basis. But finally, I had to admit defeat, and say "aye" to the need for reading glasses. I bought some cheap glasses at a local pharmacy. Now I have three pairs of them scattered all over the boat. And being a sailor I'm happy to say "aye, glasses" instead of "eyeglasses."

The mind molasses is more problematic. After the accident, when I went through a battery of tests to discover the level of damage to my brain, one of my biggest problems was in the area defined as "mental processing speed." Dr. Rubino explained it by saying that I was now like an old, slow DOS desktop computer. Just what I wanted to hear—I am an Apple person; it was bad enough I had to be like an old, slow computer, but a DOS machine? Not even Windows 1.0? Or an old Macintosh II?

Serious decreases in mental processing speed are fairly typical in TBI patients, and can manifest in ways that range from vaguely annoying—having trouble coming up quickly with a word, for example—to fairly dangerous. The first time I tried to drive a car after I arrived in Florida I almost had another serious accident when I didn't respond to a red light and ran the intersection, almost hitting another car.

I told Dr. Rubino what had happened.

"You're DRIVING?" he said, incredulously. "You shouldn't be driving. When I think you're ready we'll give you a test to gauge reaction time and processing speed. Until then, stay out from behind the wheel."

Eventually Rick McCawley, who was not only a cognitive therapist but a psychometrician (a neuropsychological test-giver), gave me a series of tests in his office where I had to respond to changing lights and my reaction times were recorded. Thankfully I passed and was given the green light to start driving again.

I have had to come to terms with the fact that my thinking will never be as quick as before the accident, although I have healed well enough to perform most tasks of daily living, such as driving. When I complain to friends or doctors about my sometimes foggy cognition, which usually manifests itself as memory and organizational problems, people just laugh and try to make light of it and tell me I'm just aging like everybody else. I know they mean well, but it is at those moments that I feel most like screaming, "You don't understand!" because the aftereffects of TBI are not like the slight drop in cognition experienced by most people as they age. One day I was doing fine and then, zap! and the next day my brain is functioning like I imagine it functions for someone with early-stage Alzheimer's. I know people mean well, and there is undoubtably some truth to my brain getting slower as I get older, but usually I just wish they would say, "I understand," instead of trying to tell me that I really don't have a cognition problem, that I'm just like everyone else.

Because I'm not like everyone else; I'm a TBI survivor, with a brain that will never be the same, a brain that is sometimes slow as molasses.

Twister

Baby
Bahamian
Boa.

~

WALKING ALONG THE CRUSHED CORAL road in Black Point in the Exumas, Meg and I spied a small grey-green snake lying motionless in the road. It looked like a garter snake, but we had not seen any snakes in the Bahamas and did not even know what kinds of snakes lived in the islands. Meg reminded me of the Bahamian Boa we had read about, an endangered species that lives on a select few Bahamian islands. As the small snake suddenly came to life and twisted its way across the road towards the brush with an undulating, squirming motion, I cried out, "It's a baby Bahamian boa!" and a new tongue twister was born. (Try saying it three times fast.)

I've always loved tongue twisters, such as "rubber baby buggy bumpers" and "she sells seashells by the seashore." There is something so wonderfully naive and childlike about them. They bring back memories of childhood days when something so simple as a bunch of jumbled-up words can bring one to a convulsion of giggling, uproarious laughter. As a writer I love that words have such power to make people burst into fits of happiness. And as a TBI survivor I love that these words could even come to me, that I could remember them, that I could spell them and put them together in a way that makes sense. I had come a long way from not being able to spell "world" backwards, from a time when words made me cry instead of laugh. I had come a long way from those days of sitting and staring at the computer screen, waiting for words that would never come.

I have no idea what kind of snake it really was, if it was really a Bahamian Boa, but I like the word play on twist—the wiggling motion of a snake—and tongue twister—the rolling, weaving, bobbing flow of life, the rolling, weaving, bobbing flow of words.

SEASONS

Spring

Green
Dream.

~

SPRINGTIME CAN BE SO BEAUTIFUL, so magical, especially after a long, dark cold winter, that time seems suspended in the air along with the smells of the earth waking from a long winter slumber. That day I was hit by the car was a gorgeous spring day, and it seemed like a dream then, and even more so like a dream now. Perhaps all of our life is like that as it slides into the past, into memory, and becomes nothing but a dream, a remembered time.

This spring, one moment it was winter, with grey skies, grey empty tree branches and cold biting winds blowing in from the northwest. Then suddenly it was spring. Bam. The trees seemed to bud and burst into full leaves overnight; the flowers pushed up from the ground and opened their petals, and we walked the dogs by the water's edge in full, glorious warm sunshine. I was reminded of the two schools of Zen—Rinzai and Soto—the first emphasizing sudden enlightenment and the second gradual enlightenment. Things in life can happen suddenly, or gradually, and either is equally valid, equally green, equally dreamlike.

Summer

Reach
the beach.

~

COUPLE YEARS AFTER I MOVED back to Long Island I landed a job as an estate manager for a very wealthy family in the Hamptons. I had been originally hired as their private yacht captain, but the owner was impressed with my organizational skills and offered me the estate manager position. The estate's employees included two chefs, a chauffeur, an office manager/bookeeper, a live-in tutor for the owners' son, a half-dozen housekeepers and several gardeners. Some of the staff lived on the estate, and others arrived every morning at the crack of dawn so the house and grounds would be ready when the owners started their day. My job was like running a small luxury hotel.

The estate had a grass tennis court; paddle tennis court; heated outdoor pool with statuary; an indoor pool in a separate all-glass building that included a gym, sauna, steam room, water slide, showers and hot tub; a huge fountain to rival anything in Rome or Paris; a greenhouse; beautiful gardens, trees and acres of lawns. The three-story main house had so many bathrooms and bedrooms that I lost count; a separate staff wing with rooms and apartments for the live-in staff; fabulous collections of modern art and ancient artifacts from the Far East; a wine cellar; and a sophisticated computer system that ran everything from the lighting, heat and phones to music and video throughout the house. The huge gourmet kitchen had every conceivable modern appliance, all built to look like a classic French country kitchen. A separate carriage house contained the estate manager's apartment, which was situated above a garage housing a collection of antique cars.

Whenever one project or renovation was finished, it would give the owners happiness for a few days, and then that happiness would fade and another new project was conceived. They always wanted more. There was an army of interior decorators, lighting designers, computer programmers, pool technicians, lawn tennis specialists, kitchen designers, audiovisual technicians, phone technicians, acoustic specialists, tree specialists, garden designers, fountain specialists, architects, art consultants, painters, carpenters, contractors, classic car specialists, personal trainers and tutors who were constantly coming and going every day. One time we even had to fly in a technician from Germany to fix the giant flat screen television that rose out of a secret compartment at the foot of the bed in the master suite. A huge part of my job was coordinating the service people's schedules with the schedules of the owners, opening the electric service gate, then escorting the workers through the house or grounds so as not to disturb the family, while making sure the latest project was completed to the owners' exacting standards.

All this lavish wealth came with its own set of problems: the family constantly felt that vendors or servants were taking advantage of them or stealing from them, which was sometimes true but mostly not—most of the workers were loyal and hardworking. It was also sometimes difficult for the owners to know who their real friends were and who were just hangers-on. There were perceived social slights, mostly imagined. There were good moments, but overall there was an almost constant undercurrent of anxiety, anger, hurt, jealousy and unhappiness permeating the house.

The estate was near a beautiful ocean beach and the wife complained to me that the previous summer before I was hired she had only gone to the beach once because she couldn't leave the estate—there was just too much going on that needed her attention and she couldn't trust the previous estate manager to do things right. She told me in no uncertain terms that it would be part of my job to make sure she was able to go to the beach more often. I didn't say anything to her, but what she didn't understand was that she could have easily just grabbed a towel and a book and gone to the beach anytime she wanted; things would never be exactly "right" in an estate so large and complex. The only thing stopping her was her own mental image of what was important: she thought owning all these things and having all these projects would bring her happiness. But instead she was one of the most unhappy women I'd ever met; her material possessions had taken over her life.

It is up to each and every one of us to let go: of possessions, of hurts real or imagined, of greed, anger, anxiety and desire, of physical and psychological ills, so that we may each reach the paradise that is exemplified by a towel, sand, sun, laughter and salty ocean waves on a summer day. No one else can reach nirvana for us.

Fall

Leaves,
Breathe.

~

IN THE NORTHEASTERN U.S., FALL is a magical time, the air
turns crisp and cold and the leaves turn myriad shades of gold,
orange and yellow, like some mythical treasure trove. A wealth
of golden riches that was hidden is suddenly revealed. There is a
clarity to the air. It reminds me of what Zen calls "encountering the
absolute," when you suddenly realize the true golden nature of the
world around you.

After a year in Florida going through rehab it felt good to be back
in the Northeast when fall came. I would take long walks in the woods
with Henry, breathing in that crispness, watching the grassy fields and
trees turn to gold. The autumnal light slants differently, and everything takes on a magical glow. There were vineyards behind my house,
and Henry and I would walk the rows of grapevines and marvel at the
beauty of the purplish-red, fully ripened grapes, ready to be picked.

One of the lingering effects of the accident was that I had seriously
damaged my sense of smell. The medical term is anosmia, and while

it doesn't sound very dramatic, as disabilities go, it was very frustrating. Some smells, like body odor, I could no longer detect at all. Other scents, like citrus, I could still vaguely smell.

Sometimes this was comic, as when I got in an elevator in New York with my friend Michael and several strangers, and when we got to our floor and disembarked Michael wrinkled up his nose and said, "Phew! Can you believe that? I thought I was going to gag!" He was incredulous when I asked what he was talking about. "You didn't smell that?" he asked. "Somebody let one rip in there!"

I hadn't smelled a thing. My disability was actually an advantage.

But other times it could be dangerous, especially when coupled with other neurological problems like my faulty short-term memory. Shortly after I had moved into my rental, I put a teakettle on the stove so I could have a cup of tea. Somehow I was distracted by the television, or the phone—I don't remember exactly—and forgot I was making tea. The kettle boiled dry and the electric coils on the stove and the kettle became so hot that they fused together. The paint on the teakettle began to bubble and smoke, but since I couldn't smell, I had no idea there was a problem until I saw smoke coming from the kitchen. Fortunately I was able to turn off the stove and put out the fire, but I had to replace the stove's coil and it took me a day of scrubbing the stovetop to remove the burn stains. The outcome could have been much worse.

Another problem was that I would get "phantom" smells: I would smell things that just weren't there. One time I was driving to rehab when I was convinced that I smelled something burning, except that there was no smoke and no warning light on the dashboard. I waved frantically to the car next to me at a stoplight, and when the woman rolled down her window I explained that I couldn't smell, but I thought my car was on fire. Did she smell anything? She must have thought I was nuts, but she politely leaned out her window, sniffed the air and pronounced me safe—no odor of any kind emanating from my car.

So walking with Henry in the woods or fields that first autumn, I rejoiced not only in the beautiful sights, but also the smells, because even though they were very faint, I could just discern the sweet odor of fermenting grapes that had fallen off the vines, or the fecund odor of decomposing vegetation. I would breathe deeply, thankful that I could smell *something*, and revel in the magnificence of the cycle of decay and rebirth.

Winter

Snow,
Blowing.

~

ON A COLD, BLUSTERY WINTER day in the mountains of Vermont, there was a certain peace and comfort for me to these seemingly stressful conditions. The snow just was. It just blew. There was no judging the snow. It had no malicious intent, or any benevolent intent. It was not trying to help or hinder; it was just nature being nature. Where some people might have been scared by the blizzard-like conditions, or worried about skidding off the road, I just watched the white whorls fill the air.

Part of the reason I felt comfort was the snow reminded me of my childhood growing up in Buffalo, or my college days in the Adirondacks, and all the times I have spent outdoors in the winter, skiing or hiking in the mountains. But I think I also felt a kinship with the transitory, impermanent nature of the swirling flakes. I was like them, just one snowflake in a million, yet still myself, unlike any other snowflake. I was alone, feeling at one with the raw simple power of nature, at one with the snow, blowing unfettered across the landscape.

ONE HAND SLAPPING

Cats

Hissing...
Pissing.

~

AT THE TIME I WROTE this bit of sibilant silliness, we had not yet moved onto Nirvana full-time and were still living in a house with six cats, in the winter in the northeastern U.S. Enough said. I love cats and have had various cats and kittens since I was a child, but six cats was a bit much. The excessive (to me) number was an accident of timing and one of those side issues one doesn't hear much about in our modern age of divorce and remarriage and blended families. I had two cats that I'd gotten as kittens for Chas and Niall when I returned from rehab and was trying to create a "normal" life for my boys. We had found the kittens at a local greenhouse, where they were the unwanted offspring of the greenhouse's semi-feral cats. Each boy got to pick out a kitten from the many kittens running wild beneath the trays of flowers, and so each boy ended up with a pet, even though mostly they were my pets, since my boys didn't live with me and only visited during the summer and a few holidays. Chas named his cat Daisy, for the flowers she was sleeping under when he found her.

Niall named his cat Sasha. This was all before I started dating Meg, and well before I moved in with Meg. She already had three cats, and then someone had given her another one for safekeeping before we moved in together. The "friend" never did retrieve that cat.

If I wanted to be a modern Hemingway, I'd have a clowder of cats wandering around my home while I write. But Hemingway lived in Cuba and Key West, where the cats could live outside on the grounds of his estate and not be all cooped up in one small house where they would get stressed and fight and piss all over the house.

Six cats in one house didn't work very well. The cats would jump up on my desk in the basement when I wasn't there and piss on my stacks of papers. Meg even found cat pee on her laptop once. We never caught them in the act, so weren't sure which one(s) were to blame, although we suspected all of them. It was a totally unacceptable situation.

Moving onto Nirvana, we had to find homes for the cats. There was no way we were going to deal with kitty litter and cats peeing on things in such a small space. Eventually we did find good homes for them all, although my children were very upset about losing some of their animals (we still had Henry and Owen, our Welsh corgi), and I was very upset as well. It was one of the most difficult and heart-wrenching decisions of my life. The cats, in spite of their hygiene problems, had also been members of the family, and had often curled up in my lap, purring happily, or slept with Chas and Niall, keeping them company, or slept at the foot of my bed. I loved the cats just as much as my boys loved them, and they had been part of rebuilding a new life, a new home.

Modern Poetry

Depressing,
Distressing...

~

MEG GAVE ME A CD anthology of modern poets she thought I would like, but as I put the CD in the stereo and listened, I found the poems all too depressing, full of laments and darkness. Darkness is certainly part of the human experience, but after listening to the CD I longed for some joy, some appreciation of this world, some appreciation of life. Months later I heard Billy Collins, former U.S. Poet Laureate, being interviewed and talking about how all poetry is really about death, and I thought, "How depressing!" The greatest writers and philosophers have known that the human experience is about both death *and* life. Shakespeare wrote tragedies *and* comedies. One of my favorite Zen sayings, posted on the Zendo bulletin board along with a picture of a Japanese monk's intense face glowering from under bushy black eyebrows, is "Life and Death are Matters of Great Importance." My Zen friend Katri, who died of breast cancer, had a saying: "I don't have cancer, I have life!"

Wind

Crying,
Sighing.

~

T HE BUDDHA TAUGHT THAT ALL life is suffering. Many people
have misunderstood that teaching as being especially morbid,
depressing and disheartening. But as awful as that may sound,
it was his insight into the human condition, and it was just a
first step. Most of us, a great deal of the time, are tuned into the sadness
of life: the loss of a loved one, the inexorable march of old age and death.
The Buddha also taught something very exciting and life-affirming and
joyous: he taught that there is a way for human beings to rise above suffering, to find joy and happiness in the midst of the human condition.

I have spent a great deal of my life in nature, whether living,
working or playing on the ocean, or hiking, climbing or skiing in the
mountains, and the wind is an ever-present companion. Few people
would describe the wind as making a joyous noise. To most it moans,
or sighs, or cries. The mournful sound of the wind in the rigging, or
day after day of wind blowing at mountain cabin walls, can quiet even
the most ardent optimist. One of the great movies of all time is "Black

Narcissus," in which a group of Catholic nuns, sent to the Himalayas for missionary work, are nearly driven insane by the constant howling of the winds. The crying of the wind can mirror, magnify and heighten the crying of the human soul.

And yet if we are willing to move beyond, to let go of suffering, the wind can take us places beyond sighing and sadness. The wind can take us to that second step. In "Islands in the Stream," Hemingway's narrator writes about the main character, Thomas Hudson, as he sits on his boat in the Bahamas:

> The wind was blowing heavily and had blown now, day and night, for more than fifty days. It had become a part of the man and it did not make him nervous. It fortified him and gave him strength and he hoped that it would never stop. We wait always for something that does not come, he thought. But it is easier waiting with the wind than in a calm or with the capriciousness and malignancy of squalls.

During the winter we spent on Nirvana in the Bahamas the wind howled day after day after day. It was one of the windiest winters anyone could remember; the wind was the topic of conversation in every store, bar, restaurant, boat and church. In the beginning it drove me crazy; I kept hoping for the wind to stop, or at least die down to a gentle breeze, so we could have a nice, quiet, peaceful night at anchor. Yet after several weeks, I couldn't imagine living without it. The wind felt a vital part of me, a necessary and welcome part of the world. I had moved beyond suffering from it, learned to embrace the wind and see its beauty. I could see the gusts dancing across the surface of the bay as they approached, feel Nirvana heel slightly when they hit, or veer wildly on her anchor chain like a hooked fish suddenly changing direction. I could hear the high-pitched whistling in the rigging, or the rushing of a blast of air as it hit the furled sails. When the wind finally died, the air grew almost too hot, and the flies came out, and we wished the wind would return.

Warriors

Big Men,
Amen.

~

I WAS SITTING IN A SPORTS bar in Portsmouth, Virginia, waiting for a good weather window so that Henry and I could continue south in Nirvana while Meg finished her fall semester teaching obligations. (I think I'll start calling it Po–rtsmouth.) I was watching a professional football game on the bar's big-screen television, watching 300-pound men throw themselves into each other with reckless abandon. As I sat there joints stiff from living on a cold, damp boat, I felt all of my fifty years, and because I still struggle with the residual repercussions of a Traumatic Brain Injury I was feeling a bit bummed that I can no longer participate in any sports where my head might get hit. No touch football with friends, no senior-league sports, and when skiing I now always wear a helmet. And yet since the accident I haven't always been smart enough to realize the importance of coddling my brain. All TBI survivors struggle with the feeling that we want our lives to be the same as they were before the accident, we don't want to admit defeat, to confront the reality that our life will never be the same. One of the stupider things I did after my recovery was try to go wakeboarding one summer day with my sons. In my own youth I had been an expert slalom waterskier, and when I got older I had tried wakeboarding a few times and liked it. The speeds were slower, and it didn't require the upper body strength that slalom water-skiing called for. It was a water sport that a middle-aged body could enjoy. Before the accident I had even tried teaching Chas how to wakeboard a few times off the back of our seventeen-foot motorboat.

Several years after the accident, we were sitting on Nirvana, anchored in Cutchogue Harbor on a beautiful, warm July day. One of the kids' friends came by in his motorboat and asked if we all wanted to try wakeboarding. Why not? I thought. I'd be careful, and doing something athletic with my sons seemed like fun. Chas had forgotten how to wakeboard, if he'd ever even really known, and Niall had never tried it. I looked forward to helping them make this rite of passage, and, okay, I'll admit it, there was a certain macho bravado to showing the kids that their father still had it in him.

I got up on the second or third try and was having a great time, slowly wakeboarding across the bay, when I hit a wave and went flying, hitting the water head first. I came up sputtering, confused, not quite remembering where I was. It hadn't been a bad fall; it had actually been a very easy, gentle fall, but just the shock of hitting the water must have bounced my brain around, and with my brain, there is no longer any margin for error. The boy driving the boat circled around and asked if I wanted to try it again, but I politely declined and climbed back on the boat, not saying anything to my boys about how I felt, not wanting to alarm them. For the next several days I felt spacey, confused and head-achy, but fortunately I recovered fairly quickly. I have not been foolish enough to try anything like that again. I don't even dive head first off Nirvana, instead lowering myself gently down the ladder into the water.

The cumulative effect of head injuries is something that is just beginning to be understood due to the high prevalence of multiple concussions among professional football players, those same big men I enjoyed watching on the big high-definition TV screen in Portsmouth. These giant, seemingly invincible warriors are being laid low in alarming numbers by an invisible malady—recurring concussions and head injuries that often leave them with dementia and cognitive decline as they age, long after they have left the sport.

I've often wondered how much the severity of my own symptoms was caused by previous incidents. When I was ten years old I was riding my bike down a steep hill near our house when I caught a wheel on some gravel and went flying. I was found by a neighbor who was a doctor, who cleaned my cuts—the skin on my right leg and arm had been scraped away and I had a nasty road rash—and then took me home so my mother could take me to the hospital, where they further cleaned my bloody, raw skin, applied ointment and wrapped my arm and leg in gauze. I don't remember any specific head injury, but in those days no one wore helmets, and medical professionals were not as sensitive to the possibility of concussions, so I wouldn't be surprised if any bump on the head would have been dismissed as nothing to worrying about.

Another time at about roughly the same age I was skiing with some friends, and we used shovels to build a jump on the ski hill out of snow. We had been watching the Winter Olympics, and didn't understand that Olympic ski jumpers used a different type of binding where the heel lifts free so they can lean forward, and also that the landing is incredibly steep so the jumpers don't land hard on a flat surface. We built our little jump in a place where the run-in was steep, but the landing was flat, icy and hard. I took the first crack at the jump, went flying into the air, couldn't lean forward, and came down with a loud thud on my back, neck and head (no helmet—nobody wore helmets back then). I lay there, seeing stars, unable to move, my friends gathered around me not knowing what to do, until an adult skied up, asked what was going on and then finally helped me to my feet. Again, no one was worried about head injuries or concussions.

I was a typical energetic, rambunctious boy. Once I got hit in the head with a rock while playing army with a group of boys in a vacant lot. The resulting wound needed a trip to the hospital for stitches. Another time I fell waterskiing and nearly knocked myself out when my head hit the ski. Another time I was playing varsity football as a defensive end and tried to tackle the quarterback as he was throwing a pass. The tip of the football went full force into the bridge of my nose, breaking my nose and causing me to see stars. Another time I was playing lacrosse and was blindsided by a defenseman; my head hit the ground and even though I was wearing a helmet, I couldn't get up for several minutes. Did the coaches or myself or anyone else worry about a concussion? No, both times I went back in the game after a few minutes.

As an adult, although I was supposedly smarter and more mature, there were still a few times when I fell skiing and hit my head, or smacked my head on the boom when sailing, or banged my head under the sink while trying to fix a leaking drain, cursing and sporting an ugly egg-shaped bruise for days afterwards. How many of those times had I imperceptibly damaged my brain, adding to the cumulative effects of repeated, minor brain trauma? How many of those incidents contributed to my continuing problems with cognition after the accident?

Because of the research being done on professional football players and other athletes, we now know that the cumulative effects of multiple head injuries can be devastating. You just have to look at Muhammad Ali to know this sad truth. So what do we do about this problem? Do we ban violent sports? Especially for kids? Or do we get smarter about how we play those sports, about what kind of equipment we use, about protecting our precious brains?

Yes, I am a Buddhist, and yes, I believe in peace, but I grew up playing violent, contact sports: high school football, high school hockey, high school lacrosse, college lacrosse—and have done many things that most people consider aggressive "macho" activities: extreme skiing, sailing boats across oceans, rock climbing. And I enjoyed those sports and activities. Part of being a Buddhist is learning to appreciate the world for what it is, and I have come to accept that being a man sometimes means being fueled by testosterone, enjoying "manly" activities. And sometimes engaging in manly activities means you get hurt.Being a Buddhist means to be totally aware. The Buddha's name means "the awakened one." Watching those men on the television screen, I was reawakened to the joy a man feels when he knocks someone down on the sports field, or bashes his body into someone else.

Several months before I had been reminded of that joy by a friend of mine, Mark, a co-captain with me of our high school lacrosse team, who still plays lacrosse in a senior league. Mark had stopped to visit us on Nirvana on his way to a senior lacrosse tournament. We were sitting in Claudio's Clam Bar, on the pier next to Nirvana in Greenport, having a couple beers, and Mark was describing to me being driven into the ground at age fifty by an opposing player. He was complaining about it, but there was also an element of exhilaration in his voice, and I knew he was still playing at his age because the rough nature of the sport made him happy. His story reminded me of other friends: a surgeon who played hockey well into his sixties for that adrenaline, hard-charging rush, in spite of potential injury to his life-giving hands; my friend Michael who still plays hockey as a goalie at age fifty, letting people shoot hard rubber projectiles at him and knock him down in the crease; my fifty-two-year-old friend Neil who is an acupuncturist and Tai Chi teacher, but still enjoys riding his off-road motorcycle on mountain trails in the Rockies near his home.

As odd as it may seem, there is ancient precedent for the convergence of Eastern spirituality and male athletic fierceness. According to legend, Bodhidharma, the Indian Buddhist monk who brought Buddhism to China sometime around 500 CE, was also an Indian martial arts master who taught martial arts to the monks in the Shaolin Temple in Northern China, the birthplace of kung fu. Martial arts were an important skill for traveling monks like Bodhidharma to protect themselves from bandits, thieves and warlords, and would have also been an important self-defense art to protect monasteries and monks who left the protection of the monastery for their traditional rounds of begging. Some stories even say that Bodhidharma was appalled to find the monks in a feeble state from all the time they spent sitting around meditating, so he prescribed a daily regimen of exercise to whip them into shape. Bodhidharma came from the Indian tradition with its emphasis on yoga—caring for the body as a vessel for the mind—and he would have taught that keeping the body fit was important to spiritual practice. Not only that, he'd just finished traveling more than 3,000 miles, mostly on foot, from Southern India to Northern China, and he would have been in incredible shape. He would have had no patience for slackers.

Modern scholars have cast doubt on the legend of Bodhidharma as the founder of kung fu. The real truth is lost to history and is probably an amalgam of influences. But *kalari*, the most ancient known form of martial arts and an art that makes extensive use of stick fighting, much like kung fu's emphasis on staff fighting, originated in Southern India. It is highly likely that Bodhidharma, as a prince in a royal family, would have been schooled in *kalari,* as well as having learned yoga and meditation as a Buddhist monk.

But the precedent goes even further back than Bodhidharma. The Buddha himself was also a prince in a royal family, and was born into the warrior caste. As such he would have been schooled in athletics and the warrior arts, and would have been required to pass certain tests of warrior skill before being allowed to marry. He was a skilled horseman and is said to have been so physically strong that a king asked him to become a general in the king's army. This warrior background carried on throughout the Buddha's life, culminating in his enlightenment. The language of war has traditionally been used to describe the night the Buddha spent sitting underneath the bodhi tree, after meditating for forty-nine days, when legend has it that he spent the entire night battling the forces of Mara—the Hindu devil—to achieve enlightenment. Mara is said to have appeared riding an elephant, waving his thousand arms, surrounded by leagues of minions carrying weapons and assuming various frightening poses. Mara's army included sloth, torpor, lust, aversion, hunger, thirst, craving, cowardice, doubt, hypocrisy, stupidity, false glory, conceit and Mara's three beautiful daughters, who tried to seduce the thirty-five-year-old ascetic. But the Buddha fought them all night, aided by his own collection of gods and angels, with the battle raging back and forth, until at dawn the earth finally came to the Buddha's aide with a mighty roar, driving off Mara and his followers.

Being ferocious in everyday life and being ferocious in pursuit of nirvana like two legs walking in the same direction but still moving independantly, taking turns stepping forward to reach the same goal.

One afternoon I was meeting with my divorce lawyer, Bridget Tartaglia, and we were discussing how to handle some recent attack from my soon-to-be-ex-wife and her lawyer. One of the reasons I liked Bridget is that even though she was smart and tough, she was also compassionate, looking for ways to solve problems and bring parties together, rather than always following the traditional American legal dictum of being adversarial. To give a sense of what kind of person Bridget is, one day at the courthouse I was looking for her and asked an imposing, gun-toting guard if he had seen Bridget, and his stern face immediately lit up with a big smile. "You're a client of Bridget? Everyone here loves Bridget!"

On this afternoon in her office Bridget was pushing for a calm response to this latest attack, while I was pushing for a more forceful response. She was surprised by my position. "But you're a Buddhist," she said. "I thought that meant you were a pacifist."

"No," I said, "I'm an activist, an activist for peace, for love—an activist for fairness and compassion. There are times when you have to fight for what's right. You just use different weapons. You use the strength of peace and gentleness, the strength of an immovable oak tree, the strength of setting strong boundaries."

There are people who think that even using words such as "fight" or "weapons" or "battle" is wrong, that using such language promotes violence. There are people who believe that sports like football, lacrosse and hockey are deplorable pastimes, encouraging brutality, and there is some validity to both those views. And there is the fact that violent sports can cause brain injuries. But there is also the reality of a world where big animals like lions attack other animals and then relax into a post-activity state of peaceful lethargy, a world where young strapping marines and big armies protect us from bandits and psychopaths, keeping the peace and sometimes sacrificing their own brains and lives in the process. A world where battling life's challenges like TBI, divorce, sloth, torpor, lust, aversion, hunger, thirst, craving, cowardice, doubt, hypocrisy and stupidity can bring about an enlightened world view. A world where teenage boys learn to channel their natural aggressions onto the sports field, not in the school hallways, leaving them better students, better citizens, better human beings.

As I watched those giant men throw themselves about with apparent disregard for their own health, partly for my enjoyment and for the enjoyment of everyone in the bar, the stadium—everyone watching on TV across the country—I was inspired to say a prayer for them, for their brains, for their future, for their families. I was moved to say a prayer for all the brave soldiers who are returning from Iraq and Afghanistan with life-changing Traumatic Brain Injuries from bullets and bombs. I thought of my friend Bob, the young Marine TBI survivor, who keeps telling me that he would go back to combat in a heartbeat if he could, because he misses that action, that camaraderie of other men.

As I sat there, I was acutely aware of the truth of struggle, the truth of testosterone, the validity and honesty of people who enjoy brawny, rugged, tough activities, and all I could say was:

"Big Men, Amen."

Corgi Nirvana

Scratch ear,
Lick rear.

~

WE HAVE TWO DOGS, HENRY, the golden retriever, and
Owen, a Welsh corgi. Henry is ten and Owen is three
and they definitely have the elder dog/puppy thing
going: Owen jumps all over Henry who patiently puts
up with it. They live in a dog's nirvana: we feed them, give them water,
give them treats, take them to the beach for swimming, take them for
runs, and they get fawned over like a newborn baby by anyone who
comes aboard Nirvana. They get to jump up on the bunk, lie around
whenever and wherever they want, and have three teenage boys and
a twenty-one-year-old girl to play with them. The dogs never have
to hunt for their own food, worry about a roof over their head (or a
keel under their feet), pay any bills or fret about being to work on time.
Their only "job," which they do quite well, is to protect Nirvana and
her inhabitants by barking loudly whenever anyone comes too close.

One day Owen was doing what dogs do best: he barked at a motorboat that was zooming nearby, then, when the danger had passed, he sat

back, scratched behind his ear, turned and licked his rear and, now perfectly content, he laid his head down on his paws. What could be more natural, at least to a Corgi?

In Zen, there are stories of intense, strict Zen masters who would slap a student across the face to shock them out of their complacent, rational thoughts, to get them to "Wake Up!" That is the essence of "One Hand Slapping." Just when you thought you had these po and this book all figured out, just when you thought you understood all this "beauty of the world we live in" stuff, here comes a po about a dog licking its butt. Huh?

My mother's cousin Joanna Macy once spent a year living in Sri Lanka to study the principles of Sarvodaya Shramadana Sangamaya, a Buddhist self-help movement that aimed to teach poor Third World people how to help themselves through a combination of personal, spiritual, economic and cultural development. While she was there, she spent a week at a vipassana retreat center (vipassana is a form of Buddhist meditation that concentrates on the mind and body). In her memoir "Widening Circles," she tells the story of being taught to contemplate the "loathsomeness of the body" by a Bengali meditation master named Munindraji. In this practice, one contemplates the thirty-two "impurities" that come from the human body, including such things as blood, sweat, urine, pus, bile and so on. "There is nothing coming out of the body," he told her, "that is not disgusting."

Having borne three children, she rebelled against this teaching. Exasperated at the sexist bent of the master's lesson, she left the room and went outside to pace back and forth under the palm trees, muttering, "Oh, Munindra, I'll show you three things that came out of my body that aren't disgusting." He had dope-slapped her good.

Later, when she had calmed down, she spoke to Munindraji directly, and he told her that the meditation on the foulness of the body is for special situations, for those getting too high on bliss, enraptured by samadhi, or union with the divine. Eventually she realized that this tender man who so revered all forms of life was a gentle, generous teacher whose love of all things went right to his bones.

This is in that tradition. Just when you've gotten too blissed out by stories of sailing, love and the cooing of doves, time to contemplate a corgi's more repulsive habits. Just like Munindraji, however, this is still a loving, life-affirming view of the world. Corgi nirvana: It's real. It's life. It's gross.

LAST PO

Writer's Wisdom

Surprise,
Don't proselytize.

~

MY WRITING TEACHER IN COLLEGE was a wonderful man named Clark Blaise. Although he has written a number of excellent books, from novels to short story collections to memoirs to nonfiction, he is, unfortunately, not well-known outside the writing community. Within that small world, however, he is considered one of the best teachers of his generation. He was the preeminent student of one of the towering figures of literature, Bernard Malamud, and went on to found the International Writing Program at Iowa University in the seventies, which was one of first programs to bring writers from Third World countries into a Master's-level program, which led to a flowering of ethnic fiction in the U.S. His roommate at Iowa and lifelong friend was Raymond Carver, the short story writer. Clark went on to teach at Skidmore College, where I met him, and at several other schools. As Clark's wife, Bharati Mukherjee, herself an accomplished writer, once remarked to me, "At one time or another Clark has taught many of the big names in modern literature."

I had lost touch with Clark after college, but just before my accident I found him. We corresponded briefly, and then our communication was put on hold as I dealt with the aftereffects of being hit by a car. Several years later I was overjoyed to learn he was now teaching at Southampton College near my home on Eastern Long Island. We reconnected and a friendship that had taken a twenty-five-year hiatus was rekindled. We had lunches and dinners together; sometimes I would stop by his house and be surprised to find this literary lion watching college football; he was still a big fan of Iowa. When he retired from Southampton College, I threw a small dinner party to celebrate his years of teaching, all the students he had helped and all the writers he had influenced. Since my new home was still sparsely furnished, I bought new special dinner plates for the occasion—festive French hand-painted red and yellow earthenware in an abstract pattern—and made a scallop dish from my Aunt Leslie's cookbook. Meg was there (we were not yet living together), as were my friend Steve Wick and his wife Debbie. Steve is a Pulitzer Prize-winning journalist for Newsday who has published two books. Bharati was her usual elegant, Indian-American self, lending an air of exotic Brahman sophistication, and Clark and Bharati's small white and gray dog, a Papillon named Faustine, romped around, playing with Henry and peeing on the floor in her excitement. So the dog peed on the floor, who cared? I was alive, with old friends, a new love and my writing mentor. I was alive in my new home, in a house full of writers. I had survived to build a new life.

So when I finished the original manuscript for "Passage to Nirvana," Clark was one of the first people I sent it to. One of his critiques was that I shouldn't have to proselytize for the form that I had invented (the original introduction was almost apologetic in its attempt to explain the po). His comments made me think back to his lessons in the classroom, where a dozen students sat around a large wooden table, with Clark at the head like a family patriarch. Let the work speak for itself, he would say, let the work surprise and engage the reader.

So while I wrote this po, it really came from Clark. This is the second po in the book that came from my teachers (see "Core Koan"). There is so much emphasis in our culture on youth that we sometimes lose sight of the fountain of wisdom available to us from our elders, the surprises they have in store for us.

Survivor's Sagacity

Mind,
Mine.

~

PASSAGE TO NIRVANA IS ONLY one person's journey, one person's story of surviving Traumatic Brain Injury, divorce and the death of loved ones. And yet on another level it is everyone's story. We are all survivors in our own way. We all have our own mental afflictions and abilities; we are all human beings, struggling with the mysteries of our own mind.

Why do we act the way we do? What causes us to choose a certain mate? A certain kind of work? To choose certain friends? To interact with friends and family in certain ways? The mind is a deep, deep mine of emotions, thoughts, memories and creativity. It is also a minefield, tripping up even the most inward-looking of us, just when we thought we had it all figured out.

In my own case a nasty divorce started me down the road of learning more about the deep mine of my own mind, and the minds of others, through both Zen and psychotherapy, and a Traumatic Brain Injury and its treatment—literally losing my mind and gaining it back—gave me insight into the human brain and one's own mind that few people will ever experience.

There is a great deal of difference between brain and mind. As part of my accident I learned about the brain and its workings from my doctors, therapists and various books and web sites: the frontal cortex, the amygdala, the cerebellum, the hippocampus, the limbic system, the vestibular system, the thalamus, neurons, axons, myelin sheaths, neurotransmitters and much more. But learning about mind is much more subtle, difficult and mysterious. Mind is the province of psychologists, bartenders, boats, dogs and Zen masters.

"Passage to Nirvana" is my attempt to relate some of what I learned not about all the pieces and parts of the brain, but about the human mind, an attempt to relate a journey from ignorance to illumination, that others might benefit from this knowledge. It is my story of how I became not just a survivor, but a thriver, someone who is not just clinging to the sides of the lifeboat, hanging on for dear life, but someone who has learned how to pull themselves over the gunwales, step the mast, hoist the sails and head for home.

The word "thrive" comes from the Old Norse word *prifask*, which literally meant to "grasp to oneself," and that is an apt description for anyone wanting to become not just a survivor, but a thriver. At some point one needs to grasp life, to seize it and clutch it to one's chest; at some point one needs to not only grasp to oneself, but to grasp oneself.

In the end the greatest knowledge I gained is not that the human mind is a deep mine (it is), or a minefield (that too), but that my mind is uniquely my own, with its own history, memories, feelings, thoughts, hopes, handicaps and fears. My mind is mine.

Uroboros

Begin
again.

~

THIS FINAL PO IS EMBLEMATIC of the great circle of life, in which every ending is a new beginning, every death a beginning of a new life. Uroboros is the term for an ancient symbol depicting a serpent or dragon swallowing its tail and forming a circle. The uroboros is widely considered a metaphor for the infinite circle of existence, and can be found in many ancient cultures on every continent, ranging from the Aztecs in Mexico to the Yoruba in Africa to Hindu folk myths in India to Norse mythology in Europe. The actual word means "tail devourer" and comes from the Ancient Greeks, who acquired the symbol from Egypt via the Phoenicians. I like that the *ensō,* the Zen calligraphic brushstroke circle of enlightenment, is really nothing more than a stylized, abstract uroboros.

Although there is no snake in it, one of my favorite songs that captures this idea is the American spiritual classic "Will The Circle Be Unbroken," with its timeless lyrics:

Will the circle be unbroken?
By and by Lord, by and by.
There's a better home awaitin'
In the sky, Lord,
In the sky.

Perhaps it is the positive, simple melody, perhaps it is the idea of the "unbroken circle" in the lyrics—perhaps it is a combination of the two. But whatever it is, that song strikes a chord in me and sends shivers down my spine whenever I hear it. I don't necessarily agree that there is a better home awaiting us somewhere else—an integral part of finding joy in life is learning that we are living in a paradise right here, right now, if we can only open our eyes to it. But the song does capture the Zen belief in reincarnation and karma—the unbroken circle—strong testaments to the truth that every ending is also a new beginning.

It is one thing to discuss this idea in abstract terms, quite another to actually internalize this vital truth. The older most of us get, the more our lives change, the more we become aware of the reality not just of death, but of rebirth. In my own life there have been many endings that were new beginnings: an acrimonious divorce, a terrible accident, the death of a loved one. These life-changing experiences allowed me to find a new love, a new path, a new understanding of myself and my relationship with the world. I would not trade these experiences for all the riches on Wall Street (there are a few riches left on Wall Street, I think, even after the great recession of 2008–2009).

I am convinced that my mother's death was a new beginning for her, not out of some sense of false hope, but because years of silent meditation have allowed me to sense this truth of the universe: every ending is a new beginning, as horrible as that ending may seem. Every ending isn't a conclusion but a part of the voyage of discovery; every beginning is a continuation of the odyssey.

Let this be the last po, for now, for this book, as it closes this life chapter and opens a new one, whatever that may be.

BRICOLAGE

RUMBLE IN THE JUMBLE

First, We Teach All the Lawyers

~

NOT ALL THINGS RELATED TO a debilitating brain injury inspired a po. Some things were just too draining, too unappetizing, things that—to me at least—did not lend themselves to creative, poetic treatment. But there were a jumble of things that still needed to be said, subjects that needed to be wrestled with, rumbled with and finally overcome. Things like lawyers, judges, bill collectors, enemy doctors, lawsuits and insurance companies. These things inevitably become a major part of any TBI survivor's story. Voyaging through the labyrinth legal paths is frightening and confusing for TBI patients and their families. In my own case the huge amount of time, psychic energy and stress from dealing with the legal shit drained me, but it was something I had to cope with.

The health care and legal systems in the United States are not set up to help TBI patients. In fact they are the exact opposite. We do not provide government health care for accident victims; instead our system is based on the premise that the victim will sue somebody—a car wash owner, a car owner, a car wash attendant, a homeowner—and the defendant's insurance coverage will pay for the victim's medical expenses, lost wages, pain and suffering, etc.

It almost goes without saying that those people being sued and their insurance company will fight back. They will hire high-powered lawyers to prove that the victim is a liar, a cheat, a faker. The last thing in the world a TBI survivor or their family needs is to be expending time and energy fighting with gargantuan insurance companies, an uncaring government and ruthless law firms in a David versus Goliath battle. Victims and caregivers should instead be expending their precious resources on healing, but that's not the way the system is rigged. I spent a huge amount of time in lawyers' offices, courtrooms and enemy doctors' offices, but the effect was much more far-reaching than just taking up my time. As Dr. Rubino said to me, "Stress is the enemy; it will harm the healing process." And yet the stress of fighting with these myriad enemies on many different fronts was draining, the effects lasting for days, weeks, even months—far beyond the actual time spent in enemy territory.

It didn't help that I had a vindictive soon-to-be-ex-wife to deal with. While my story is one individual's story, it is not unique. Many TBI survivors find themselves abandoned by family or friends because the personality changes often wrought by TBI can severely try even the most patient and understanding family members. But going through a difficult divorce at the same time one is trying to heal did not exactly help my personal healing either.

The first lawyer I encountered was almost a caricature of the ambulance chaser lawyer. I don't remember how he found me, but he showed up in the hospital and sat by my bed, talking to me and my sister about the accident. He did not seem like a bad guy, and he lived in the same town I did and we had mutual friends. I think a friend had told him about my accident. He was a sole practitioner and within days of the accident he was in contact with the insurance company, claiming to represent me. Thankfully, when I heard about this in Florida I was thinking clearly enough to call this lawyer and tell him that he was not representing me, not yet anyway. I was concentrating on meeting with doctors and therapists and getting my recovery underway. Lawyers would have to wait. As messed up as my thinking was, from previous dealings with lawyers as a businessman, I knew enough to shop around for the right lawyer to represent me.

Also since I was comfortable dealing with high-powered law firms, lawyers didn't intimidate me or confuse me with their legal mumbo jumbo. But this episode does makes me wonder about TBI victims and families who have little experience with the legal world and who are preyed on by shysters and ambulance chasers. This particular lawyer was fairly well respected, and might have done a good job, but still, his somewhat disingenuous "representation" of me left me wondering.

My divorce process had already begun, and I had a local matrimonial lawyer who had a good reputation as being a tough advocate for her clients. My father called this lawyer to tell her what had happened and that the divorce would have to be put on hold. My father is an intelligent, usually even-keeled businessman who over the years has dealt with more than his fair share of professionals: lawyers, accountants, bankers, investment professionals—and he was flabbergasted by the response, which was to paraphrase, "Tough luck. Your son needs to get up here and keep moving forward on the divorce." My father tried to explain to her that I was in no shape to travel, in no shape to appear in court, that I had a serious head injury, that my doctors had, for the time being, expressly forbid me from getting involved with stressful situations, like a divorce courtroom. Her response was as uncaring and unsympathetic as before.

My father couldn't believe it. In all his years he said he had never met a lawyer so rude, so uncaring for a client. He didn't tell me all this until about two months later when I had my own problems with this lawyer. He didn't want to insert himself into my personal affairs.

After two fruitless months of trying to deal with this divorce lawyer, I had had enough. She kept pushing me to come back to Long Island for a four-way sit-down conference with Belinda and her lawyer, kept pushing me to come back for "family therapy" that might help us resolve the issues. I kept explaining to her that I had been down that road already, it hadn't worked, and in any event my doctors had told me to avoid stress and nothing could be more stressful than traveling all the way back to Long Island and then sitting down in a room with my wife and her lawyer.

But my own lawyer wouldn't listen to me, wouldn't listen to my doctors' instructions, and when I said no, I wouldn't come back, she dropped me. It was my turn to be flabbergasted. Instead of understanding the complexities of my case, brought on by a serious head injury, and acting accordingly, she had just tried to pigeonhole me into her usual way of operating. I don't think she was a terrible person; on her office walls were framed newspaper articles about her charity work on behalf of children. She was either unwilling or unable to make changes to her modus operandi, unable to understand how a Traumatic Brain Injury might affect her client. Lawyer number one that needed teaching.

Her dropping me as a client left me even more stressed out. I was now being sued for divorce, with no legal representation, living 1,200 miles away, not fully able to understand what was going on legally thanks to a Traumatic Brain Injury.

In the meantime I had found a lawyer to represent me in my accident lawsuit, John Flaherty, of Congdon Flaherty & O'Callaghan, one of the largest and best personal injury law firms on Long Island. John had been recommended to me by another lawyer friend; both he and his firm had a reputation for being honest, thorough, fair advocates for their clients, and had a good reputation with the insurance companies. In fact, they sometimes even represented the insurance companies in complex cases. They were not ambulance chasers.

John recommended a firm he knew that did matrimonial work, and soon I had a new divorce lawyer, Bridget Tartaglia. Bridget was as understanding and compassionate as Costello was not, and I now felt that I had two lawyers, Flaherty and Tartaglia, who were on my side, my own personal advocates to help me navigate the hazardous reefs and shoals of the legal world, much like a large ship takes on a pilot to help bring them into an unfamiliar harbor. While the stress was not gone, at least thanks to good legal representation it was somewhat alleviated.

When I was released from rehab and returned to Long Island full time, I was able to begin working with John on my lawsuit. There were numerous meetings to go over my medical history, the accident, my rehab and medical care. There were depositions, reams of legal documents to read and digest, and then, finally, meetings with the insurance company's lawyers. There would be an attempt to settle out of court, to spare everyone the hassle and cost of a full-blown trial.

At our first meeting I sensed I was in trouble. The opposing lawyer was a grossly overweight man, who from his weight, pasty white skin, dark circles under his eyes and general demeanor, appeared to have some serious health problems. I had been keeping myself in shape, was trim, fit, tanned. I looked much healthier than he did. How was this guy going to agree that I had serious, long-term health problems, when I appeared on the surface to be better than he was? Telling him not to judge a book by its cover was probably not going to work.

Eventually we settled out of court. The money was not nearly what I had hoped for, or needed, but I needed the money. I couldn't wait. I'll never know exactly what this lawyer thought, and his job was to make sure his client, the insurance company, paid as little as possible, but I do think if he had a better understanding of the effects of TBI, the insurance company might have been willing to settle for a slightly higher number. Lawyer number two that needed educating.

Meanwhile my divorce had started up. Here again there would be an attempt to settle out of court. There were many meetings between my lawyer and my wife's lawyer, and many meetings "in chambers" with the judge in New York's Supreme Court. I never met the judge. It was one of the most bizarre processes I have ever encountered. I kept asking my lawyer why I couldn't just meet the judge and plead my case; in person he would certainly see the difference between my wife's behavior and my behavior and rule in my favor re: custody, support, etc. But apparently that would only happen with a full-blown trial. The judge only wanted to rule on the facts, and never met Belinda or myself.

However, according to my lawyer, this particular judge was a smart man who had been confronted with several cases that involved TBI patients, and he went back to school, on his own, and took a course in TBI so that he could better understand and make educated rulings regarding people who suffered from TBI. While I certainly didn't get everything I wanted in the divorce, the judge's rulings were for the most part fair and understanding. Kudos to lawyer number three; he had educated himself.

While I thought that would be the end of it, I should have known better. Several years after the divorce, I again found myself in court. My now ex-wife was suing me, claiming that I should be paying more in child support, that there was nothing wrong with me, that I should be making more money. This time we ended up in Family Court in Riverhead, a much smaller, less prestigious court than Supreme Court. For the first time, I found myself in front of an actual magistrate, a woman who was hostile to me from the start. I answered all her questions truthfully, but several times she made snide, cutting remarks as I was talking, such as when I was describing my employment as a private yacht captain and then estate manager for a wealthy family.

"So after captaining their boat they put him to work as a gardener or something," she said to my lawyer, the implication being that I had quit the job because I had been forced to do work that was somehow beneath me. I tried to object, tried to tell her that actually I had been their estate manager, a very prestigious job, but that I had been forced to quit because the stress of the job brought on increasing headaches, confusion and other cognition problems, but she cut me off. She didn't want to hear it. In her eventual ruling against me, she wrote that I was "not credible." Basically she called me a liar.

I was incensed. Who was this woman? How dare she pass judgment on me, when she knew nothing about me, the struggles I had been through, how hard I had worked to repair my brain, how hard I had tried to begin working again, to find a meaningful career so I could support myself and my family? How dare she call me a liar? But there was nothing I could do. She had not learned more about TBI before making a ruling, as the Supreme Court judge had done.

I should have known better; she was obviously not of the caliber of a Supreme Court Judge. Still, she had power over me. I'd like to believe that this woman, too, could be educated—lawyer number four—but she may be too ignorant or too unwilling to learn. Some people are just born that way. A Buddhist would say its that judge's karma from a previous life. A modern geneticist might say her lack of compassion is in her genes. I prefer to think that yes, people are born a certain way, but they still have the capacity to learn, change and grow, much like the child molester I had worked with in prison (see "Atonement").

One of the Buddhist precepts is not to elevate oneself above others by talking about other's faults, and so perhaps I am breaking that precept in talking about some of these lawyers' faults, but as a writer I know of no other way to highlight this aspect of TBI other than to tell the story, no other way to educate lawyers and judges, to educate this particular judge, so that perhaps next time someone comes before her with a brain disorder—or any disorder for that matter—she will think twice before rushing to judgment.

A TBI Patient A Day

Keeps The Doctors In Hay

~

I WAS LUCKY TO HAVE EXCELLENT doctors. From Dr. James Davis, the head of Neurology at Stony Brook, to Dr. Rubino and the other physicians at Neuroscience and Spine Associates (NASA) in Naples, to various doctors that kept me healing after my return to Eastern Long Island. They were all compassionate, intelligent and genuinely caring individuals. I do not know why each one of them chose medicine as their profession; perhaps some did it for the intellectual challenge, some because they were fascinated with the human brain, some may have even become doctors for the money, but in the end they all were kind, understanding people who took an interest in me, my life and making sure I healed.

But there was another class of doctor who were, in their own way, as evil as my other doctors were good. I'm talking about the quacks who prostitute themselves for the insurance companies.

Much of my care and treatment was being paid for by my automobile insurance company. I was fortunate to have a good company, Aetna, and a good insurance agent, a lifelong friend, Eric Clauss, who owned his own small insurance agency and who made sure that Aetna was living up to its obligations. For the most part there had been very little hassle with Aetna, even though my case was complex. New York State is a no-fault auto insurance state. In other words, it didn't matter whose fault the accident was; my own auto insurance company paid the bills so that I could receive immediate treatment without having to wait years for the outcome of a lawsuit, and then the insurance company sued the other party later to recover their money, if the other party was at fault (which in this case they clearly were).

However, this meant that Aetna was shelling out tens of thousands of dollars, and they wanted to make sure their money was, at best, well-spent, and at worst, not going to a fraudulent claim. As a businessperson, I can understand their need to control costs, but as a TBI patient, let's just say their methods sucked.

After several months of rehab, I received a notice that Aetna wanted me to see another neurologist for a second opinion. I was given the name of the doctor and the time of the appointment. I wasn't overly worried. I knew my case was real, my injuries real, my doctors excellent. This was, I was assured by Eric, only a formality, a way for Aetna to keep fraud to a minimum, and I had no problem with that. I understood their concerns.

I arrived at the doctor's office a few minutes early, and soon I sensed something was wrong. At NASA the waiting room was always full—old people, young people, people in wheelchairs, people who were seemingly healthy, caregivers, family members, children. NASA had a staff of three receptionists/secretaries, several doctors and an assortment of therapists who were all bustling about, popping in and out of the waiting room, smiling, laughing, joking with patients and generally creating a positive, collegial, soothing atmosphere. At this new neurologist's office, I was the only one in the waiting room. There was a single receptionist behind a glass window. The office was in a new office building, and the waiting room was clean, the furniture expensive, the building's grounds well-manicured. But there was no life, no hum and, most importantly, no patients other than myself.

I was ushered through a hallway into the doctor's office, where a nervous, large middle-aged man with dark hair sat behind his desk. His medical degree hung on the wall behind him. It was from a good U.S. medical school, not some foreign school for students who didn't have what it takes to make it in a U.S. medical school. He explained that he was there to help me, to be my friend, but his whole mannerism was so unctuous as to put me immediately on my guard. I would just do my best, get through this and then get the hell out of there. I felt immediately stressed, under attack, and felt my anxiety coming on. Not a good thing for a TBI patient.

He proceeded to give me the usual battery of neuropsychology tests, which I knew only too well from having been tested on a regular basis at NASA. As we continued through the tests, he became more and more agitated, until he finally exploded, yelling at me, "Hurry up! What's taking you so long?! We don't have all day!"

I was flabbergasted. I was doing my best, but these tests were hard for me. I would get confused, have trouble remembering, coming up with answers. That was my whole problem: cognition. I had a Traumatic Brain Injury. Every other contact I had with the medical community had been caring and considerate, and here this jerk was yelling at me about something I was already hypersensitive about, my inability to think quickly. I finished the tests and left, thankful to be out of there, literally shaking with fear and anxiety. What would his report be? Would I suddenly lose my insurance payments? What would happen to my recovery program?

A few days later I was at NASA's offices, meeting with Dr. Stephen Schengber, the neuropsychologist, and he said to me, "I was surprised to see in your chart that you've been to see Dr. _____ "

"The insurance company made me go see him to get a second opinion. He was a total jerk." I told Dr. Schengber about my experience.

"Yes, we've had a lot of complaints about him," he said.

I must have "passed" the exam, because there were no further communications from Aetna; they continued paying for my treatment without any problems.

When I returned to Eastern Long Island the lawsuit began against the car wash for their negligence. Although my auto insurance had paid most of my medical bills, they were suing the car wash's insurance company to regain their losses, and I was suing the car wash for future medical costs and other unknown future problems (like not being able to work at the same level I had before the accident).

The car wash's insurance company sent me to see their own doctor to be examined. Again I was given a time and place, although this time

I had an ally who was to meet me at the doctor's office, a young lawyer from the law firm representing me.

As usual, I had trouble finding my way, following directions, although part of the reason I had trouble finding this doctor's office was that it was in a tiny, dingy room in a rundown building. I was used to finding doctor's offices in shiny glass and metal professional medical parks, or small upscale office buildings. I drove right by the address several times before I realized it was the location of my appointment.

In the office, there were no other patients, and a brusque, older man with an accent examined me. From his last name I believed he was Russian, but I wasn't sure. He gave me a standard physical—hitting my knee with his reflex hammer, asking me to touch my finger to my nose, etc. He didn't once ask about my cognition, or give any neuropsychological tests to measure memory or mental processing speed or other TBI-related afflictions. It was a cursory exam, and then he told me I could go. That was it. He had done absolutely nothing that would have determined if my injuries were real or imagined. It took him all of fifteen minutes. But I'm sure he billed the insurance company a hefty sum.

And his report? I never saw the whole thing, but I do remember something about his report saying that my injuries were not severe. In my defense I had reams of reports from real doctors that would have overwhelmed his opinion if the lawsuit ever went to trial, which it never did, so his report became mostly irrelevant.

I understand the insurance company's need to keep from being conned by people falsely claiming to have been injured, but they were instead being conned by a different kind of con artist—doctors who are so bad they couldn't even get their own patients, doctors who were "doctors" in name only, who were trying to hurt people by denying them coverage, not helping them.

Did the insurance companies know this? I'm sure they did. It's all part of the game; they needed to find an "expert" to take their side and try to reduce their liability. But the good doctors, the real experts, are busy helping patients and making good money doing so; they don't need to get involved with shilling for the insurance companies. It is a byproduct of our adversarial legal/health care system, but it doesn't seem to be the ethical thing to do. It was a waste of time and money, and caused me more stress in the middle of my recovery, at the same time my doctors kept drumming into me, "Avoid stress, avoid stress, avoid stress ... remember that stress is the real enemy to your recovery."

So there are two kinds of injury con men, and to my mind the doctors are the sleazier of the two. With an injury faker, well, you mostly get lowlifes trying to game the system; they may be faking injuries, but they aren't faking who they are. They are sleazeballs being sleazeballs. But a person pretending to be an upstanding medical doctor who is really just a fraud, who is hurting patients rather than helping them, is doing more than just faking a specific incident, they're faking something much bigger, faking who they really are, and harming the medical profession and patients in the process.

But for those doctors, their fakery keeps paying their salaries, keeps feeding them their hay.

Dry Finance

~

You never miss the water until your well runs dry.
– Traditional Folk Saying

ACCIDENTS, ESPECIALLY TRAUMATIC BRAIN INJURIES, can have a profound and devastating effect on one's financial health. Some people are lucky, and have ample savings, excellent health insurance, excellent disability insurance and perhaps even financially secure family members who will help them out. But not everyone has this perfect alignment of financial stars, especially as more and more people go without health insurance in modern-day America.

My father had owned his own business, and had been very successful throughout his adult life. His company was profitable and provided a good living for his family. Growing up we rarely wanted for anything. We took family ski vacations, family sailing vacations, belonged to several private clubs. When it came time for college, although I was expected to work and contribute to my college costs, there was plenty of money for tuition at a first-rate private college. But my father's business was still a small business, which required his full attention to keep it running effectively. He had people who worked for him, but he was the sole executive and decision maker. Without him, there was no one to run the business. When my mother had her accident, most of my father's attention turned to her care. He had no choice. Although he tried to keep things going, without his steady hand on the tiller his business foundered rapidly. Buffalo was already a depressed city, with major economic problems, and there was no margin for error when running a small business. Without a full-time owner, my father's company quickly sank and closed its doors for good.

Fortunately my father was able to keep his and my mother's health insurance, but even so, the costs of my mother's care were huge, and insurance wouldn't pay for the level of care she needed. At the hospital, the doctor in charge of her recovery after she regained consciousness said to my father, "Mr. Carlson, whatever you do, don't put her in a nursing home. They'll just park her in a corner in her wheelchair and ignore her. She needs stimulation, people talking to her, working with her. Do not—I repeat do not—put her in a nursing home."

And yet that's all the insurance company would pay for. Anything beyond that—home care, extensive outpatient physical therapy—would have to come out of my father's pockets. The real estate boom was still at its peak. He mortgaged their house, which was paid for free and clear, and used the money to pay for my mother's care.

In my case I was lucky to have good car insurance, but I didn't have medical insurance or disability insurance. My wife and I had joint health insurance through her company, and she had canceled my health insurance without giving me ample warning to get my own. Since individual health insurance is so expensive, I had been researching my options, but had not yet picked a plan when my accident hit. A classic case of bad timing. And disability insurance is prohibitively expensive for most people, including someone just starting a freelance writing business.

My auto insurance paid most of my medical bills, but without the ability to work and without any disability insurance, bills quickly piled up. I tried to keep expenses to a minimum, but still needed money to live on, and money to send my wife to help pay the household bills and children's expenses. I borrowed money from my father, from my aunt, but the stress of not having my own money took its toll, especially after I returned from Florida and began starting over.

My lawsuit had not been settled. I borrowed money to rent a house, buy pots and pans, chairs and a bed, etc. I set up a home office to try getting back to work. Ikea became one of my best friends.

I had always believed in myself, in my ability to succeed, but I didn't fully understand the obstacles I now faced. If you've injured your brain, by definition you've damaged the part of you that would understand the problems you face. It's very different from hurting your back, or getting cancer, or breaking a leg. As my inability to work dragged on, I couldn't borrow more money, the bills started to pile up, I had no income. I thought about applying for Social Security disability benefits and consulted with a Social Security attorney, but I still wanted to believe that I could work, could be a productive member of society. I did not want to be "disabled." The attorney explained that the process took a long time, and that invariably people were rejected the first time, and then had to appeal. It seemed to me that I was better off concentrating my energies on continuing my rehab/healing process so that I could work. I decided to forgo the Social Security route.

One afternoon I was in the parking lot of the local supermarket. I'd spent a fruitless day trying to write, trying to connect with old clients, and needed a break. I ran into a friend, Charlie Riley, who was the editor-in-chief of We magazine, a lifestyle magazine for people with disabilities. A few years before I had written a feature article for News-day about the senior hockey league he played in.

"How's it going?" he asked. "I heard about the accident."

"Oh, things are going all right."

"You look good."

"Yeah, that's the problem. I'm still having trouble concentrating and writing, but everybody thinks I'm fine."

"That's why in the disability community we refer to Traumatic Brain Injury as 'The Invisible Disability.' Hang in there; if there's anything I can do to help, let me know."

Over the next few months bills continued to pile up, notices and calls from collection agencies grew more frequent. The stress kept getting worse. The boys arrived for Christmas vacation, and I tried to put the best face on things, to just have a good time with my kids, to give them a home and a father and a childhood. We bought red aprons and made Christmas cookies, covering ourselves in flour. We went to the nearby Christmas tree farm and cut down our own tree. On Christmas Eve, I needed some cash to buy groceries and drove up to the drive-thru ATM. I put my card in the slot and tried to withdraw money, but the card wouldn't work. That's strange, I thought, there should be several thousand dollars in my account. I went into the branch, where the manager informed me that American Express had filed a lien against my account, so it was frozen. My head started pounding; how was I going to buy groceries? Feed the kids? Enjoy Christmas? I had no money. Everything was closing for the holidays. There was no time to straighten things out with American Express, the bank. What was I going to do?

I went back to the car, trying not to alarm the boys, but Chas could tell something was amiss.

"What's wrong, Dad?"

"Nothing," I lied. "Everything's fine."

Thankfully I was able to borrow some money and get through the crisis, but events like that just added to the stress level, leaving me drained, confused and having a hard time enjoying Christmas with my children.

Meanwhile the lawsuit dragged on. The car wash's lawyers were doing their best to claim nothing was wrong with me, but there was too much medical evidence proving otherwise. Finally, after much legal wrangling, they made an offer to settle the lawsuit. It was well below what I wanted and thought I deserved. I met with John Flaherty, my lawyer, and he said, "We could not accept their offer and go to trial, but there is no guarantee you'll get anything more. If you were drooling and in a wheelchair, then it wouldn't be a problem. But you look fine, you sound fine, and a jury of non-medical professionals aren't going to understand or care about all the medical evidence. They can't see your memory problems, your cognition problems, your problems not being able to write. Also, you had the bad luck of having the accident in a very conservative county, with lots of farmers and blue collar workers who are known for not giving large jury awards in personal injury cases. If this had happened in Brooklyn or the Bronx, you'd get hundreds of thousands more, but that's life. Be thankful you didn't get a Traumatic Brain Injury falling in your own bathtub. You'd get nothing. You have to make a decision about whether you want to accept their offer or go to trial."

I was out of money. I didn't have much choice. We made the deal. The money they offered was just enough to pay off some bills and short-term debts and leave enough of a cushion that I had time to get back to work to support myself, or so I thought. I still didn't understand how difficult it would be for a TBI survivor to find work. And the settlement, while helpful, left me with substantial unpaid long-term debts.

Many head injury patients struggle with the long-term financial effects of their accidents and disabilities. My own history shows the debilitating financial burdens TBI places on both caregivers—my father—and victims. Eight years after the accident I still struggle financially. On my cell phone I've programmed collection agencies' phone numbers so that when my phone rings, the display shows "collection agency" and I know not to answer.

It is a vicious circle: the difficulty in thinking clearly makes it difficult to work, and the lack of work causes a shortage of money and the constant threat of penury causes untold stress, and the stress causes serious cognition problems, which make it more difficult to think clearly.

All you can do is keep working hard, keep going back to the well, hoping for a little luck, a break in the weather, a little rain, a little water seeping into the well to give some relief until the drought finally ends.

Ann Carlson's Eulogy

~

I gave the eulogy for my mother at Westminster Presbyterian Church in Buffalo, New York, where hundreds of people attended the memorial. It was originally written in very short paragraphs, with plenty of white space between paragraphs, much like a script, to remind me to go slow, to let the words resonate with the audience, but I have reformatted it here to make it easier to read in book form. As a TBI survivor, reading line by line with space between the lines also made it easier to find my way without losing my concentration.

I was worried that the section on the bardo might be a bit much for a conservative WASP audience, but was amazed and heartened at how many people came up to me after the service to tell me how beautiful and moving they had found that part of the eulogy.

WELCOME! WHAT A BEAUTIFUL, GLORIOUS day! As I was driving to the church, I was overwhelmed by the beauty of the pink blossoms on the trees, the shining green budding leaves and the golden sunshine. All signs of rebirth after a long, cold, gray winter—nature's way of teaching us about resurrection and rebirth. God often uses nature to teach us important lessons. So welcome! What a beautiful, glorious day ... in so many ways.

That's something I learned from Mom—always seeing the joy in every situation. If she were here right now—and I believe she is—that's what she'd want, for all of us to realize what a marvelous day this is. So welcome! It's wonderful to see so many friends, family, so many familiar faces, all come to pay their respects. That's something else Mom taught—she was good at teaching by example—she taught that you should welcome people into your home, your place of worship, your circle of friends. At one point in her life, Mom likely welcomed you with an open, loving heart, and here, today—this church filled with people—is the result.

So thank you so much for coming. That's something else Mom was good at: saying thank you for whatever came her way. Rejoicing in people: friends, family, strangers—celebrating their lives—appreciating life! Mom would appreciate that all of you made the effort to be here, although she'd think the whole thing was a bit much, because she also had a modesty, a sense of humor and a sense of "let's just get on with things."

But she'd be very touched. And she'd say thank you not just for coming, but for being such good friends to her in life, and in death. No woman is an island, to turn the phrase a bit, and you all helped her be who she was, as she helped you be who you are. If she could she'd say thank you so much for being her coworker, sports partner, fellow volunteer, husband, child, grandchild, sister, cousin, niece, nephew, and above all, friend. Since she can't say it, I'll say it for her: Thank you all very, very much.

There are so many stories about Mom, and what made her special, that I could go on for hours, but I'll tell you a few short stories to help illustrate what kind of a person she was:

When I was a teenager, I got into trouble, as many teenagers do, and was suspended from school for six weeks. It was quite a scandal, and I'm sure it hurt her deeply, but I don't remember her ever scolding me or coming down really hard on me.

Instead she used lemons to make lemonade, and took charge in her usual resolute way, and made sure I got my homework done and met with teachers. She took me to lunch at the Albright-Knox Art Gallery, because she knew how much I loved art. She treated me with unconditional love and compassion, instead of anger, even though I'm sure she was angry about what I had done. She allowed me to make my own mistakes and learn from them. She listened to what my interests were, and encouraged them. She treated me like a fellow human being, instead of a knuckleheaded kid.

And she treated everyone the same way. Sure, she could get upset with family and friends—after all she was only human—but it didn't last long before her unconditional love took over.

That's something else Mom taught—unconditional love, God's love, a mother's love, a grandmother's love. She set a very high standard—but I still try to follow her example and I know many of you do, as well.

Most of you have your own stories like these about Ann Carlson, so I'm going to tell you a story you may not know: her life after her accident. Many people have called her accident a tragedy, and on many levels it was a tragedy, but even as severely injured as she was, Mom kept giving lessons about how to live life.

Because of my own accident, I lived with her for the last year, and it was a truly amazing experience. She knew who she was, where she was, how much her body had failed her. Yet she never gave up.

She struggled through therapy and wheelchairs and lack of speech and muscle control with an unflagging optimism that was amazing for all to see. Much the same way she had struggled against cancer several years before—and won.

This time, she won in a different way. Friends would come to visit, and her eyes would light up and a big smile would cross her face, and the people that had come to cheer her up would end up being cheered up themselves, saying things like, "She recognized me!" or "She smiled at me!" How amazing that as sick as she was, she could still bring joy to people's lives. She still found a way to teach by example, still found a way to make lemonade.

Mom taught us all something very special in her final year and a half: we cannot judge the quality of a human life. A human life is a human life, a precious thing, in whatever form it takes.

That was Ann Carlson's life, it took many forms: sportswoman, businesswoman, daughter, mother, grandmother, student, teacher, volunteer, patient, friend — it was a wonderful, precious life.

Let us today appreciate it as much as she did.

We'd like to do something a bit different now. One of Mom's cousins and lifelong friends is Joanna Macy, who is well-known for being one of the first Western women to become a Tibetan Buddhist scholar and teacher. I called Joanna as Mom lay dying, and asked her what I could do to help Mom, and she said, "Don't forget about the importance of the bardo."

The Tibetans are considered to be one of the most knowledgeable religions when it comes to death and dying, and they believe the bardo is the place between life and death, the place where souls rest before they move on. Modern science seems to agree with this ancient wisdom. As we are able bring patients back from near death, survivors tell tales of seeing bright lights, hearing voices and other wonderous things.

Mom died a day later, and over the next week our family agreed on a date for Mom's service: May 9th, today.

The most important day in the bardo is the forty-ninth day after a person dies, when the soul leaves the bardo for its next life: heaven, rebirth, resurrection. Tibetans traditionally gather on this day to pray for the deceased, to help them on their journey.

I had a strange feeling, so I checked the calendar, and caught my breath as I realized that May 9th is the forty-ninth day since mom died. Coincidence? Perhaps. But as the famous scientist Werner von Braun (another person of German heritage—Mom would have liked that) is supposed to have said, "Nature does not know extinction, only transformation."

So we ask all of you to join together in a minute of silence to help send Mom on her way, to wish her well in your thoughts, to tell her what a good friend she was, to say goodbye to her, to pray for her, to tell her everything is going to be all right, to open up your heart to her with unconditional love — whatever you choose.

She will hear you, and send her love back, I promise. Because that's Ann Carlson. Please, let us pray.

(Minute of Silence)

ABOUT THE PO

Simple Blings

~

THERE IS POWER IN SIMPLICITY: a child's smile, a golden sunrise, the smell of fresh-baked bread, the ringing of a church bell, a mother's love. So as I wrote I posed myself a simple question: What is the smallest, simplest combination of words that has the power to tell a story, evoke an emotion, create a complete world? Like a Rothko painting, the opening notes of a Beethoven symphony or a mourning dove's soft cry, what basic combination of colors, shapes, sounds or words can part the shadowy veils that obscure true understanding? What is the most elemental marriage of words that can achieve absolute clarity?

I did not ask this question lightly. Much of my interest in Eastern spirituality had been an interest in searching for the essence of truth, which I believe to be both simple and profound. Zen, with its emphasis on simplicity, had seemed to me to be the most elemental of beliefs, the practice most willing to shed the unnecessary, the spiritual path most willing and able to wield the razor-sharp sword to cut through the bullshit and get directly to the heart of the matter.

In many ways, "Passage to Nirvana" is a Zen book, with references to Zen masters past and present, Zen spirituality, the Zen arts and my time spent at the Ocean Zendo. But this is also a book about living, about children, family, TBI, nature and self. It is a book about seeing and appreciating the world in a certain way. It is a book about healing and love.

I was born and raised in the United States, not the Far East, and my schooling was firmly rooted in Western religious, philosophical and artistic traditions. Within that rich Western tradition, as far back as I can remember, I've always been drawn to the elemental: simple Protestant churches, the brushstrokes of abstract expressionism, the minimalist paintings of the 1960s, the music of John Cage, the spare staging of Beckett, the lean short stories of Jack London or Hemingway. It is simply who I am, something in my DNA. Ever since I was a child I have been enchanted by the austere. Where others might relish the complex layering of rococo architecture, for example, I find myself drawn to the clean lines of the Bauhaus school. Where some might thrill to the intricate constructions of Dali's surrealism, I was drawn more to the simple paintings of Magritte. In literature I chose Vonnegut over the Victorians. Writing short stories in college, I took as my inspiration crisp and incisive writers such as Raymond Carver, as opposed to more long-winded authors such as Fitzgerald or Updike. In poetry, I admired Gary Snyder, whose lean style owed much to haiku and Chinese influences, and other beat poets such as Robert Creeley and Lawrence Ferlinghetti, as opposed to the long rambling nature of Kerouac's "Mexico City Blues," or the more lengthy traditional poetry of the English romantic poets.

On the rare occasions I have worn jewelry, I have gone for the unpretentious: a plain gold wedding band, a single piece of black coral on a black leather cord around my neck. Bling is not my thing.

In music, I remember during the same period attending an open-air rock festival in Toronto, with The Police as the headliners and Talking Heads as one of the lead-in acts. I had gone specifically to see the Talking Heads, the group being an avant-garde band popular in the artistic community, and thought The Police too pop, too commercial. But I was in for a surprise: although I admired the Talking Heads and their multilayered sound with a stage full of musicians, I found when The Police came on stage that I appreciated even more the music produced by their pure elemental form: a drummer, a bass and a guitar.

The apparent lack of complexity in Eastern art forms and Western minimalism would, at first glance, seem to relegate their existence to the mundane; certainly to many people these unadorned works of art lack the sophistication to warrant meaningful consideration. Yet these art forms are like a Trojan Horse: let down your guard for a moment, allow them through your defenses—Western mind-walls built up by years of rational thought conditioning—and once inside these simple expressions of the human spirit will unleash an entire army of feeling, emotion and understanding that will break down those mind-walls from within, not from without.

I knew the story I had to tell was complex: how to give a true sense to people with fully functioning brains what it feels like have a brain that isn't firing on all cylinders? How to explain to people struggling with the stresses and challenges of modern life what it feels like to have gained a sense of peace, in spite of overwhelming difficulties? I put my faith in simplicity. I took my lesson from the artists, writers, musicians, spiritual leaders and others who had touched me. I put my faith in minimalism: extremely short poems and short essays. I put my faith in the po.

Less is Amour

~

LEONARDO DA VINCI SAID, "POETRY is painting that is felt rather than seen." Da Vinci understood that a poem is an emotional illustration in the way that a painting is a visual illustration. The challenge for the po, like all minimalist art forms, is to ensure that while the po is constructed with concise and exacting brevity, the idea behind it is a magnum opus, imbued with a depth and breadth of feeling overwhelming in its magnitude, much in the way that a simple white pearl glows from within, containing the essence of the universe. But what is it that da Vinci was trying to get us to see? What are poets trying to get us to feel? Da Vinci may not be thought of as a minimalist, but the "Mona Lisa" is one of the great minimalist artworks of all time, evoking an entire world of feeling with a simple woman's smile.

This book is a dichotomy: there is lengthy prose, but also the world's shortest poems expressed with a minimalist visual sensibility, giving the words room to breathe, in the same way that a modern painting is given a large section of a wall to itself. The poems are the essence of the pearl. I like to think of the po as the equivalent of a simple ikebana, a Japanese flower arrangement, with just a delicate white flower and slender brown branch rising out of a simple raku vase.

Ancestor Wordship

~

D
A VINCI, ZEN, HAIKU, IKEBANA, Snyder—it all sounds so highbrow, but much of the sensibility of these po comes from more workaday influences. In my years as a magazine editor I would sometimes be forced to take a 3,000-word story and suddenly condense it to 300 words as the layout changed, all within the space of a few hours, working late into the night under deadline pressure, fueled by pizza and coffee, while the managing editor kept drumming her fingers and the FedEx man waited impatiently by the front desk knowing that I would rush to hand him the envelope at 11:59 p.m. just before the midnight deadline. In my advertising work I would be asked to write extremely short advertising copy, sometimes as few as five or six words for a full-page newspaper ad. I became an expert at cutting "excess" words.

Then there is my father. A great fan of Ogden Nash, he would recite to me bits of Nash's subversively clever rhyming short poetry when I was a boy (such as "Candy is dandy but liquor is quicker"), referring to him tongue-in-cheek as "Ogden Trash." One of the bits my father liked to recite, which was supposedly the world's shortest poem and which I (and he) assumed was Nash's handiwork, was this:

LEE CARLSON

Fleas

Adam
Had 'em.

Years later however, with children of my own, I decided to look up this ditty on the web and found that its original title had been "Lines on the Antiquity of Microbes" and that it hadn't been written by Nash at all, but by Strickland Gillian (1869–1954), a U.S. poet mainly remembered for his rhyme (particularly the final couplet) often quoted on Mother's Day:

The Reading Mother

I had a Mother who read to me
Sagas of pirates who scoured the sea,
Cutlasses clenched in their yellow teeth,
"Blackbirds" stowed in the hold beneath.

I had a Mother who read me lays
Of ancient and gallant and golden days;
Stories of Marmion and Ivanhoe,
Which every boy has a right to know.

I had a Mother who read me tales
Of Gêlert the hound of the hills of Wales,
True to his trust till his tragic death,
Faithfulness blent with his final breath.

I had a Mother who read me the things
That wholesome life to the boy heart brings—
Stories that stir with an upward touch,
Oh, that each mother of boys were such!

300

You may have tangible wealth untold;
Caskets of jewels and coffers of gold.
Richer than I you can never be—
I had a Mother who read to me.

As luck would have it, I did grow up with a mother who read to me, and am all the wealthier for it. My mother helped instill in me a love of reading, of writing, of words. Ever since I was a child, on up through adulthood, I could count on receiving at least one book from her at Christmas and on my birthday. She loved to read herself, and I have fond memories of her reading to me as a child. So to watch her after her accident, unable to read or speak, knowing that my children would never have the pleasure of having their grandmother read stories to them, was all the more painful.

Another of my "teachers" was an uneducated man who dropped out of high school, but who loved poetry all the same: Muhammad Ali, the man who used the wonderfully simple rhyming couplet, "Thrilla/ in Manilla!" to describe his boxing match against Joe Frazier in the Philippines. I remember hearing this phrase when I was a kid, and how it excited me. Those three simple words evoked an entire world so different from my childhood suburban existence: a faraway exotic land! Huge sweating gladiators! Glamorous ringside celebrities! Beautiful scantily-clad women! The phrase and all it stood for stayed with me.

Years later I was reading George Plimpton's "Shadow Box," his excellent book on the world of boxing. In it he describes how he had arranged a lunch meeting at a famous Manhattan restaurant between Muhammad Ali and the renowned poet Marianne Moore (she was so well-known that Ford Motor Company hired her to name their new E-car, but not liking her names the company chose "Edsel" instead, demonstrating that one should always stick with professional wordsmiths, but that's another story). Plimpton knew that Ali was hooked on poetry and would probably enjoy meeting Moore. He also knew Moore was a great sports fan and believed Moore would enjoy meeting Ali. He was right. At their first meeting, the two wrote a poem together about Ali's upcoming fight with Ernie Terrell, although Ali did most of the writing, having greater experience than Moore with performing under pressure in public:

A Poem on the Annihilation of Ernie Terrell

After we defeat Ernie Terrell
He will get nothing, nothing but hell,
Terrell was big and ugly and tall
But when he fights me he is sure to fall.
If he criticize this poem by me and Miss Moore
To prove he is not the champ she will stop him in four,
He is claiming to be the real heavyweight champ
But when the fight starts he will look like a tramp
He has been talking too much about me and making
    me sore
After I am through with him
He will not be able to challenge Mrs. Moore.

Their collaboration endured; Moore went on to write the liner notes to Ali's spoken-word album, "I Am the Greatest!" Moore later wrote Plimpton that Ali "has an ear, and a liking for balance ... comic, poetic drama, it is poetry ... saved by a hair from being the flattest, peanuttiest, unwariest of boastings." She also wrote a wonderful short poem about Ali:

Is there something I have missed?
He is a smiling pugilist.

Later in the book, Plimpton wrote about Ali's poem that, in Plimpton's opinion, should have supplanted "Adam / Had 'em" as the world's shortest poem. Ali's poem was:

Me,
Whee!

Plimpton said in a later videotaped interview that Ali came up with the poem while addressing the Harvard graduating class, when someone in the crowd yelled out, "Give us a poem!" thanks to his well-known propensity for short verse, such as:

> On the war in Vietnam, I sing this song:
> I ain't got no quarrel with them Viet Cong.

I agree with Plimpton that Ali's "Me/Whee!" KO'd Gillian's "Fleas" for the championship title of world's shortest poem. What I find especially fascinating is that since Ali's was an oral poem, there have been at least three different interpretations. Is the poem:

> Me,
> Whee!

(an ego-athlete statement about Ali, the greatest) or:

> Me,
> We.

(a statement of universal multiracial solidarity) or:

> Me.
> *Oui.*

(similar to version one, but showing a more sophisticated, man of the world temperament)?

I like the "Me,/Whee!" version best. It seems the most true, the most real, the most in tune with Ali's sensibilities. The "Me, / We" version seems too trite, too much like a political statement invented by self-serving politicizers trying to capitalize on the Ali legacy to make a statement about race or world peace. Grand, wonderful themes, to be sure, but not the poetry of the young, freewheeling iconoclast, the man who could do anything, the young man that was Muhammad Ali. And the French version? Highly unlikely, although he traveled extensively thanks to his boxing. Ali was more worldly than many give him credit for and insisted that his daughter speak three languages by the time she was six years old, but I still doubt that's what he was thinking when he came up with this impromptu rhyme. Whatever the correct interpretation, Ali's place in history as an historical world champion in short poem writing—and his place as an influence on subsequent generations of short poem writers—seems secure.

Is all this rumination on my own history and the history of other short poetry writers really necessary to the enjoyment of the "world's shortest poems" in Book II? Not entirely; I believe the po can stand well enough on their own. But I also believe in honoring our ancestors, our influences and our own past. We seem as a society to have lost much of that tradition. In our modern culture with its emphasis on youth, respecting the wisdom of our forebears has gone out of favor. One of the elements of Zen Buddhism I greatly appreciate is the 2,500 year tradition behind the teachings. In the Ocean Zendo on Saturday mornings there is a moment where the long lineage of teachers who handed down the Buddha's teachings, from the Buddha himself to modern living teachers, is chanted in unison as a way of paying homage to these wonderful beings. While I've never sat down and chanted "Basho, da Vinci, Gillian, Nash, Soen, Dad, Mom, Ali, Moore, Plimpton, Police, Snyder" (sounds like a Monty Python skit), I do believe that understanding where short poetry comes from—honoring its ancestors—and having gratitude for that path is an important practice.

Poan Study

~

I N ZEN THERE IS A long tradition of what is called koan study.
Koans are well-known in the West but not well understood.
Koans are questions, stories or statements that are used in meditative practice as aides to achieving clarity, understanding and
eventually enlightenment. The most famous koan is probably, "What
is the sound of one hand clapping?" (There is some disagreement about
the proper translation, which can also be, "What is the sound of the
single hand?" or "Two hands clap and there is a sound; what is the
sound of one hand?") But there are thousands of other koans, and most
are longer than the simple "one hand clapping," although as a testament
to the power of brevity, this is the koan that is best known in the West.

In our hectic, fast-paced modern world who has time to contemplate traditional poetry? Who has time to read Ovid or Keats
or Whitman or Ginsberg and spend quiet hours ruminating on their
meaning? (Notice how poetry keeps getting shorter and shorter? It
is possible po are the natural extension of this process.) Po are a thoroughly modern art form for our hectic, scattered, IM-ing, Twittering,
multitasking world. Do you only have thirty seconds between answering the cell phone, sending a text message, getting the report ready for
the boss or the teacher, jumping in the car on the way to the mall, etc.,
etc., etc.? Quick! Pull out "Passage to Nirvana" and find a po you like,

it only takes ten seconds to read one but you can keep thinking about it in quick snatches between all the other distractions of modern life. Think about the po for minutes, or hours or days. Keep turning it over in your mind. Po can be koans for our time.

Koan study was, for centuries, the province of the privileged few, the "answers" guarded in large dark mountain temples in China by fierce Zen priests. A controversy erupted in the Zen world nearly a thousand years ago, when a Chinese Zen monk published a book of koans with attendant "answers" or commentaries.

The reality is that no person can read the "answers" and have any sense of the truth behind the koan's meaning without years of rigorous meditation practice, but it was still a threat to the Zen hierarchy to have some of its most cherished secrets "revealed." Personally I sympathize with the monk who felt that shining an illuminating light on these mysterious koans would in the end help deepen, not cheapen, understanding.

Like koans, po can be read, viewed, contemplated and appreciated on their own merits, but the reflections that accompany each po are in the same tradition as the commentaries found in Zen koan collections such as "The Blue Cliff Record" or "The Gateless Gate." The reflections and the po together tell a story.

When I first started writing "Passage to Nirvana" I debated whether or not to include these meditations. At first I thought of just publishing the po as a simple book of poetry with a short introduction. Would the po have more power and mystery without any "answers" to their meanings? The most important reason I decided to include the reflections was that I felt the same way I feel about koan commentaries: a little dialogue between human beings can be a powerful, illuminating tool.

Rules are Maids Unbroken

~

EVERY GENRE OF SHORT POETRY needs a set of rules in order to keep the genre, well, a genre. Without the rules the form would devolve into nothingness. For example, the rules for writing a haiku are that it be composed in three lines of 5–7–5 syllables, usually with a seasonal reference, such as snow in winter, or cherry blossoms in spring. Another short form, the sonnet, consists of fourteen lines written in iambic pentameter, and must be written in one of various standard rhyme schemes. The Arabian and Persian *ruba'i* is a four-line verse (quatrain) with the most famous being the *rubáiyát* (collection of quatrains) of Omar Khayyám.

The rules of writing a po that I devised for myself were the following:

I. A po has to be short. Really short. Ideally no more than two lines (sometimes stretched to three) with only one to three words per line. Although not a hard and fast rule, I try for no more than four words in the body of the po, with a simple one or two word title. The shorter the better (both in the body of the po and the title), with contractions allowed.

II. A po has to rhyme. The rhyme can take many forms: it can be an interior rhyme, or a loose rhyme, but it must have some rhyming ingredient, otherwise one could throw any two words in the English language together and call the result a po.

III. In grammatical construction, there should be a noun and a verb, or at least an adjective or adverb; something that connotes action, movement and a sense of time, however subtle. Again, it would be easy to just throw two rhyming nouns together, but the harder part is to suggest an entire world—including not only place (noun) but time and action as well (verb).

That's it. Just three simple rules. Nothing too complex, fancy or abstract. Rules can be tough taskmasters, tyrannical and limiting in their insatiable need for order and discipline, or they can be helpful, charming friends, like a vivacious and lively young woman, full of laughter, unbroken by the cares of oppressive authority. It depends on how strict and overbearing the rules are. The rules I made for po are, I believe, in the more positive, helpful vein; the idea behind the po rules is the same idea as haiku, or Mondrian's grid paintings: the idea that simple form limitations can free up an artist to create a work of beauty. Rules can give you a boundless freedom.

Okay, I lied a little. There is one more rule. A big rule, an important rule. The one overarching principle for a po is that the words must be symbols for something much bigger, much deeper than a few simple words would at first blush suggest. It would be easy to write thousands of short poems that were just doggerel. This rule does not preclude humor, or joy, or lightness of being however, since those are deep human emotions as well.

Having a vaguely subversive nature, I also made another rule for po: rules are made to be broken. So if something really works, then throw the previous edicts out the window.

There are several po that are examples of this. In "Zen Love" there is no rhyme of any kind, but the difference of the po's structure and the idea behind "Zen Love" allow it to work. "Spring" breaks my rules, but in a different way. There is an adjective and a noun, but no verb. The lack of a verb suggests a kind of magical moment when time stands still, which dovetails nicely with the feeling of the po. Sometimes it's as important to know what to leave out as it is to know what to put in.

Po-ssibilities

~

ONE OF THE REASONS I'VE always loved travel is for the mystery: Where will you end up? What unexpected side roads will pull you away from the main path? What characters will you meet? What adventures will you have? Will you return exhilarated or exhausted? Or both? We already know how this trip turned out; the narrator survived a series of misfortunes and lived to write about it. "Passage to Nirvana" gives at least partial answers to many questions: How did he survive? What paths did he wander down? To what extent did he recover? Could he ever go home again? Was he enlightened or extinguished? Is there life after divorce and Traumatic Brain Injury? But there are still many mysteries to be discovered. Trust me.

For me, the most interesting question still to be answered is what will become of the po? What will their reception be? What influence will they have? I hope you enjoyed them. Their difference from "normal" prose or poetry can be both wonderful and strange. You can read them when you have time, or have no time at all. You can read the po by themselves, or read them with the reflections. Read them alone or share them with a friend (or friends). Use them as you wish. Once you read one, it is yours; the po takes on your own meaning, your own subtle interpretation, your own reflection.

It becomes colored with all the wonderful humanity and life experience that you bring to it.

One of the first agents I showed the manuscript to wrote me and said, "The problem with me is that—believe it or not—I actually want to EDIT some of the po."

I think he believed I would be offended by this, but I was exhilarated. I wrote him back, saying that:

> I'm happy to know that you felt like editing some of the po. That's what is supposed to happen; they engage you on a gut level, draw you in, make you feel like they are yours, like you own them and have a part in their creation and can make changes to them. As a reader, they have hooked you; they have done their job. They are so short that in some ways they are a nearly blank slate, a canvas where the reader to project their own thoughts and feelings.

Write your own po. Write reflections on your po. Project your own thoughts and feelings. Share your po, or keep them to yourself in a locked journal hidden away in a bedside nightstand. Or send them to me at www.shortpo.com. I'd like to see what others do with the genre. Perhaps we'll publish a collection of po submitted by other writers. Or a collection of children's po. Or po on specific topics, such as animals, or work, or love. The possibilities are simply, po-etically, endless.

ENDNOTES

Brain-Damaged Memoirist's Note

~

PASSAGE TO NIRVANA IS A work of nonfiction; the events that occurred are described as truthfully as possible. The book is in many respects a memoir, and the word memoir comes from the same root as memory. A memoir is basically a memory of one's life. Readers may rightfully ask: How can an author with a serious brain injury that affected his memory write a memoir? How can the author accurately remember and recount the scenes and dialogue described in "Passage to Nirvana?"

Before my accident I had been lucky. I was one of those people you hated in school; my memory had been so good that I could attend an entire semester of a lecture class, hardly take any notes, and still ace the final exam. But my upbringing had also instilled in me a healthy Protestant work ethic, and I constantly developed and honed that memory in my work as a journalist so that I could accurately remember scenes and dialogue, along with taking good notes. While the damage to my memory was severe, the high level at which my memory functioned before the accident meant that afterwards it still had times where it functioned tolerably well, especially as I healed. As Dr. Rubino joked, "Now you'll be just like the rest of us."

In the case of "Passage to Nirvana" I was able to remember certain occasions, while not having a clue about others. When I asked my doctors why this would be, all they could tell me was that memory was still one of the great mysteries of neurology, but that in part my erratic memory might be a survival mechanism, my brain might be performing a kind of memory triage, remembering events that it deemed important to my survival and forgetting those it deemed unimportant or trivial. (See "Rothko A Gogo.") So I have written about the things I remembered best, and left alone those things I have had trouble recalling.

I also had huge volumes of medical records, police reports, lawyers' notes, photographs and my own personal notes to rely on to jog my memory, and I am indebted to family and friends whose own memories sometimes served as surrogate memories for my own.

The only place I have taken poetic license is with some of the dialogue. The conversations are remembered as best as possible, and do recount as accurately as possible the gist of the conversation, but for the most part they are not word-for-word transcriptions of what was actually said.

Lastly, I gave the manuscript to most of the people who appear in "Passage to Nirvana" for their comments, and to give them an opportunity to correct any errors or omissions of fact.

Acknowledgements

~

A S WITH MOST JOURNEYS, THERE were a number of people who helped make the trip not only possible, but successful, and who are deserving of much praise and thanks. Some helped on this specific odyssey, and others were role models who over the years helped influence the thinking and writing that went into "Passage to Nirvana."

As a Zen student who has spent years trying to extinguish ego, to get rid of "I," it felt strange writing a book with so many references to myself. So I am happy to finally be writing not about myself, but about all the wonderful people who helped bring "Passage to Nirvana" into the world.

First, there are the teachers: Austin Fox, who taught me as a young man to love poetry, even though I didn't realize it at the time; Bill Morris, the first person to teach me how to write poetry with wit, humor, brevity and a love of life; Sue Schapiro, who first taught me how to think philosophically; Clark Blaise, who taught me how to write really true prose and first showed me that being a writer was an honorable profession; Dr. Joel Smith, who first made Eastern religions come alive for me; Peter Matthiessen, who showed me by example so many things about writing and life that I could not possibly list them all, and who exhorted me to go deeper into the pain; Dorothy

Friedman, who taught me that I was stronger than I thought I was; my cousin Joanna Macy, who had a sparkle in her eyes that first led me down the spiritual path; Fred Eppsteiner of the Florida Community of Mindfulness in Naples, Florida, who taught me that Zen doesn't have to be about black robes and dark zendos; and Lisa Anderson, the owner of Studio 41 Yoga in Naples, who taught me how to restore my body while others were teaching me how to restore my mind.

Then there are the friends and family: my parents, who supported me in many ways when things weren't always going "right," and especially my father who took me in after my accident; my sisters, who have been similarly universally supportive, especially Debbie who helped in those crucial first days after the accident; my Uncle Phil, who was a wonderful sounding board and first reader; my Aunt Gretchen—my mother's sister—whose support and wonderfully positive and upbeat attitude kept reminding me of my mother and how she would have kept me focused on the positive things in life; Paula and Michael Croteau, who helped me find a house and get settled when I was finally able to be back on my own; Tom Samuels and Nancy Steelman, who got me sailing again and made me feel welcome back in the small-town community where I had lived before the accident; Russell Hearn, Neil O'Keefe and Peter Stevens, who gave their time and energy in a sweaty, steamy, dirty boatyard to get Nirvana floating again, in spite of having their own family and business obligations, and whose gung-ho attitude still amazes me to this day; Kevin Clark, who helped us get the measure of Nirvana; Renaté Eppelein, Tony Brewer, Rakeesh, Ian, Dominic, Hartmut, Ralf, Rufus, Eyes, Biggie, Shawn, Leeanne, Klaus, Martin, Fishbone and the whole St. Martin crew; Doug Messner and Michael Diliberto, who helped rescue Nirvana and me when we became stranded in Bermuda, and all my other friends and acquaintances who were there when I really needed them.

I am deeply indebted to all the medical professionals who are true embodiments of kindness and compassion and who helped me heal: Dr. James Davis, Chairman, Department of Neurology, Stony Brook University Medical School, whose gentle manner first calmed me and gave me hope, and whose own tragic early death was a great loss; Dr. Mark Rubino of Neuroscience and Spine Associates (NASA) in Naples, whose intelligence and irreverent wit kept me healing and smiling;

Dr. Stephen Schengber, the neuropsychologist at NASA whose calm and comprehensive explanations about my injuries and recovery were always welcome; Rick McCawley, M.S., the psychometrician and cognitive rehab specialist at NASA whose detail-oriented testing and rehab sessions helped get my brain working again; Earl Rectanus, Ph.D, the psychologist in Naples whose regular sessions and humor kept me going even when things looked bleakest; Meredyth Arnott, the bright and energetic vestibular therapist whose bounce in her step helped rid me of vertigo and put the bounce back in my step; Barbara Seifert, R-A.C.S.W., B.C.D., the psychologist whose unflagging patience, insight and intelligence for more than five years not only helped me learn and heal, but gave me continuity and a safe place while the rest of my world was a psychological minefield; Susan Meyer, the acupuncturist who did her damnedest to recover my sense of smell and keep my chi flowing; and finally the many other doctors, nurses and therapists I came in contact with during my journey that are too numerous to list, but who are saints just the same.

I'd also like to thank my friend Eric Clauss, who helped me navigate intricacies of insurance coverage for my medical bills, and John Flaherty and Bridget Tartaglia, who helped me navigate the legal storms resulting from TBI and divorce. Lawyers often get a bum rap, but they were both compassionate yet firm.

Much gratitude goes out to the writers and friends who read drafts of the manuscript and gave me valuable feedback, disproving the adage that writing is a solitary, lonely pursuit: Kristan Andersen, Suzy Becker, Clark Blaise, Fred Eppsteiner, Peter Matthiessen, Neil O'Keefe, Earl Rectanus, Dana White, and especially Meg Bennett.

"Passage to Nirvana" would never have slid down the ways without the generous financial support of the following patrons: Thomas Adler, Thomas Alfano, Kristan Andersen and Robin Bronstein, Elizabeth Andersen, Noel Andersen, Brian Andrews, Kira Bacak, Ray Ball, Pat Barber, Seth R. Bershadsky, Judith Bigham, Lester Black, Clark Blaise, Jessica Celano Brason, Todd Brason, Jennifer Bronstein, Christopher Burdick, Charles and Jackie Carlson, Molly Sanders Clauss, Missy Cleary, Amy and Spaulding Coffey, Ed and Mary Coffey, Lina Coffey, Aaron Cohen, Nonnie Coovert, Skip Cornelius, Mary Ann Costello, Peter Cutler, Claire Day, Brian Dillon, Doug Doolittle, Keith Dunlap,

Lee Joscelyn Duval, Chip Fay, Bill Fenton, Mike Finkel, Geoffrey Flickinger, Matt Flickstein, Sara Flitner, Ellen Unher Frick, Scott Friedman, Carol Geyer, Lauren Grant, Tom Gustin, Sam Hershey Hafey, Scott and Connie Hambley, Russell Hearn, Marty Heitner, James P. Hettrick, Liz Smith Hitchcock, Greg Holbrook, the Doug Hopkins family, Laura Hopkins, Karen Johnson, David Kelleran, Bob Klipstein, Bruce Knapp, Christopher Kuehn and Aida Reyes-Kuehn, Josh Lerman, Peter Lewis, John and Nancy Linder, Peter Linder, Tim McClive, Anne and Mark McDonald, Earl McMillen III, Erica Siegfried Machado, Karen Magee, Tad Magee, Peter Marlette, Gayle Marriner-Smith, Rafe Martin, Doug and Sharon Messner, Michael Mihaley, Michael Miracle, the Moog family, Mary Foster Morgan, John Munschauer, Gretchen Nymoen, Dick O'Hern, Neil O'Keeffe, Tom Pile, Jane Anne Pincus, Mark Pincus, Robert Pincus, Cal and Debbie Puffer, Mary Quinn, Evelyn Ramunno, Cindy Rand, Tracy K. Rice, Andrew Rogers, Elizabeth K. Rogers, Cindy Deatly Ross, Karla Ross, Jack Ruh, Tom Samuels, John Schelp, Rainer Schoenbach, Tim Schreier, Stephen Schwartz, Marcie Shealy, Corinne Slade, Scotti Slater, George Smith, Karl Spangenberg, Molly Stevens, Peter Stevens, Jeff Street, Pierre Tagliabue, Neil Tetkowski, Barbara Tschamler, Bernard M. Turchiano, Melissa C. Umbsen, Fam van de Heyning, Mindy Vitale, David Waldron, Dan Ward, John D. Williams Jr., Carl Yerkovich and Thomas H. Yorty.

Of course, we need to acknowledge the contributions of the lady Nirvana, who has a soothing, nurturing soul and personality all her own, while still being a demanding mistress.

And last but certainly not least, my children, who have been, and continue to be, my greatest teachers and inspiration.

Suggestions for Further Reading

~

A HUGE BODY OF LITERATURE RELATING to Zen is available to interested readers, as is a large library of books on boats and the sea, since both subjects are as old as mankind's quest for knowledge, as old as Buddha and Homer. There is a smaller collection of writing about Traumatic Brain Injury, since it is a relatively new field, as well as a growing body of work in a comparatively new genre, the memoir about overcoming personal tragedy. Although it could be argued that two of the books which lay claim to being the earliest novels—"Don Quixote" and "Robinson Crusoe"—are structured as memoirs about overcoming personal tragedy (insanity and shipwreck, respectively).

There are many magnificent books in each category that are not listed here, but these are some of my favorites, books that influenced "Passage to Nirvana" in some way.

MEMOIR
"The Snow Leopard," by Peter Matthiessen
Winner of the National Book Award, this chronicle of Matthiessen's search for meaning in the Himalayas after his wife's death from cancer is one of the best memoirs about loss, Zen and looking deep inside oneself while also looking clearly at the world around you.

"The Year of Magical Thinking," by Joan Didion
This moving memoir won the National Book Award. It covers the year following the sudden death of Didion's husband from a heart attack, as well as her daughter's collapse and hospitalization from a brain stroke.

"Zen and the Art of Motorcycle Maintenance," by Robert M. Pirsig
While the author considered this a work of philosophy, what has made it a modern classic is the book's description of the author's coming back to life and reflecting on life's values while on a cross-country motorcycle trip after a bout with mental illness.

"A Heartbreaking Work of Staggering Genius," by Dave Eggers
Both his parents die, suddenly leaving Eggers in charge of his younger, preadolescent brother, trying to create some sort of normal life for them both. Told with a frenetic energy, disjointed time sequence and wry, closely observed humor that showed new possibilities for the "proper" way to write a memoir about personal loss.

"I Had Brain Surgery, What's Your Excuse?" by Suzy Becker
This offbeat look at having brain surgery, complete with the author's whimsical cartoon drawings, addresses the very scary issues regarding loss of cognition and brain function.

"My Stroke of Insight," by Jill Bolte Taylor
A Harvard-trained neuroanatomist suffers a severe stroke in roughly the same area where I had bleeding in the brain from my TBI. Her experience and insights are remarkably similar to my own. Her scientific training led her to look at her experience from a medical standpoint, much in the same way my background as a creative writer led me to examine my own experience through the lens of creative writing.

TRAUMATIC BRAIN INJURY
"Head Injury: The Facts," by Dorothy Gronwall
Basic no-nonsense guide for the nonprofessional, including family members, victims and caregivers. Covers everything from what happens to the brain in a head injury, to hospital stays, to what happens after the patient leaves the hospital.

"Living with Brain Injury: A Guide for Families," by Richard C. Senelick
Another good book for the layperson, this covers such topics as how to pick a good rehabilitation hospital and the exciting, relatively new concept of neural plasticity in recovery.

"Brainlash: Maximize Your Recovery from Mild Brain Injury," by Gail Denton, Ph.D.
Just like the title suggests, this book is full of down-to-earth practical advice for TBI sufferers. Covers almost every topic imaginable from driving to anger to sex.

"Coping with Mild Traumatic Brain Injury," by Dr. Diane Roberts Stoler and Barbara Albers Hill
Dr. Stoler is a successful psychologist who sustained a Traumatic Brain Injury in a car accident. This life-changing event led her to devote much of her practice to TBI. Her excellent book gives examples, advice and suggestions for coping with the aftereffects of TBI, from academic problems to financial issues.

BUDDHISM & ZEN

"Narrow Road to the Interior," by Matsuo Basho
One of the best-loved books of Japanese literature, the equivalent of "Adventures of Huckleberry Finn," written by a real wandering Zen poet, not a fictional wandering rascally boy, although the two personality types are not dissimilar. The story of a five-month, 1,233 mile journey by foot, combining prose and poetry into a single, cohesive whole.

"Endless Vow: The Zen Path of Soen Nakagawa," by Kazuaki Tanahashi
The story of one of the first great Japanese Zen masters to teach in America, including collections of his poetry and letters.

"Zen for Americans," by Soyen Shaku
A collection of lectures originally delivered to Americans between 1905–1906 by the first Zen master to visit the United States. Wonderfully insightful teachings tailored to the unique cultural sensibilities of a Western audience. The first and still one of the best books about Zen Buddhism in English.

"Zen Mind, Beginner's Mind," by Shunryu Suzuki
Considered one of the "bibles" of modern Zen. A collection of dharma talks given in the 1960s by the founder of the San Francisco Zen Center. Suzuki Roshi was one of the first Japanese monks to found a congregation in the United States.

SAILING, BOATS & THE SEA
"The Cruise of the Snark," by Jack London
In 1907, at the height of his fame, London and his wife Charmian built a forty-five-foot sailboat and set sail for the South Pacific from San Francisco. A wonderfully written sailing travelogue penned by an author at the zenith of his powers.

"The Log of the Sea of Cortez," by John Steinbeck
An account of a marine animal specimen-collecting trip Steinbeck took with his longtime friend and marine biologist Ed Ricketts, model for the Doc character in Steinbeck's "Cannery Row," and a misfit crew of commercial fisherman. A sea story told with humor, wit, wisdom and beautiful writing about beautiful places by one of America's best writers.

"My Old Man and the Sea," by David and Daniel Hays
A he-said, he-said memoir by a father-son team who use a voyage aboard their small sailboat from New England around Cape Horn as a way of discovering the world and each other.

"Wanderer," by Sterling Hayden
A famous movie star defies a court order and takes his small children to the South Pacific aboard his old wooden schooner with a ragtag crew in an attempt to get away from his twisted Hollywood life.

"Gift From the Sea," by Anne Morrow Lindbergh
Often described as a "woman's book," this short but brilliant reflection on modern living really speaks to everyone. Although not technically a memoir, the pain of the killing of her first-born infant by kidnappers twenty years before, the devastation caused by World War II and the strain of a difficult marriage to one of the world's most famous men led her to search for peace and simplicity on Florida's Captiva Island.

Resources

~

THANKS TO THE INTERNET, ONE can find just about anything or anyone with a few clicks of a mouse, but as a shortcut, here is contact information for a number of important resources on Traumatic Brain Injury, Buddhism, Zen and boats. Some are mentioned in the text, some not.

TRAUMATIC BRAIN INJURY
Brain Injury Association of America
http://www.biausa.org/
Founded in 1980, the Brain Injury Association of America (BIAA) is a national organization for individuals, families and professionals who are affected by Traumatic Brain Injury. BIAA has a network of more than forty state affiliates, and hundreds of local chapters and support groups across the country. BIAA provides information, education and support.

BrainLine.org
http://www.brainline.org/
BrainLine.org is a web site produced by WETA, a public television station in the Washington, D.C., area. The website is partially funded by the Defense and Veterans Brain Injury Center and is, as of this writing, the best source for information about TBI on the Internet.

LEE CARLSON

National Institute of Neurological Disorders and Stroke
http://www.ninds.nih.gov/disorders/tbi/tbi.htm
The Traumatic Brain Injury web site of the National Institute of Health. Mainly an information site, with up-to-date information on research, clinical trials and treatment, and good links to other organizations.

Center for the Study of Traumatic Encephalopathy
http://www.bu.edu/cste/
Traumatic Encephalopathy is the near-twin of TBI, best known as the neurological disease suffered by professional football players, boxers and other athletes who suffer repeated concussions. Whereas TBI can be the result of a single, traumatic accident, TE is the result of multiple small incidents. But the neurological results are often the same.

Family Caregiver Alliance
http://www.caregiver.org/
Although not specifically a TBI-focused organization, FCA offers programs at the national, state and local levels to support and sustain caregivers, including caregivers of TBI patients.

BUDDHISM & ZEN
There are many excellent Zen groups throughout the U.S. that can be found on the web. While reading about Zen Buddhism can be helpful, there is no substitute for actual hands-on experience with a Zen group and teacher. Following is a highly personal list of Zen and Buddhist organizations.

The Zen Peacemakers
http://www.zenpeacemakers.org/
The home of Zen master Bernie Glassman, The Zen Peacemakers is a global network that integrates Zen practice, social action, interfaith work and the arts.

Joanna Macy
http://www.joannamacy.net/
Joanna is a scholar of Buddhism and deep ecology. She travels widely giving lectures and workshops in the Americas, Europe, Asia and Australia.

Florida Community of Mindfulness
http://floridamindfulness.org/
Teacher Fred Eppsteiner has built a community of lay practitioners on
Florida's Southwest Coast that is a model of modern nonsectarian Buddhist practice.

White Plum Asanga
http://www.whiteplum.org/
Has an excellent listing of contact information for Zen groups around
the U.S. and the world.

New York Buddhist Vihara
http://www.newyorkbuddhist.org/
The home of the Venerable Kurunegoda Piyatissa Maha Thero, a Ther-
avada Buddhist monk from Sri Lanka. He is an executive committee
member of the World Conference on Religion and Peace and a faculty
member of the New School in Manhattan.

SAILING, BOATS & THE SEA
US Sailing
http://www.ussailing.org
Adult sailing schools have proliferated in the past decades. US Sailing
has an excellent web site full of information, including a listing of thousands of learn-to-sail organizations.

DIVORCE
Divorce is at epidemic levels in the U.S., and basically the whole thing
sucks, especially for children. Yet I know of very little that is being
done to fight this societal scourge. Most web sites only offer legal information, not advice on how to prevent divorce or how to deal with the
psychological aftermath. Many sites are thinly veiled ads for law firms.
The best divorce resources are friends, family, a therapist, a meditation
teacher, a good lawyer and/or your local bartender. Good luck.

About the Author

~

Lee Carlson is.

He lives.

He loves.

He writes.

He is a Zen Buddhist.

He lives on a sailboat, somewhere.

Colophon

THE BODY TEXT IS SET in a modern variant of Bembo, a revival of a typeface designed by Venetian Francesco Griffo in 1495. The face was first used in "de Aetna," a sixty-page travelogue considered to be the first modern book, printed by the Aldine Press in Venice. Aldine's anchor and dolphin imprint seems a fitting ancestor for a book that includes a boat named Nirvana.

"De Aetna" details a journey to Mount Aetna written by the young Italian poet Pietro Bembo, who later gained fame as secretary to Pope Leo X, as well as lover to the infamous Lucrezia Borgia, femme fatale of the Italian Renaissance court. (The poet Lord Byron called the correspondence between Borgia and Bembo "the prettiest love letters in the world.") The de Aetna typeface was widely admired in Renaissance Europe. Bembo is considered a good choice for expressing classic beauty in typography, producing text that is extremely consistent in color and texture. The typeface as set in "Passage to Nirvana" uses extra leading, giving the page—and the book—an open, ethereal feeling.

falo aliquando fubexefa uentos admiferit aeftuantes, per quos idonea flammae materies incenderetur. Habes, unde incendia oriantur Aetnae tuae: habe nunc quómodo etiam orta perdurent: in quo quidem nolo ego te illud admirari, quod uulgus folet: magnú effe fcilicet tantas flammas, tam immen fos ignes poft hominum memoriam fem per habuiffe, quo aleretur: quid eft enim magnum ipfi magiftrae rerum omniú, et parenti naturae? quid arduum; quid illa tandem non poteft? qui ftellas; qui folem; qui coeli conuexa; qui terras omnes, ac maria; qui mundum deniq; ip fum, quo nihil eft admirabilius, uel po tiusextra quem nihil eft, quod admireris; faepe fine admiratione intuemur; iifdem nobis effe, Aetna miraculum poteft? caue fistam imprudens fili; ut tu id putes:nam fi naturam refpicimus; nihil in Aetna eft, quod mirum uoces: fi rem.